The Interpersonal World of the Infant

THE INTERPERSONAL WORLD OF THE INFANT

A View from Psychoanalysis and Developmental Psychology

DANIEL N. STERN

Basic Books, Inc., Publishers / New York

Library of Congress Cataloging in Publication Data

Stern, Daniel N.
The interpersonal world of the infant.

Bibliography: p. 278
Includes index.
1. Infant psychology. 2. Psychoanalysis.
3. Developmental psychology. I. Title. [DNLM:
1. Child Development. 2. Child Psychology.
3. Infant. 4. Psychoanalysis—in infancy & childhood.
WS 350.5 S839i]
BF719.S75 1985 155.4'22 85-47553
ISBN 0-465-03403-9

Printed in the United States of America
Designed by Vincent Torre
87 88 HC 9 8 7 6 5

For Susan

CONTENTS

PREFACE

THE PATHS LEADING toward my writing this book have been many and interwoven. When I was a resident in psychiatry and in psychoanalytic training, we were always asked to summarize each case with a psychodynamic formulation, that is, an explanatory historical account of how the patient became the person who walked into your office. The account was to begin as early as possible in the patient's life, to include the preverbal and preoedipal influences operating during infancy. This task was always an agony for me, especially trying to tie the infancy period into a coherent life account. It was agonizing because I was caught in a contradiction. On one side, there was the strong conviction that the past influences the present in some coherent fashion. This fundamental assertion of all dynamic psychologies was one of the things that made psychiatry, for me, the most fascinating and complex of all the branches of medicine. Psychiatry was the only clinical discipline for which development really mattered. But on the other side, my patients knew so little about their earliest life histories and I knew even less about how to ask about them. So I was forced to pick and choose among those few facts about their infancies that best fit the existing theories and from these selected pickings come up with a coherent historical account. The formulations for all of the cases began to sound alike. Yet the people were very different. This exercise was like playing a game with limited moves—or worse, smacked of intellectual dishonesty—in an endeavor that otherwise adhered so closely to what felt to be true. The earliest months and years of life held a firm and prominent place in the theories, but occupied a speculative and obscure role in dealing with a real person. This contradiction has continued to disturb and intrigue me. Addressing this contradiction is one of the major tasks of this book.

A second path began when I discovered the current research in developmental psychology. It promised new approaches and tools for finding out more about that earliest period. And I used those tools for the next fifteen years, together with the clinical approach. This book attempts to create a dialogue between the infant as revealed by the experimental approach and as clinically reconstructed, in the service of resolving the contradiction between theory and reality.

There was a third path—one that supports the argument that the present is best understood with knowledge of the past. When I was seven or so, I remember watching an adult try to deal with an infant of one or two years. At that moment it seemed to me so obvious what the infant was all about, but the adult seemed not to understand it at all. It occurred to me that I was at a pivotal age. I knew the infant's "language" but also knew the adult's. I was still "bilingual" and wondered if that facility had to be lost as I grew older.

This early incident has a history of its own. As an infant, I spent considerable time in the hospital, and in order to know what was going on, I became a watcher, a reader of the nonverbal. I never did grow out of it. So when halfway through my residency I finally discovered the ethologists, it was with great excitement. They offered a scientific approach to the study of the naturally occurring nonverbal language of infancy. And this struck me as the necessary complement to the analysis of verbal self-report as described by the dynamic psychologies. One has to be "bilingual" to begin to solve the contradiction.

Some may say that research or theory that is determined by highly personal factors should not be trusted. Others will say that no one in their right mind would bother with the arduous business of research without a history of personal reasons. Developmentalists would have to cast their lot with the latter.

The most recent path leading directly to the writing of this book has been influenced by several colleagues and friends to whom I am indebted. They have read all or portions of the manuscript at various stages, offering the kinds of suggestions and criticisms that help both to encourage and to reshape a book. In particular, I am most grateful to Susan W. Baker, Lynn Hofer, Myron Hofer, Arnold Cooper, John Dore, Kristine MacKain, Joe Glick, and Robert Michels.

Three groups have been helpful in shaping specific aspects of this book. For a period of time I was privileged to join in regular meetings with Margaret Mahler and her colleagues Annamarie Weil, John McDevitt, and Anni Bergman. While they will probably not agree with many of the conclusions I have drawn, the discussions we had en route to divergent conclusions were always enriching and deepened my theoretical understandings. The second group, put together by Katherine Nelson to study the crib talk of one child, included Jerome Bruner, John Dore, Carol Feldman, and Rita Watson. Discussions were invaluable in thinking about the interaction between the preverbal and verbal experiences of a child. The third group was brought together by Robert Emde and Arnold Sameroff at the Center for Advanced Study in the Behavioral Sciences to study developmental psychopathology. Discussions with Alan Sroufe, Arnold Sameroff, Robert Emde, Tom Anders, Hawley Parmelee, and Herb Leiderman helped in struggling with the problems of how relational problems get internalized.

I would also like to acknowledge the ubiquitous contributions of the many people who have worked in our Laboratory of Developmental Processes during this period: Michelle Allen, Susan Baer, Cecilia Baetge, Roanne Barnett, Susan Evans, Victor Fornari, Emily Frosch, Wendy Haft, Lynn Hofer, Paulene Hopper, Anne Goldfield, Carol Kaminski, Terrel Kaplan, Kristine MacKain, Susan Lehman, Babette Moeller, Pat Nachman, Carmita Parras, Cathy Raduns, Anne Reach, Michelle Richards, Katherine Shear, Susan Spieker, Paul Trad, Louise Weir, and Yvette Yatchmink.

I also wish to thank those outside of our laboratory with whom I have had the opportunity to collaborate—namely, John Dore at CUNY and Bertrand Cramer in Geneva.

I am especially indebted to Cecilia Baetge for the preparation of this manuscript at all phases and for her administrative skill in making the writing of a book and conducting the rest of my professional life possible.

Jo Ann Miller, my editor at Basic Books, has been wonderful in her encouragement, criticism, ideas, patience, impatience, and deadlines, all mixed together with sensitivity and exquisite timing. Nina Gunzenhauser's clarity of mind and good sense in copy editing were indispensable.

Much of the research related to this book was supported by the Herman and Amelia Ehrmann Foundation, the William T. Grant Foundation, the Fund for Psychoanalytic Research, the National Foundation of the March of Dimes, the National Institute of Mental Health, and Warner Communications, Inc.

Finally, I want to thank all of the parents and infants—my ultimate collaborators—who have let us learn from them.

PART I

THE QUESTIONS AND THEIR BACKGROUND

Chapter 1

Exploring the Infant's Subjective Experience: A Central Role for the Sense of Self

ANYONE CONCERNED with human nature is drawn by curiosity to wonder about the subjective life of young infants. How do infants experience themselves and others? Is there a self to begin with, or an other, or some amalgam of both? How do they bring together separate sounds, movements, touches, sights, and feelings to form a whole person? Or is the whole grasped immediately? How do infants experience the social events of "being with" an other? How is "being with" someone remembered, or forgotten, or represented mentally? What might the experience of relatedness be like as development proceeds? In sum, what kind of interpersonal world or worlds does the infant create?

Posing these questions is something like wondering what the universe might have been like the first few hours after the big bang. The universe was created only once, way out there, while interpersonal worlds are created, in here, every day in each new infant's mind. Yet both events, at almost opposite frontiers, remain remote and inaccessible to our direct experience.

Since we can never crawl inside an infant's mind, it may seem pointless to imagine what an infant might experience. Yet that is at the heart of what we really want and need to know. What we imagine infant experience to be like shapes our notions of who the infant is. These notions make up our working hypotheses about infancy. As such, they serve as the models guiding our clinical concepts about psychopathology: how, why, and when it begins. They are the wellspring of ideas for experiments about infants: what do they think and feel? These working theories also determine how we, as parents, respond to our own infants, and ultimately they shape our views of human nature.

Because we cannot know the subjective world that infants inhabit, we must invent it, so as to have a starting place for hypothesis-making. This book is such an invention. It is a working hypothesis about infants' subjective experience of their own social life.

The proposed working theory arises now, because the enormous research advances of the recent past have put in our hands whole new bodies of information about infants, as well as new experimental methods to inquire about their mental life. The result is a new view of the infant as observed.

One aim of this book is to draw some inferences about the infant's subjective life from this new observational data. This has not been done before, for two reasons. On the one hand, developmentalists, who are creating this new information, generally work within the tradition of observational and experimental research. In keeping with that approach, they choose not to make inferential leaps about the nature of subjective experience. Their emphasis on objective phenomena, even in clinical matters, is in line with the phenomenological trend now prevalent in American psychiatry, but it places severe limits on what can be embraced as clinical reality—objective happenings only, not subjective happenings. And just as importantly, this approach remains unresponsive to the basic questions about the nature of the infant's experience.

Psychoanalysts, on the other hand, in building their developmental theories continually make inferences about the nature of the infant's subjective experiences. This has been both a liability and a great strength. It has permitted their theories to embrace a larger clinical reality that includes life as subjectively experienced (and that is why it works clinically). But they have made their inferential leaps on the basis of reconstructed clinical material alone, and in the light of older and outdated views of the infant as observed. The new observational data has not yet been fully addressed by psychoanalysis, although important attempts in that direction have begun (see, for example, Brazelton 1980; Sander 1980; Call, Galenson, and Tyson 1983; Lebovici 1983; Lichtenberg 1981, 1983).

I have worked for some years as both a psychoanalyst and a developmentalist, and I feel the tension and excitement between these two points of view. The discoveries of developmental psychology are dazzling, but they seem doomed to remain clinically sterile unless one is willing to make inferential leaps about what they might mean for the subjective life of the infant. And the psychoanalytic developmental theories about the nature of infant experience, which are essential for guiding clinical practice, seem to be less and less tenable and less interesting in light of the new information about infants. It is against this background, which I know to be shared by many others, that I will attempt to draw inferences about the infant's subjective social experience from this new data base. The aims of this book, then, are to use these inferences to describe a working hypothesis of the infant's experience and to evaluate their possible clinical and theoretical implications.

Where can we start inventing infants' subjective experience of their own social life? I plan to start by placing the sense of self at the very center of the inquiry.

The self and its boundaries are at the heart of philosophical speculation on human nature, and the sense of self and its counterpart, the sense of other, are universal phenomena that profoundly influence all our social experiences.

While no one can agree on exactly what the self is, as adults we still have a very real sense of self that permeates daily social experience. It arises in many forms. There is the sense of a self that is a single, distinct, integrated body; there is the agent of actions, the experiencer of feelings, the maker of intentions, the architect of plans, the transposer of experience into language, the communicator and sharer of personal knowledge. Most often these senses of self reside out of awareness, like breathing, but they can be brought to and held in consciousness. We instinctively process our experiences in such a way that they appear to belong to some kind of unique subjective organization that we commonly call the sense of self.

Even though the nature of self may forever elude the behavioral sciences, the sense of self stands as an important subjective reality, a reliable, evident phenomenon that the sciences cannot dismiss. How we experience ourselves in relation to others provides a basic organizing perspective for all interpersonal events.

The reasons for giving the sense of self a central position, even—or especially—in a study of the preverbal infant, are many. First, several senses of the self may exist in preverbal forms, yet these have been relatively neglected. We comfortably assume that at some point later in development, after language and self-reflexive awareness are present, the subjective experience of a sense of self arises and is common to everyone, providing a cardinal perspective for viewing the interpersonal world. And certainly a sense of self is readily observable after self-reflexive awareness and language are present. A crucial question for this book is, does some kind of preverbal sense of self exist before that time? There are three possibilities. Language and self-reflection could act simply by *revealing* senses of the self that had already existed in the preverbal infant, that is, by making them evident as soon as the child can give an introspective account of inner experiences. Alternatively, language and self-reflection could *transform* or even *create* senses of the self that would only come into existence at the very moment they became the subject matter of self-reflection.

It is a basic assumption of this book that some senses of the self do exist long prior to self-awareness and language. These include the senses of agency, of physical cohesion, of continuity in time, of having intentions in mind, and other such experiences we will soon discuss. Self-reflection and language come to work upon these preverbal existential senses of the self and, in so doing, not only reveal their ongoing existence but transform them into new experiences. If we assume that some preverbal senses of the self start to form at birth (if not before), while others require the maturation of later-appearing capacities before they can emerge, then we are freed from the partially semantic task of choosing criteria to decide, a priori, when a sense of self *really* begins. The task becomes the more familiar one of describing the developmental continuities and changes in something that exists in some form from birth to death.

Some traditional psychoanalytic thinkers dismiss the whole issue of a preverbal subjective life as outside the pale of legitimate inquiry on both the methodological and the theoretical grounds just mentioned. They are joined in this position by many developmental experimentalists. Legitimate inquiry about human experience would, in that view, preclude the study of its very origins.

And that is exactly what we wish to study. Accordingly, it must be asked, what kind of a sense of self might exist in a preverbal infant? By "sense" I mean simple (non-self-reflexive) awareness. We are speaking at the level of direct experience, not concept. By "of self" I mean an invariant pattern of awarenesses that arise only on the occasion of the infant's actions or mental processes. An invariant pattern of awareness is a form of organization. It is the organizing subjective experience of whatever it is that will later be verbally referenced as the "self." This organizing subjective experience is the preverbal, existential counterpart of the objectifiable, self-reflective, verbalizable self.

A second reason for placing the sense of self, as it may exist preverbally, at the center of this inquiry is the clinical one of understanding normal interpersonal development. I am mostly concerned with those senses of the self that are essential to daily social interactions, not to encounters with the inanimate world. I will therefore focus on those senses of the self that if severely impaired would disrupt normal social functioning and likely lead to madness or great social deficit. Such senses of the self include the sense of agency (without which there can be paralysis, the sense of non-ownership of self-action, the experience of loss of control to external agents); the sense of physical cohesion (without which there can be fragmentation of bodily experience, depersonalization, out-of-body experiences, derealization); the sense of continuity (without which there can be temporal disassociation, fugue states, amnesias, not "going on being," in Winnicott's term); the sense of affectivity (without which there can be anhedonia, dissociated states); the sense of a subjective self that can achieve intersubjectivity with another (without which there is cosmic loneliness or, at the other extreme, psychic transparency); the sense of creating organization (without which there can be psychic chaos); the sense of transmitting meaning (without which there can be exclusion from the culture, little socialization, and no validation of personal knowledge). In short, these senses of the self make up the foundation for the subjective experience of social development, normal and abnormal.

A third reason for placing the sense of self at the center of a developmental inquiry is that recently there have been renewed attempts to think clinically in terms of various pathologies of the self (Kohut 1971, 1977). As Cooper (1980) points out, however, it is not that the self has been newly discovered. The essential problem of the self has been crucial to all clinical psychologies since Freud and for a variety of historical reasons has culminated in a psychology of the self. It has also been central to many of the dominant strains in academic psychology (for example, Baldwin 1902; Cooley 1912; Mead 1934).

The final reason to focus upon the sense of self in infancy is that it fits with a strong clinical impression about the developmental process. Development occurs in leaps and bounds; qualitative shifts may be one of its most obvious features. Parents, pediatricians, psychologists, psychiatrists, and neuroscientists all agree that new integrations arrive in quantum leaps. Observers also concur that the periods between two and three months (and to a lesser degree between five and six months), between nine and twelve months, and around fifteen to eighteen months are epochs of great change. During these periods of change, there are quantum leaps in whatever level of organization one wishes to examine, from electroencephalographic recordings to overt behavior to subjective experience (Emde, Gaensbauer, and Harmon 1976; McCall, Eichhorn, and Hogarty 1977; Kagan, Kearsley, and Zelazo 1978; Kagan 1984). Between these periods of rapid change are periods of relative quiessence, when the new integrations appear to consolidate.

At each of these major shifts, infants create a forceful impression that major changes have occurred in their subjective experience of self and other. One is suddenly dealing with an altered person. And what is different about the infant is not simply a new batch of behaviors and abilities; the infant suddenly has an additional "presence" and a different social "feel" that is more than the sum of the many newly acquired behaviors and capacities. For instance, there is no question that when, sometime between two and three months, an infant can smile responsively, gaze into the parent's eyes, and coo, a different social feel has been created. But it is not these behaviors alone, or even in combination, that achieve the transformation. It is the altered sense of the infant's subjective experience lying behind these behavioral changes that makes us act differently and think about the infant differently. One could ask, which comes first, an organizational change within the infant or a new attribution on the part of the parent? Does the advent of new infant behaviors such as focal eye contact and smiling make the parent attribute a new persona to the infant whose subjective experience has not as yet changed at all? In fact, any change in the infant may come about partly by virtue of the adult interpreting the infant differently and acting accordingly. (The adult would be working within the infant's proximal zone of development, that is, in an area appropriate to infant capacities not yet present but very soon to emerge.) Most probably, it works both ways. Organizational change from within the infant and its interpretation by the parents are mutually facilitative. The net result is that the infant appears to have a new sense of who he or she is and who you are, as well as a different sense of the kinds of interactions that can now go on.

Another change in sense of self is seen at about age nine months, when suddenly infants seem to sense that they have an interior subjective life of their own and that others do too. They become relatively less interested in external acts and more interested in the mental states that go on "behind" and give rise to the acts. The sharing of subjective experience becomes possible, and the subject matter for interpersonal exchanges is altered. For example, without using any words, the infant can now communicate something like "Mommy, I want you to look over here (alter your focus of attention to match my focus of attention), so that you too will see how exciting and delightful this toy is (so that you can share my subjective experience of excitement and pleasure)." This infant is operating with a different sense of self and of other, participating in the social world with a different organizing subjective perspective about it.

Given the sense of self as the starting point for this inquiry into the infant's subjective experience of social life, we will examine the different senses of self that appear to emerge as the maturation of capacities makes possible new organizing subjective perspectives about self and other. And we will examine the implications of such a developmental process for clinical theory and practice. The following is a summary of the major points of our examination.

Infants begin to experience a sense of an emergent self from birth. They are predesigned to be aware of self-organizing processes. They never experience a period of total self/other undifferentiation. There is no confusion between self and other in the beginning or at any point during infancy. They are also predesigned to be selectively responsive to external social events and never experience an autistic-like phase.

During the period from two to six months, infants consolidate the sense of a core self as a separate, cohesive, bounded, physical unit, with a sense of their own agency, affectivity, and continuity in time. There is no symbiotic-like phase. In fact, the subjective experiences of union with another can occur only after a sense of a core self and a core other exists. Union experiences are thus viewed as the successful result of actively organizing the experience of self-being-with-another, rather than as the product of a passive failure of the ability to differentiate self from other.

The period of life from roughly nine to eighteen months is not primarily devoted to the developmental tasks of independence or autonomy or individuation—that is, of getting away and free from the primary caregiver. It is equally devoted to the seeking and creating of intersubjective union with another, which becomes possible at this age. This process involves learning that one's subjective life—the contents of one's mind and the qualities of one's feelings—can be shared with another. So while separation may proceed in some domains of self-experience, new forms of being with another are proceeding at the same time in other domains of self-experience. (Different domains of self-experience refer to experiences that occur within the perspective of different senses of the self.)

This last point highlights a more general conclusion. I question the entire notion of phases of development devoted to specific clinical issues such as orality, attachment, autonomy, independence, and trust. Clinical issues that have been viewed as the developmental tasks for specific epochs of infancy are seen here as issues for the lifespan rather than as developmental phases of life, operating at essentially the same levels at all points in development.

The quantum shifts in the social "presence" and "feel" of the infant can therefore no longer be attributed to the departure from one specific developmental task-phase and the entrance into the next.

Instead, the major developmental changes in social experience are attributed to the infant's acquisition of new senses of the self. It is for this reason that the sense of self looms so large in this working theory. The sense of self serves as the primary subjective perspective that organizes social experience and therefore now moves to center stage as the phenomenon that dominates early social development.

Four different senses of the self will be described, each one defining a different domain of self-experience and social relatedness. They are the sense of an *emergent self,* which forms from birth to age two months, the sense of a *core self,* which forms between the ages of two and six months, the sense of a *subjective self,* which forms between seven to fifteen months, and a sense of a *verbal self,* which forms after that. These senses of self are not viewed as successive phases that replace one another. Once formed, each sense of self remains fully functioning and active throughout life. All continue to grow and coexist.

Infants are seen as having a very active memorial and fantasy life, but they are concerned with events that actually happen. ("Seductions," as Freud first encountered them in clinical material, are real events at this stage of life. There are no wish fulfilling fantasies.) The infant is thus seen as an excellent reality-tester; reality at this stage is never distorted for defensive reasons. Further, many of the phenomena thought by psychoanalytic theory to play a crucial role in very early development, such as delusions of merger or fusion, splitting, and defensive or paranoid fantasies, are not applicable to the infancy period—that is, before the age of roughly eighteen to twenty-four months—but are conceivable only after the capacity for symbolization as evidenced by language is emerging, when infancy ends.

More generally, many of the tenets of psychoanalysis appear to describe development far better after infancy is over and childhood has begun, that is, when speech is available. This observation is not meant as a disconfirmation of psychoanalytic theory; it is a suggestion that psychoanalytic theory has been misapplied to this earlier period of life, which it does not describe well. On the other hand, academic working theories that describe the infancy period do not give adequate importance to subjective social experience. The emphasis in this account on the development of the sense of self is a step in the direction of gradually finding theories that better fit the observable data and that will ultimately prove of practical import in dealing with subjective experience.

Finally, one of the major clinical implications of the proposed working hypothesis is that clinical reconstructions of a patient's past can best use developmental theory to help locate the origin of pathology in one of the domains of self-experience. Since the traditional clinical-developmental issues such as orality, autonomy, and trust are no longer seen as occupying age-specific sensitive periods but as being issues for the life span, we can no longer predict the actual developmental point of origin of later-emerging clinical problems involving these issues, as psychoanalysis has always promised. We can, however, begin to make predictions about the origins of pathology in the various domains of self-experience. The result is a greater freedom in therapeutic exploration.

These, then, are the general outlines of the working theory that will result from making clinically informed inferences from the newly available infancy data. Because the different senses of the self are so central to this account, separate chapters of part 2 of this book are devoted to describing how each new sense of self comes about, what maturing capacities and abilities make it possible, what new perspective it adds to the infant's social world view, and how this new perspective enhances the infant's capacity for relatedness. Part 3 then looks at some clinical implications of this working theory, from differing viewpoints. Chapter 9 looks at the "observed infant" with a clinical eye. Chapter 10 reverses that perspective and looks at the reconstructed infant of clinical practice with the eye of an observer of infants. And the last chapter looks at the implications of this developmental viewpoint for the therapeutic process of reconstructing a patient's past.

First, however, it seems essential to explain in greater detail the nature of my approach and its problems. Chapter 2 will address those issues, in particular the advantages and limitations of combining data from experimental and clinical sources; the rationale for placing the sense of self at the center of a developmental account of social experience; and the conceptualization of the developmental progression of senses of the self.

Chapter 2

Perspectives and Approaches to Infancy

THE PICTURE of infant experience suggested in this book has both differences from and similarities to the pictures currently drawn by psychoanalysis and developmental psychology. Since the approach I have adopted borrows methods and findings from developmental psychology and insights from clinical practice, it is important to discuss in greater detail the assumptions of each discipline and the problems of using both approaches together.

The Observed Infant and the Clinical Infant

Developmental psychology can inquire about the infant only as the infant is observed. To relate observed behavior to subjective experience, one must make inferential leaps. Clearly, the inferences will be more accurate if the data base from which one is leaping is extensive and well established. The study of intrapsychic experience must be informed by the findings of direct observation, as the source of most new information about infants continues to be naturalistic and experimental observations. But at best, the observations of an infant's available capacities can only help to define the limits of subjective experience. To render a full account of that experience, we require insights from clinical life, and a second approach is needed for this task.

In contrast to the infant as observed by developmental psychology, a different "infant" has been reconstructed by psychoanalytic theories in the course of clinical practice (primarily with adults). This infant is the joint creation of two people, the adult who grew up to become a psychiatric patient and the therapist, who has a theory about infant experience. This recreated infant is made up of memories, present reenactments in the transference, and theoretically guided interpretations. I call this creation the *clinical infant,* to be distinguished from the *observed infant,* whose behavior is examined at the very time of its occurrence.

Both of these approaches are indispensable for the present task of thinking about the development of the infant's sense of self. The clinical infant breathes subjective life into the observed infant, while the observed infant points toward the general theories upon which one can build the inferred subjective life of the clinical infant.

Such a collaboration was not conceivable before the last decade or so. Up to that point, the observed infant concerned mostly nonsocial encounters: physical landmarks like sitting and grasping or the emergence of capacities for perceiving and thinking about objects. The clinical infant, on the other hand, has always concerned the social world as subjectively experienced. So long as these two infants involved different issues, they could go their own ways. Their coexistence was nonproblematic, and their collaborative potential was small.

But this is no longer the case. Observers of infants have recently begun to inquire about how and when infants might see, hear, interact with, feel about, and understand other persons as well as themselves. These efforts are bringing the observed infant in line with the clinical infant to the extent that both concern versions of the infant's lived social experience, including the infant's sense of self. Their coexistence now invites comparisons and cooperation.

The problem raised by drawing upon these two differently derived infants is, to what extent are they really about the same thing? To what extent do they share common ground, so that they can be joined for one purpose? At first glance, both viewpoints appear to be about the real infant's social experience. If this is so, then each should be able to validate or invalidate the claims of the other. However, many believe that the two versions are not at all about the same reality and that the conceptualizations of one are impervious to the findings of the other. In that case, there would exist no common meeting ground for comparison, and possibly not even for cooperation (Kreisler and Cramer 1981; Lebovici 1983; Lichtenberg 1983; Cramer 1984; Gautier 1984).

The dialogue between these two views of infancy and how they may influence one another is a secondary theme of this book. The way in which they together can illuminate the development of the infant's sense of self is the primary theme. For both purposes, it is important to examine each view more fully.

A clinical infancy is a very special construct. It is created to make sense of the whole early period of a patient's life story, a story that emerges in the course of its telling to someone else. This is what many therapists mean when they say that psychoanalytic therapeutics is a special form of story-making, a narrative (Spence 1976; Ricoeur 1977; Schafer 1981). The story is discovered, as well as altered, by both teller and listener in the course of the telling. Historical truth is established by what gets told, not by what actually happened. This view opens the door for the possibility that any narrative about one's life (especially one's early life) may be just as valid as the next. Indeed, there are competing theories, or potential narratives, about what early life was actually like. The early life narratives as created by Freud, Erikson, Klein, Mahler, and Kohut would all be somewhat different even for the same case material. Each theorist selected different features of experience as the most central, so each would produce a different felt-life-history for the patient.

Viewed in this way, can any narrative account ever be validated by what was thought to have happened in infancy? Schafer (1981) argues that it cannot. He suggests that therapeutic narratives do not simply explicate or reflect what may actually have happened back then; they also create the real experience of living by specifying what is to be attended to and what is most salient. In other words, real-life-as-experienced becomes a product of the narrative, rather than the other way around. The past is, in one sense, a fiction. In this view, the notion of mutual validation between the clinical (narrated) infant and the observed infant is out of the question. No meeting ground exists.[1]

Ricoeur (1977) takes a less extreme position. He does not believe, as does Schafer, that no meeting ground for external validation exists. If that were so, he argues, it would "turn psychoanalytic statements into the rhetoric of persuasion under the pretext that it is the account's acceptability to the patient that is therapeutically effective" (p. 862).

Ricoeur suggests that there are some general hypotheses about how the mind works and how it develops that exist independently of the many narratives that could be constructed—for example, the developing sequence of psychosexual stages or the developing nature of object- or person-relatedness. These general hypotheses can be potentially tested or strongly supported by direct observation or by evidence existing outside of any one particular narrative and outside of psychoanalysis. One advantage of Ricoeur's position is that it provides the clinical infant with greatly needed independent sources of information to help examine the implicit general hypotheses that go into the construction of the life narrative. The observed infant might be such a source.

I am in full agreement with Ricoeur's position, which provides much of the rationale for proceeding as I do in this book, but with the understanding that this position applies to metapsychology, or the constraints of developmental theory, not to any one patient's reconstructed felt-history.

There is a third consideration that bears on this issue of contrasting, partially incompatible viewpoints. The current scientific Zeitgeist has a certain persuasive and legitimizing force in determining what is a reasonable view of things. And at this moment the Zeitgeist favors observational methods. The prevailing view of the infant has shifted dramatically in the past few years and will continue to shift. It will ultimately be a cause for uneasiness and questioning if the psychoanalytic view of infancy becomes too divergent and contradictory relative to the observational approach. As related fields, presum-

1. The two infants live at different levels of epistemological discourse. For Schafer, therefore, the issue of the validity of a narrative is strictly an internal matter. The issue is never a question of whether the life narrative was observably true back when, but of whether the life story "appear(s) [to the narrator] after careful consideration to have the virtues of coherence, consistency, comprehensiveness, and common sense" (p. 46).

ably about the same subject matter even though from different perspectives, they will not tolerate too much dissonance, and it currently appears that it is psychoanalysis that will have to give way. (This position may seem overly relativistic, but science advances by shifting paradigms about how things are to be seen. These paradigms are ultimately belief systems.) Thus, the mutual influence between the observed and the clinical infants will result both from a direct confrontation about those specific issues that the two views can contest, as implied by Ricoeur, and from the evolving sense of the nature of infancy, to which both views contribute. This process will gradually determine what feels acceptable, tenable, and in accord with common sense.

The observed infant is also a special construct, a description of capacities that can be observed directly: the ability to move, to smile, to seek novelty, to discriminate the mother's face, to encode memories, and so on. These observations themselves reveal little about what the "felt quality" of lived social experience is like. Moreover, they tell us little about higher organizational structures that would make the observed infant more than a growing list of capacities that is organized and reorganized. As soon as we try to make inferences about the actual experiences of the real infant—that is, to build in qualities of subjective experience such as a sense of self—we are thrown back to our own subjective experience as the main source of inspiration. But that is exactly the domain of the clinical infant. The only storehouse of such information is our own life narratives, what it has felt like to live our own social lives. Here, then, is the problem: the subjective life of the adult, as self-narrated, is the main source of inference about the infant's felt quality of social experience. A degree of circularity is unavoidable.

Each view of the infant has features that the other lacks. The observed infant contributes the capacities that can be readily witnessed; the clinical infant contributes certain subjective experiences that are fundamental and common features of social life.[2]

The partial joining of these two infants is essential for three

2. The potential dangers of adultomorphizing are real. Therefore, it is important that the subjective experiences chosen are not those seen exclusively or particularly in adult psychopathological states, nor those that come to be acceptable and reasonable only after much psychodynamic self-exploration. They should be apparent to anyone and a normal part of common experience.

reasons. First, there must be some way that actual happenings—that is, observable events ("mother did this, and that . . .")—become transformed into the subjective experiences that clinicians call intrapsychic ("I experienced mother as being . . ."). It is this crossover point that involves the participation of both the observed infant and the clinical infant. While the two perspectives do not overlap, they do touch one another at certain points to create an interface. One can never understand the genesis of psychopathology without this interface. Second, the therapist who is better acquainted with the observed infant may be in a position to help patients create more appropriate life narratives. Third, the observer of infants who is better acquainted with the clinical infant may be prompted to conceive of new directions for observation.[3]

Perspectives on the Subject Matter of Development

THE PSYCHOANALYTIC PERSPECTIVE

Developmental psychology views the maturation of new capacities (such as hand-eye coordination, recall memory, and self-awareness) and their reorganization as the appropriate subject matter of developmental shifts. For the sake of clinical utility and a subjective account, psychoanalysis has had to take a further step and define the progressive reorganizations in terms of larger organizing principles of development, or mental life. Freud's developmental progression from oral to anal to genital stages was seen as the sequential reorganization of drive, or the nature of the id. Erikson's developmental progression from trust to autonomy to industry was seen as the sequential reorganization of ego and character structures. Similarly, Spitz's progression of organizing principles concerned a sequential restructuring of ego precursors. Mahler's developmental progression

3. Even those who are decidedly committed to the approach of psychopharmacology will ultimately (when further advances in neurochemical understanding have been made and assimilated) have to re-confront or confront for the first time the level of subjective experience in the light of their new understandings. At the moment, the level of subjective experience may seem like a thing of the past from the chemical viewpoint, but soon enough it will be the wave of the future, if and when (and only if and when) chemical psychiatry fulfills its promise.

from normal autism to normal symbiosis to separation-individuation concerned the restructuring of ego and id, but in terms of the infant's experience of self and other. Klein's developmental progression (depressive, paranoid, and schizoid positions) also concerns the restructuring of the experience of self and other, but in a very different manner.

The developmental account described in this book, in which new senses of the self serve as organizing principles of development, is closest to the accounts of Mahler and Klein in that its central concern, like theirs, is for the infant's experience of self and other. The differences lie in what the nature of that experience is thought to be, in the order of the developmental sequence, and in my focus on the development of the sense of self, not encumbered with or confused with issues of the development of the ego or id.

Psychoanalytic developmental theories share another premise. They all assume that development progresses from one stage to the next, and that each stage is not only a specific phase for ego or id development but also specific for certain proto-clinical issues. In effect, developmental phases concern the infant's initial dealing with a specific type of clinical issue that can be seen in pathological form in later life. This is what Peterfreund (1978) and Klein (1980) mean by a developmental system that is both pathomorphic and retrospective. More specifically, Peterfreund speaks of "two fundamental conceptual fallacies, especially characteristic of psychoanalytic thought: the adultomorphization of infancy and the tendency to characterize early states of normal development in terms of hypotheses about later states of psychopathology" (p. 427).

It is in this way that Freud's phases of orality, anality, and so on refer not only to stages of drive development but to potential periods of fixation—that is, to specific points of origin of pathology—that will later result in specific psychopathological entities. Similarly, Erikson sought in his developmental phases the specific roots of later ego and character pathology. And in Mahler's theory, the need to understand later clinical phenomena such as childhood autism, symbiotic psychosis of childhood, and overdependency initially led to postulating the occurrence of these entities in some preliminary form earlier in development.

These psychoanalysts are developmental theorists working backward in time. Their primary aim was to aid in understanding the development of psychopathology. This in fact was a task of therapeutic urgency, a task that no other developmental psychology was dealing with. But it forced them to position pathomorphically chosen clinical issues seen in adults in a central developmental role.

In contrast, the approach taken here is normative rather than pathomorphic and prospective rather than retrospective. While disruptions in the development of any sense of self may prove to be predictive of later pathology, the different senses of self are designed to describe normal development and not to explain the ontogeny of pathogenic forms (which does not mean that ultimately they may not be helpful in that task).

Psychoanalytic theories make yet another assumption, that the pathomorphically designated phase in which a clinical issue is being worked on developmentally is a sensitive period in ethological terms. Each separate clinical issue, such as orality, autonomy, or trust, is given a limited time slot, a specific phase in which the designated phase-specific clinical issue "comes to its ascendancy, meets its crisis, and finds its lasting solution through a decisive encounter with the environment" (Sander 1962, p. 5). In this way each age or phase becomes a sensitive, almost critical, period for the development of a single phase-specific clinical issue or personality feature. Freud's, Erikson's, and Mahler's sequences are examples par excellence. In such systems, each issue (for example, symbiosis, trust, or orality) ends up with its own distinct epoch. The result is a parade of specific epochs, in which each of the most basic clinical issues of life passes by the grandstand in its own separate turn.

Do these clinical issues really define age-specific phases? Does the succession of different predominant clinical issues explain the quantum leaps in social relatedness that observers and parents readily note? From the point of view of the developmental psychologist, there are serious problems with using clinical issues to describe developmental phases meaningfully. The basic clinical issues of autonomy and independence provide a good example.

How does one identify the crucial events that might define a phase that is specific to the issues of autonomy and independence? Both Erikson (1950) and Freud (1905) placed the decisive encounter for this clinical issue around the independent control of bowel functioning at about twenty-four months. Spitz (1957) placed the decisive encounter in the ability to say "no" at fifteen months or so. Mahler

(1968, 1975) considered the decisive event for autonomy and independence to be infants' capacity to walk, to wander away from mother on their own initiative, beginning at about twelve months. The timing of these three different decisive encounters disagrees by a whole year, half the two-year-old child's life. That is a big disagreement. Which author is right? They are all right, and that is both the problem and the point.

In fact, there are other behaviors that can equally well be identified as criteria for autonomy and independence. The interaction between mother and infant as carried on with gaze behavior during the three- to six-month period, for instance, is strikingly like the interaction between mother and infant as carried out with locomotor behaviors during the twelve- to eighteen-month period. During the three- to five-month period, mothers give the infant control—or rather the infant takes control—over the initiations and terminations of direct visual engagement in social activities (Stern 1971, 1974, 1977; Beebe and Stern 1977; Messer and Vietze, in press). It must be recalled that during this period of life the infant cannot walk and has poor control over limb movements and eye-hand coordination. The visual-motor system, however, is virtually mature, so that in gazing behavior the infant is a remarkably able interactive partner. And gazing is a potent form of social communication. When watching the gazing patterns of mother and infant during this life period, one is watching two people with almost equal facility and control over the same social behavior.[4]

In this light, it becomes obvious that infants exert major control over the initiation, maintenance, termination, and avoidance of social contact with mother; in other words, they help to regulate engagement. Furthermore, by controlling their own direction of gaze, they self-regulate the level and amount of social stimulation to which they are subject. They can avert their gaze, shut their eyes, stare past, become glassy-eyed. And through the decisive use of such gaze behaviors, they can be seen to reject, distance themselves from, or defend themselves against mother (Beebe and Stern 1977; Stern

4. The same can of course be said of any dyad of infant and caregiver. Throughout this book, "mother," "parent," and "caregiver" are generally used interchangeably to mean the primary caregiver. Similarly, "the dyad" denotes infant and primary caregiver. The exceptions should be fairly obvious: references to breast-feeding, to specific cases, and to research focusing on maternal behavior.

1977; Beebe and Sloate 1982). They can also reinitiate engagement and contact when they desire, through gazing, smiling, and vocalizing.

The manner in which infants regulate their own stimulation and social contact through gaze behavior is quite similar, for the generic issue of autonomy and independence, to the manner in which they accomplish the same thing nine months later by walking away from and returning to mother's side.[5] Why, then, should we not consider the period from three to six months also as phase-specific for the issue of autonomy and independence, both as displayed in overt behavior and as experienced subjectively?[6]

Mothers know quite well that infants can assert their independence and say a decisive "NO!" with gaze aversions at four months, gestures and vocal intonation at seven months, running away at fourteen months, and language at two years. The basic clinical issue of autonomy or independence is inherently operating in all social behaviors that regulate the quantity or quality of engagement. The decision, then, as to what constitutes a decisive event that makes autonomy or independence *the* phase-specific issue appears to have more to do with maturational leaps in cognitive level or motor capacities that are outside the considerations of autonomy and independence *per se.* It is these abilities and capacities that are the real desiderata in each theoretician's definition of a phase. And each theoretician uses a different criterion.

Those who are persuaded that there do exist basic clinical issues, time-locked specific phases, would argue that all clinical issues are of course being negotiated all of the time, but that there is still the feature of predominance, that one life-issue is relatively more prominent at one life period. Certainly, at a given point in development the new behaviors that are used to conduct ongoing issues can be more dramatic (for example, the forms that autonomy and independence take in the "terrible twos"), and these new forms can also require more socializing pressure that attracts much more attention

5. Messer and Vietze (in press) point out that the dyadic gazing patterns become far less regulatory of the interaction at one year, when infants have acquired other ways (such as locomotion) of regulating the interaction and their own level of tension.

6. One could argue that not until twelve months do infants have sufficient intentionality, object permanence, and other cognitive capacities to make the notion of autonomy or independence meaningful. But one could also argue that not until eighteen to twenty-four months do infants have enough symbolic functions or self-awareness to make these notions meaningful. Both arguments have been made.

to them. But the need for more socializing pressure is largely culturally determined.[7] The "terrible twos" are not terrible in all societies.

It therefore seems likely that a relative predominance of protoclinical issues in a particular age period is illusory and emerges from theoretical, methodological, or clinical needs and biases in conjunction with cultural pressures. It is in the eyes of the beholder, not in the infant's experience. Further, if one picks out one basic life-issue and devotes a developmental epoch to its decisive resolution, the picture of the developmental process will necessarily be distorted. It will portray potential clinical narratives, not observable infants. There are no convincing grounds, from the observational point of view, for considering basic clinical issues as adequate overall definers of phases or stages of development.[8]

Clinical issues are issues for the life span, not phases of life. Consequently, clinical issues fail to account for the developmental changes in the social "feel" of the infant or in the infant's subjective perspective about social life.

There is an additional problem with making these traditional clinical-developmental issues the subject matter of sequential sensitive phases of life. In spite of the fact that these views have been prevalent for many decades, there have as yet been no prospective longitudinal studies that support the very clear predictions of these theories. Psychological insults and trauma at a specific age or phase should result in predictably specific types of clinical problems later on. No such evidence exists.[9]

7. Sameroff (1983) provides a systems-theory model for explaining the interaction between society and the parent-infant dyad in determining "predominance" of an issue, that is, how events at the societal level can make an issue more salient for the dyad.

8. Pine (1981) has offered a compromise accounting for the fact commonly observed by mothers that infants are "in" many clinical issue-specific phases at the same time (for example, attaching, while becoming autonomous, while developing mastery). He suggests that the infant has many significant "moments" in any day or hour when different clinical issues are dominant. The problem with this solution is twofold. Significant "moments" appear to be chosen partly on the basis of preconception about the predominant phase (that is, circularly), and such moments are organized around high-intensity experiences. The privileged organizing capacity of high-intensity compared to medium- or low-intensity moments is an open empirical issue. Nonetheless, the impressions that led Pine to this particular solution attest to the widespread recognition of the problem.

9. One of the problems with the implicit or explicit predictions that psychoanalytic theory has made about the ontogeny of pathology is that they were perhaps too specific. Recent thinking about developmental psychopathology (Cicchetti and Schnieder-Rosen, in press; Sroufe and Rutter 1984) stresses that the manifestations of pathology may be very different at

THE PERSPECTIVE OF CLINICALLY ORIENTED DEVELOPMENTALISTS

For those who observe infants directly, there certainly do appear to be phases of development. These phases, however, are not seen in terms of later clinical issues, but rather in terms of current adaptive tasks that arise because of maturation in the infant's physical and mental capacities. The result is a progression of developmental issues that the dyad must negotiate together for adaptation to proceed. It is from this perspective that Sander (1964) has described the following phases: physiological regulation (zero to three months); regulation of reciprocal exchange, especially social-affective modulation (three to six months); the joint regulation of infant initiation in social exchanges and in manipulating the environment (six to nine months); the focalization of activities (ten to fourteen months); and self-assertion (fifteen to twenty months). Greenspan (1981) has evolved a somewhat similar sequence of stages, except that his stray further from readily observable behavior and incorporate some of the abstract organizing principles of psychoanalysis and attachment theory. The stages he proposes are thus more heterogeneous: homeostasis (zero to three months); attachment (two to seven months); somatopsychological differentiation (three to ten months); behavioral organization, initiative, and internalization (nine to twenty-four months); and representational capacity, differentiation and consolidation (nine to twenty-four months).

Most observers of parent-infant interactions would agree that such descriptive systems more or less capture many of the important developmental changes. While several specifics of these descriptive systems are arguable, the systems are helpful clinically in evaluating and treating parent-infant dyads in distress. The central point here is not the validity of these descriptions but the nature of the perspective they take. They view the dyad as the unit of focus and they view it in terms of adaptive tasks. This is at a great remove from any consideration of the infant's likely subjective experience. Infants go about their business of growing and developing, and abstract entities such as homeostasis, reciprocal regulation, and the like are not a

different ages. Even most normal developmental issues are now thought to undergo considerable transformation in manifestation across age. This has been an accumulating impression about the paradox of developmental discontinuity within continuity (Waddington 1940; Sameroff and Chandler 1975; Kagan, Kearsley, and Zelazo 1978; McCall 1979; Garmenzy and Rutter 1983; Hinde and Bateson 1984).

conceivably meaningful part of their subjective social experience. Yet it is exactly with the infant's subjective experience that we are most concerned in this inquiry.

Attachment theory as it has grown from its origins in psychoanalysis and ethology (Bowlby 1969, 1973, 1980) to include the methods and perspectives of developmental psychology (Ainsworth and Wittig 1969; Ainsworth et al. 1978) has come to embrace many levels of phenomena. At various levels, attachment is a set of infant behaviors, a motivational system, a relationship between mother and infant, a theoretical construct, and a subjective experience for the infant in the form of "working models."

Some levels of attachment, such as the behavior patterns that change to maintain attachment at different ages, can be seen readily as sequential phases of development, while others, such as the quality of the mother-infant relationship, are life-span issues (Sroufe and Waters 1977; Sroufe 1979; Hinde 1982; Bretherton and Waters, in press).

Most attachment theorists, perhaps because of their grounding in academic psychology, have been slow to pick up on Bowlby's notion that while attachment is a perspective on evolution, on the species and on the individual dyad, it is also a perspective on the subjective experience of the infant in the form of the infant's working model of mother. Only recently have researchers readdressed Bowlby's notion of the working model of the mother in the infant's mind. Currently several researchers (Bretherton, in press; Main and Kaplan, in press; Osofsky 1985; Sroufe 1985; Sroufe and Fleeson 1985) are reaching further to make the construct of attachment meaningful at the level of the infant's subjective experience.[10]

THE PERSPECTIVE OF THE DEVELOPING SENSES OF THE SELF

The present account, even in the form of a working hypothesis, shares many features with both traditional psychoanalytic theory and attachment theory. Higher order constructs are needed to serve as the organizing principles of development. In this respect, the account is completely in line with both theories. It differs from them in that the organizing principle concerns the subjective sense of self. While

10. Attachment theory is both normative and prospective. Yet interestingly it is proving to be specifically predictive—and strongly so—of later behaviors, some of which are pathological. (The research findings will be discussed in detail in chapters 5 and 9.)

Self Psychology is emerging as a coherent therapeutic theory that places the self as a structure and process at the center, there have as yet been no systematic attempts to consider the sense of self as a developmental organizing principle, although some speculations in that direction have been made (for example, Tolpin 1971, 1980; Kohut 1977; Shane and Shane 1980; Stechler and Kaplan 1980; Lee and Noam 1983; Stolerow et al. 1983). And it is not yet clear how compatible the present developmental view will be with the tenets of Self Psychology as a clinical theory for adults.

Certainly, Mahler and Klein and the object relations school have focused upon the experience of self-and-other, but mainly as the fall out of, or secondary to, libidinal or ego development. Those theorists never considered the sense of self as the primary organizing principle.

This account, centering on the sense of self-and-other, has as its starting place the infant's inferred subjective experience. It is unique in that respect. Subjective experiences themselves are its main working parts, in contrast to the main working parts of psychoanalytic theories, which are the ego and id from which subjective experiences are derived.

The Developmental Progression of the Sense of Self

As new behaviors and capacities emerge, they are reorganized to form organizing subjective perspectives on self and other. The result is the emergence, in quantum leaps, of different senses of the self. These will be outlined briefly here. In part 2 separate chapters are devoted to each.

There is, for one, the physical self that is experienced as a coherent, willful, physical entity with a unique affective life and history that belong to it. This self generally operates outside of awareness. It is taken for granted, and even verbalizing about it is difficult. It is an experiential sense of self that I call the *sense of a core self.*[11] The sense of a core self is a perspective that rests upon the working of many

11. The sense of a core self includes the phenomena that are encompassed in the term "body ego" as used in the psychoanalytic literature. However, it includes more than that, and it is conceptualized differently without recourse to the entity ego. The two are not strictly comparable. It is also more than a sensorimotor schema, since it includes affective features.

interpersonal capacities. And when this perspective forms, the subjective social world is altered and interpersonal experience operates in a different domain, a *domain of core-relatedness*. This developmental transformation or creation occurs somewhere between the second and sixth months of life, when infants sense that they and mother are quite separate physically, are different agents, have distinct affective experiences, and have separate histories.

That is only one possible organizing subjective perspective about the self-and-other. Sometime between the seventh and ninth months of life, infants start to develop a second organizing subjective perspective. This happens when they "discover" that there are other minds out there as well as their own. Self and other are no longer only core entities of physical presence, action, affect, and continuity. They now include subjective mental states—feelings, motives, intentions—that lie behind the physical happenings in the domain of core-relatedness. The new organizing subjective perspective defines a qualitatively different self and other who can "hold in mind" unseen but inferable mental states, such as intentions or affects, that guide overt behavior. These mental states now become the subject matter of relating. This new *sense of a subjective self* opens up the possibility for intersubjectivity between infant and parent and operates in a new domain of relatedness—the *domain of intersubjective relatedness*—which is a quantum leap beyond the domain of core-relatedness. Mental states between people can now be "read," matched, aligned with, or attuned to (or misread, mismatched, misaligned, or misattuned). The nature of relatedness has been dramatically expanded. It is important to note that the domain of intersubjective relatedness, like that of core-relatedness, goes on outside of awareness and without being rendered verbally. In fact, the experience of intersubjective relatedness, like that of core-relatedness, can only be alluded to; it cannot really be described (although poets can evoke it).

The sense of a subjective self and other rests upon different capacities from those necessary for a sense of a core self. These include the capacities for sharing a focus of attention, for attributing intentions and motives to others and apprehending them correctly, and for attributing the existence of states of feeling in others and sensing whether or not they are congruent with one's own state of feeling.

At around fifteen to eighteen months, the infant develops yet a third organizing subjective perspective about self and other, namely the sense that self (and other) has a storehouse of personal world knowledge and experience ("I know there is juice in the refrigerator, and I know that I am thirsty"). Furthermore, this knowledge can be objectified and rendered as symbols that convey meanings to be communicated, shared, and even created by the mutual negotiations permitted by language.

Once the infant is able to create shareable meanings about the self and the world, a *sense of a verbal self* that operates in the *domain of verbal relatedness* has been formed. This is a qualitatively new domain with expanding, almost limitless possibilities for interpersonal happenings. Again, this new sense of self rests on a new set of capacities: to objectify the self, to be self-reflective, to comprehend and produce language.

So far we have discussed three different senses of the self and other, and three different domains of relatedness that develop between the age of two months and the second year of the infant's life. Nothing has yet been said about the period from birth to two months. It can now be filled in.

During this earliest period, a sense of the world, including a sense of self, is emergent. Infants busily embark on the task of relating diverse experiences. Their social capacities are operating with vigorous goal-directedness to assure social interactions. These interactions produce affects, perceptions, sensorimotor events, memories, and other cognitions. Some integration between diverse happenings is made innately. For instance, if infants can feel a shape by touching an object, they will know what the object should look like without ever having seen it before. Other integrations are not so automatic but are quickly learned. Connectedness forms rapidly, and infants experience the emergence of organization. A *sense of an emergent self* is in the process of coming into being. The experience is that of the emergence of networks becoming integrated, and we can refer to its domain as the *domain of emergent relatedness.* Still, the integrative networks that are forming are not yet embraced by a single organizing subjective perspective. That will be the task of the developmental leap into the domain of core-relatedness.

The four main senses of self and the domains of relatedness that have been described will occupy much of this book. The four senses of the self conform in their time of emergence to the major developmental shifts that have been noted. The change in the social feel of an infant with the emergence of each sense of self is also in accord with the nature of these shifts. So is the predominant "action" between parent and child, which shifts from the physical and actional to the mental events that underlie the overt behavior and then to the meanings of events. Before examining these senses and domains further, however, we must address the issue of sensitive periods and make clear that we are dealing not only with successive phases but also with simultaneous domains of self-experience.

As the four domains of relatedness develop successively, one after the other, what happens to each domain when the next comes along? Does each sense of self remain intact in the presence of the new ones, so that they coexist? Or does the emergence of each new sense of self eclipse the existing ones, so that sequential phases wax and wane?

The traditional picture of both the clinical infant and the observed infant leans toward a view of sequential phases. In both developmental systems, the infant's world view shifts dramatically as each new stage is ushered in, and the world is seen dominantly, if not exclusively, in terms of the organization of the new stage. What happens, then, to the previous phases, to the earlier world views? Either they are eclipsed and drop out or, as Werner (1948) suggests, they remain dormant but become integrated into the emergent organization and thereby lose much of their previous character. As Cassirer (1955) puts it, the advent of a higher stage "does not destroy the earlier phase, rather it embraces it in its own perspective" (p. 477). This also happens in Piaget's system.

In these developmental progressions of phases, it is possible to return to something like an earlier phase. But special processes and conditions are needed to pull the person back, in developmental time, to experience the world in a manner similar to the way it was experienced earlier. In clinical theories, regression serves that purpose. In Werner and Kaplan's system (1963), one can move up and down the ontogenic spiral. These returns to previous and more global modes of experience are thought to occur mainly under conditions of challenge, stress, conflict, failure of adaptation, or fatigue, and in dream states, psychopathological conditions, or drug states. With the exception of these regressions, developing world views are mainly successive and sequential, not simultaneous. Current organizations of

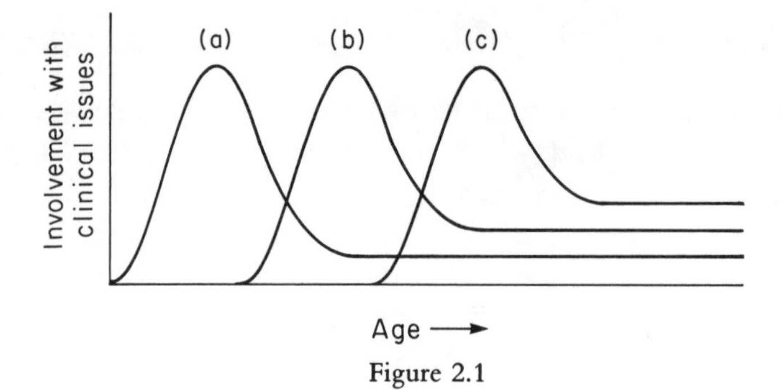

Figure 2.1

experience subsume earlier ones. They do not coexist with them. This developmental progression is schematized in figure 2.1, in which (a) could represent orality, trust, normal autism; (b) anality, autonomy; (c) genitality, and so on.

This view of development may be the most reasonable when one is considering the developmental progression of certain mental abilities or cognitive capacities, but that is not the present task. We are trying to consider the sense of self as it occurs in interpersonal encounters, and in that subjective sphere simultaneity of senses of the self appears to be closer to common experience. And no extraordinary conditions or processes need be present to permit the movement back and forth between experiences in different domains, that is, between different senses of the self.

An illustration from adult experience will help us to understand this simultaneity of senses of self. Making love, a fully involving interpersonal event, involves first the sense of the self and the other as discrete physical entities, as forms in motion—an experience in the domain of core-relatedness, as is the sense of self-agency, will, and activation encompassed in the physical acts. At the same time it involves the experience of sensing the other's subjective state: shared desire, aligned intentions, and mutual states of simultaneously shifting arousal, which occur in the domain of intersubjective relatedness. And if one of the lovers says for the first time "I love you," the words summarize what is occurring in the other domains (embraced in the verbal perspective) and perhaps introduce an entirely new note about the couple's relationship that may change the meaning of the history that has led up to and will follow the moment of saying it. This is an experience in the domain of verbal relatedness.

What about the domain of emergent relatedness? That is less

readily apparent, but it is present nonetheless. One may, for example "get lost in" the color of the other's eye, as if the eye were momentarily not part of the core other, unrelated to anyone's mental state, newly found, and outside of any larger organizing network. At the instant the "colored eye" comes again to belong to the known other, an emergent experience has occurred, an experience in the domain of emergent relatedness.[12]

We see that the subjective experience of social interactions seems to occur in all domains of relatedness simultaneously. One can certainly attend to one domain for a while to the partial exclusion of the others, but the others go on as distinct experiences, out of but available to awareness. In fact, much of what is meant by "socializing" is directed at focusing awareness on a single domain, usually the verbal, and declaring it to be the official version of what is being experienced, while denying the experience in the other domains ("unofficial" versions of what is happening). Nonetheless, attention can and does shift with some fluidity from experience in one domain to that in another. For instance, language in interpersonal service is largely the explication (in the verbal domain) of concomitant experiences in other domains, plus something else. If you ask someone to do something, and that person answers "I'd rather not. I'm surprised you asked!" he may at the same time raise his head and throw it back slightly, raise his eyebrows, and look down his nose a bit. The meaning of this nonverbal behavior (which is in the domain of core-relatedness and intersubjective relatedness) has been well rendered in language. Still these physical acts retain distinctive experiential characteristics. Performing or being the target of them involves experiences that reside outside of language itself.

All domains of relatedness remain active during development. The infant does not grow out of any of them; none of them atrophy, none become developmentally obsolete or get left behind. And once all domains are available, there is no assurance that any one domain will necessarily claim preponderance during any particular age period. None has a privileged status all of the time. Since there is an orderly temporal succession of emergence of each domain during develop-

12. These emergent experiences are descriptively disassociated from organizing perspectives. However, they are not the product of "disassociation" as a psychic process defined by psychoanalysis any more than is the initial impression of an isolated feature of a work of art viewed in the contemplative mode.

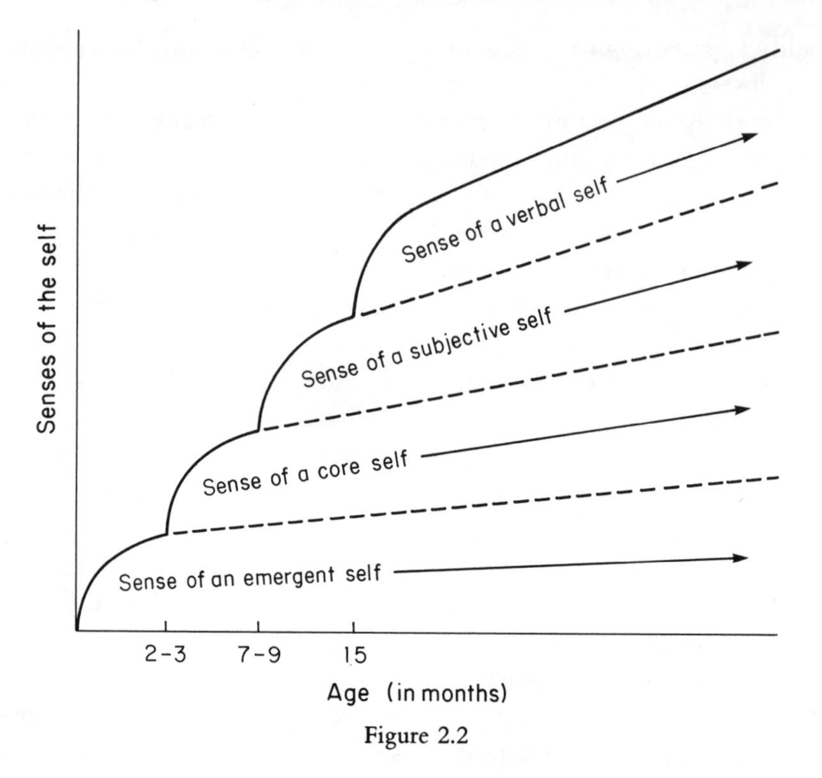

Figure 2.2

ment—first emergent, then core, then subjective, then verbal—there will inevitably be periods when one or two domains hold predominance by default. In fact, each successive organizing subjective perspective requires the preceding one as a precursor. Once formed, the domains remain forever as distinct forms of experiencing social life and self. None are lost to adult experience. Each simply gets more elaborated. It is for this reason that the term *domains* of relatedness has been chosen, rather than *phases* or *stages*.[13] The developmental situation as described is depicted in figure 2.2.

We can now return to the issue of sensitive periods. It seems that the initial period of formation for many developing psychological (and neurological) processes is a relatively sensitive one in the sense that an event occurring early will have a greater impact and its influence will be more difficult to reverse than an event occurring later. This general principle presumably applies to the formative

13. "Domains" seems preferable over "levels," because "levels" implies a hierarchical status that is accurate ontogenetically but need not pertain in the sphere of social life as subjectively experienced.

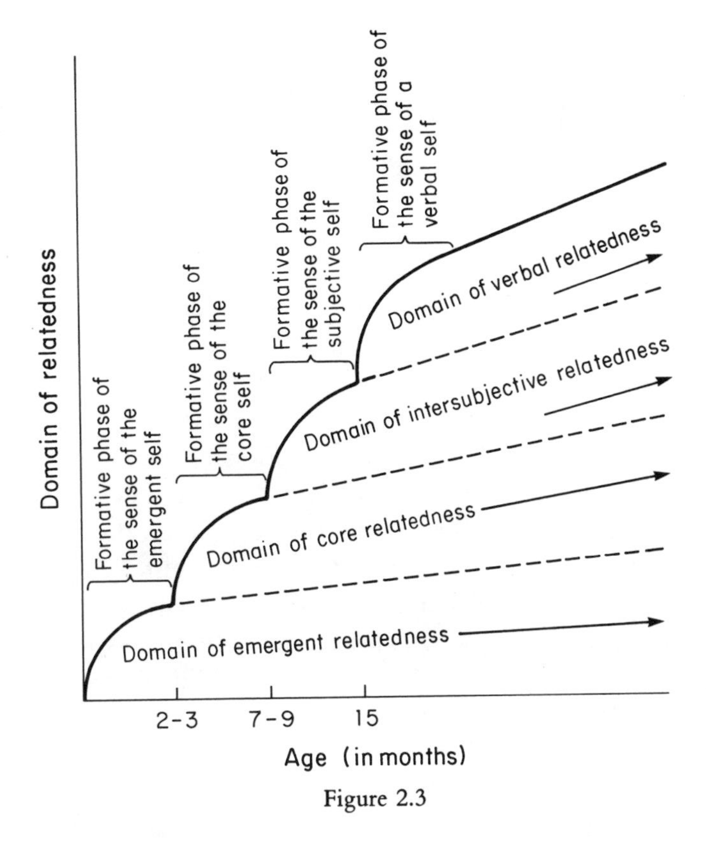

Figure 2.3

phase of each sense of the self. The timing of the formative phases is schematized in figure 2.3.

This view permits us to consider the formative phase for each sense of self as a sensitive period. The clinical implications of doing so will be considered in chapters 9 and 11.

What happens to the important clinical issues of autonomy, orality, symbiosis, individuation, trust, attachment, mastery, curiosity, and so on—the issues that occupy center stage in the therapeutic creation of the clinical infant? These clinical issues do not drop out of the picture at all. They simply hand over their role as primary organizers of subjective experience to the changing senses of self. Life-course clinical issues such as autonomy and attachment are worked on equally in all the domains of relatedness that are available at any given time. During each formative phase of relatedness, the arena of interpersonal action in which the issues get played out will change as the self and other are sensed as different. Accordingly, different forms of the same life-course issue develop in succession: for example, physical intimacy during core-relatedness, subjective (empathic-like) intimacy during intersubjective relatedness, and the intimacy of shared meanings during verbal relatedness. Thus, each life-course clinical issue has its own developmental line, and a slightly different contribution to that developmental line is made in each domain of relatedness.[14]

In summary, the subjective social life of the infant will be viewed as having the following characteristics. The infant is endowed with observable capacities that mature. When these become available, they are organized and transformed, in quantum mental leaps, into organizing subjective perspectives about the sense of self and other. Each new sense of self defines the formation of a new domain of relatedness. While these domains of relatedness result in qualitative shifts in social experience, they are not phases; rather, they are forms of social experience that remain intact throughout life. Nonetheless, their initial phase of formation constitutes a sensitive period of development. Subjective social experience results from the sum and integration of experience in all domains. The basic clinical issues are seen as issues for the life span and not as issues of developmental phases. A different contribution is made to the ontogeny of the developmental lines of all clinical issues as each domain of self-experience emerges.

With this much of the point of view and approach in hand, we can turn in the next section of this book to a closer look at the four senses of self and their four domains of relatedness. We will bring together the observational and clinical evidence that argues for this view of the development of the infant's subjective social experience.

14. This treatment of lines of development is an extreme version of the same idea put forward by A. Freud (1965). However, she did not fully abandon the notion of libidinal phase specificity. The present suggestion is a rejection of that notion. Here, all clinical issues become developmental lines, and no hidden or ultimately clinical issues remain anchored to any given developmental epochs.

PART II

THE FOUR SENSES OF SELF

Chapter 3

The Sense of an Emergent Self

THE AGE of two months is almost as clear a boundary as birth itself. At about eight weeks, infants undergo a qualitative change: they begin to make direct eye-to-eye contact. Shortly thereafter they begin to smile more frequently, but also responsively and infectiously. They begin to coo. In fact, much more goes on during this developmental shift than what is reflected by increased overt social behaviors. Most learning is faster and more inclusive. Strategies for paying attention to the world shift in terms of altered visual scanning patterns. Motor patterns mature. Sensorimotor intelligence reaches a higher level, as Piaget has described. Electroencephalograms reveal major changes. Diurnal hormonal milieu stabilizes, along with sleep and activity cycles. Almost everything changes. And all observers of infants, including parents, agree on this (Piaget 1952; Sander 1962; Spitz 1965; Emde et al. 1976; Brazelton et al. 1979; Haith 1980; Greenspan and Lourie 1981; Bronson 1982).

Until this developmental shift occurs, the infant is generally thought to occupy some kind of presocial, precognitive, preorganized life phase that stretches from birth to two months. The central questions of this chapter are, how might the infant experience the social world during this initial period? And what might be the infant's sense of self during this time? I conclude that during the first two months the infant is actively forming a sense of an emergent self. It is a sense of organization in the process of formation, and it is a sense of self that will remain active for the rest of life. An overarching sense of self is not yet achieved in this period, but it is coming into being. To understand how this conclusion was reached, it is necessary to understand the likely nature of infant experience at this age.

In the last fifteen years a revolution has occurred in observing and thereby evaluating infants. One result of this revolution is that the infant's subjective social life during the first two months has had to be reconsidered.

Observing the Young Infant: A Revolution in Infancy Research

The following description of the revolution in infancy research is intended to serve several purposes: to show some of the infant capacities that bear on forming a sense of self, capacities that no one imagined to be present so early one or two decades ago; to provide a common vocabulary and set of concepts for what is to follow; and, perhaps most important, to expand the frame of reference about infants that is commonly prevalent among clinicians and others who have not been able to keep up with the rapidly growing literature on infancy. Knowledge of the newly discovered infant capabilities will in itself do the expanding.

People have always had questions they would like to have asked of infants. What do infants see, smell, feel, think, want? Good questions abounded, but answers were scarce. How could an infant answer? The revolution in research consisted of turning the situation on its head, by asking not, what is a good question to pose to an infant? but, what might an infant be able to do (like sucking) that would serve as an answer? With this simple turn-around, the search for infant abilities that could be made into answers (response measures) began, and the revolution was set in motion.

One other change in view was required. This was the realization that newborns are not always in a state of sleep, hunger, eating, fussing, crying, or full activity. If that were the case, all potential behavioral "answers" would always be either already in action or precluded by another activity or state. But it is not the case. Starting from birth, infants regularly occupy a state called alert inactivity, when they are physically quiet and alert and apparently are taking in external events (Wolff 1966). Furthermore, alert inactivity can last several minutes, sometimes longer, and recurs regularly and frequently during wakefulness. Alert inactivity provides the needed time "window" in which questions can be put to newborns and answers can be discerned from their ongoing activity.

The issue at stake is, how can we know what infant's "know"? Good infant "answers" have to be readily observable behaviors that are frequently performed, that are under voluntary muscular control, and that can be solicited during alert inactivity. Three such behavioral answers immediately qualify, beginning at birth: head-turning, sucking, and looking.

The newborn does not have good control of his or her head and cannot hold it aloft in the upright position. But when lying on their backs so that their heads are supported, newborns do have adequate control to turn the head to the left or right. Head-turning became the answer to the following question: can infants tell the smell of their own mothers' milk? MacFarlane (1975) placed three-day-old infants on their backs and then placed breast pads taken from their nursing mothers on one side of their heads. On the other side, he placed breast pads taken from other nursing women. The newborns reliably turned their heads toward their own mothers' pads, regardless of which side the pads were placed on. The head-turning answered MacFarland's question in the affirmative: infants are able to discriminate the smell of their own mothers' milk.

Newborns are good suckers. Life depends on sucking, a behavior that is controlled by voluntary muscles. When not nursing (nutritive sucking), infants engage in a great deal of non-nutritive sucking on anything they can get hold of, including their own tongues. Non-nutritive sucking occurs during the newborn's periods of alert inactivity, making it a potentially good "answer." Infants can rapidly be trained to suck to get something to happen. It is done by placing a pacifier with an electronically bugged nipple—that is, one with a pressure transducer inside it—in the infant's mouth. The transducer is hooked up to the starter mechanism of a tape recorder or slide carousel, so that when the infant sucks at certain specified rates the recorder goes on or the carousel turns over a new slide. In that way infants control what they hear or see by maintaining some rate of sucking (Siqueland and DeLucia 1969). Sucking was used to determine whether infants are especially interested in the human voice, in preference to other sounds of the same pitch and loudness. The infants' sucking rates answered the question affirmatively (Friedlander 1970).

Newborns arrive with a visual motor system that is mature in many respects. They see reasonably well at the right focal distance, and the reflexes controlling the eye movements responsible for object fixation and visual pursuit are intact at birth. Infant looking patterns are thus a third potential "answer." Fantz (1963), in a series of pioneering studies, used infant visual preferences to answer the question, do infants prefer looking at faces rather than at various other visual patterns? They do indeed, though the reasons are complicated. (Note that all three questions asked in these studies concern interpersonal or social issues and attest to the early responsiveness of infants to their social world.)

To yoke these "answers"[1] to more interesting questions, several paradigms have been developed and elaborated. To learn whether an infant prefers one thing over another, one need only put the two stimuli in competition in a "paired comparison preference paradigm" and see which stimulus wins out for attention. For instance, if an infant is shown a symmetrical pattern in which the left side is the mirror image of the right side, and next to it is shown the same pattern lying on its side, so the top half is the mirror image of the bottom half, the infant will look longer at the left-right mirror images than at the top-bottom mirror images (see Sherrod 1981). Conclusion: infants prefer symmetry in the vertical plane, characteristic of human faces, to symmetry in the horizontal plane. (Note that parents automatically tend to align their faces to the infant's in the vertical plane.)

But suppose there is no preference for one thing over another. Can we still find out if the infant can tell them apart? To determine if infants can discriminate one thing from another, some form of the "habituation/dishabituation" paradigm is used. This method is based

1. Heart rate change and evoked potentials as psychological responses to external events also can be used as answers, either alone or to validate the behavioral answers.

on the notion that if the same thing is presented to infants repeatedly, they will respond to it progressively less. Presumably, this reaction of habituation is due to the fact that the original stimulus becomes less and less effective as it loses its novelty. In effect, the infant gets bored with it (Sokolov 1960; Berlyne 1966). If one wishes to know, for example, if infants can discriminate a smiling face from a surprise face, one presents the smiling face six or so times as the infants look at it progressively less. The surprise face of the same person is then substituted for the next expected presentation of the smiling face. If the infants notice the substitution they will dishabituate, that is, look at it a lot, as they did the smiling face at its first presentation. If they cannot tell the surprise face from the smiling one, then they will continue to habituate, that is, look at it as little as they had come to look at the smiling face after seeing it repeatedly.

These procedures tell only if infants can make a discrimination or not. They do not tell whether they have formed any concept or representation of the properties that generally make up a smile. To know that, one must take an additional step. It must be shown, for example, that an infant will discriminate a smile regardless of whose face it is on. One then can say that the infant has an abstract representation of the invariant (unchanging) properties that constitute smiles regardless of variant (changing) properties such as whose face is wearing the smile.

Using these kinds of experimental paradigms and these methods of eliciting "answers" from infants, an impressive body of information has been gathered. The examples given not only explain how one inquires about infants and hint at the capacities that infants are being found to have; they also help in laying out the information from which we can draw some general principles about infant perception, cognition, and affect that will be needed for the arguments in this chapter and elsewhere (see Kessen et al. 1970; Cohen and Salapatek 1975; Kagan et al. 1978; Lamb and Sherrod 1981; Lipsitt 1983; Field and Fox, in press). These, in brief, are:

1. Infants seek sensory stimulation. Furthermore, they do it with the preemptory quality that is prerequisite to hypothesizing drives and motivational systems.
2. They have distinct biases or preferences with regard to the sensations they seek and the perceptions they form. These are innate.

3. From birth on, there appears to be a central tendency to form and test hypotheses about what is occurring in the world (Bruner 1977). Infants are also constantly "evaluating," in the sense of asking, is this different from or the same as that? How discrepant is what I have just encountered from what I have previously encountered (Kagan et al. 1978)? It is clear that this central tendency of mind, with constant application, will rapidly categorize the social world into conforming and contrasting patterns, events, sets, and experiences. The infant will readily discover which features of an experience are invariant and which are variant—that is, which features "belong" to the experience (J. Gibson 1950, 1979; E. Gibson 1969). The infant will apply these same processes to whatever sensations and perceptions are available, from the simplest to the ultimately most complex—that is, thoughts about thoughts.
4. Affective and cognitive processes cannot be readily separated. In a simple learning task, activation builds up and falls off. Learning itself is motivated and affect-laden. Similarly, in an intense affective moment, perception and cognition go on. And, finally, affective experiences (for example, the many different occasions of surprise) have their own invariant and variant features. Sorting these is a cognitive task concerning affective experience.

This view of the young infant, made possible by the revolution in research, is mainly cognitive and determined in large part by the nature of experimental observations. But what about the young infant as viewed by clinicians or parents, and what about the more affective infant with motivations and appetites that force the infant out of the state of alert inactivity? It is here that the divergence between the observed and clinical infant may begin.

The Clinical and Parental View of the Young Infant

The vast majority of the mother's time during the infant's first two months is spent in regulating and stabilizing sleep-wake, day-night, and hunger-satiation cycles. Sander (1962, 1964) has called the primary task of this early period that of physiological regulation, and Greenspan (1981) that of homeostasis.

When the baby first comes home from the hospital, the new parents live from minute to minute, attempting to regulate the newborn. After a few days they may be able to see twenty minutes into the future. By the end of a few weeks, they have the luxury of a future that is predictable for stretches of time as long as an hour or two. And after four to six weeks, regular time clumps of three to four hours are possible. The tasks of eating, getting to sleep, and general homeostasis are generally accompanied by social behaviors by the parents: rocking, touching, soothing, talking, singing, and making noises and faces. These occur in response to infant behaviors that are also mainly social, such as crying, fretting, smiling, and gazing. A great deal of social interaction goes on in the service of physiological regulation. Sometimes parents fail to appreciate that social interactions are happening when they so realistically have their eye on the goal of the activity, such as soothing the baby; the ends seem all important, and the means to those ends go unnoticed as moments of interpersonal relatedness. At other times, parents do focus on the social interaction and act, from the beginning, as though the infant had a sense of self. Parents immediately attribute their infants with intentions ("Oh, you want to see that"), motives ("You're doing that so Mommy will hurry up with the bottle"), and authorship of action ("You threw that one away on purpose, huh?"). It is almost impossible to conduct social interaction with infants without attributing these human qualities to them. These qualities make human behavior understandable, and parents invariably treat their infants as understandable beings, that is, as the people they are about to become, by working in the infant's zone of proximal development.[2]

Parents thus view young infants on the one hand as physiological systems in need of regulation and, on the other hand, as fairly developed people with subjective experiences, social sensibilities, and a sense of self that is growing, if not already in place.

Classical psychoanalysis has focused almost exclusively on physiological regulation during this early period, while seeing right past the fact that much of this regulation was actually conducted via the mutual exchange of social behaviors. This approach has resulted in

2. While parents are consummate experts at this alignment with the future states of being of their infants, there is a related phenomenon in therapy. Friedman (1982) points out that "it is not necessary for the analyst to know the exact nature of the development he is encouraging. It is sufficient that he treats the patient as though he were roughly the person he is about to become. The patient will explore being treated that way, and fill in the personal details" (p. 12).

the picture of a fairly asocial infant, but it has also provided a rich description of the infant's inner life as it is affected by changes in physiological state. For instance, Freud (1920) saw infants shielded from relatedness by the "stimulus barrier" that protected them from having to register and deal with external stimulation, including other people. Mahler, Pine, and Bergman (1975) have viewed infants as occupying a state of "normal autism," essentially unrelated to others. In both of these views infants are related to others only indirectly, to the extent that the others influence their internal states of hunger, fatigue, and so on. In these views, infants remain in a prolonged state of undifferentiation, in which no social world exists, subjectively, to help them discover a sense of self or of other. On the other hand, the fluctuating affects and physiological tensions that befall infants are seen as the wellspring of experiences that will ultimately define a sense of self. These experiences occupy center stage for the first two months.

The British object relations "school" and H. S. Sullivan, an American parallel, were unique among clinical theorists in believing that human social relatedness is present from birth, that it exists for its own sake, is of a definable nature, and does not lean upon physiological need states (Balint 1937; Klein 1952; Sullivan 1953; Fairbairn 1954; Guntrip 1971). Currently, the attachment theorists have further elaborated this view with objective data (Bowlby 1969; Ainsworth 1979). These views consider the infant's *direct* social experience, which parents have always intuited to be part of the infant's subjective life, to be the central focus of concern.

All these clinical theories have a common assertion: that infants have a very active subjective life, filled with changing passions and confusions, and that they experience a state of undifferentiation by struggling with blurred social events that presumably are seen as unconnected and unintegrated. These clinical views have identified some of the salient experiences of internal state fluctuations and social relatedness that could contribute to a sense of self, but they have not been in a position to discover the mental capacities that might lead the infant to use these experiences to differentiate a sense of self or of other. That is where the experimental work of developmentalists makes its contribution. It permits us to look at how the infant might experience the worlds of affect and changes in tension state as well as the perceptions of the external world that accompany affect and tension changes. After all, it is the integration of all of these that will constitute the infant's social experience.

The Nature of the Emergent Sense of Self: the Experience of Process and Product

We can now return to the central question: what kind of sense of self is possible during this initial period? The notion that it exists at all at these very early ages is generally dismissed or not even broached, because the idea of a sense of self is usually reserved for some overarching and integrating schema, concept, or perspective about the self. And clearly, during this early period infants are not capable of such an overview. They have separate, unrelated experiences that have yet to be integrated into one embracing perspective.

The ways in which the relations between disparate experiences can come into being have been the basic subject matter of much of the works of Piaget, the Gibsons, and associational learning theorists. Clinical theorists have lumped all these processes together and described them metaphorically as the forming of "islands of consistency" (Escalona 1953). They describe the leaps that make up this development of organization in terms of the cognitions at each progressive step or level. They thus tend to interpret the *product* of those integrating leaps as the sense of self. But what about the *process* itself—the very experience of making the leaps and creating relations between previously unrelated events or forming partial organizations or consolidating sensorimotor schemas. Can the infant experience not only the sense of an organization already formed and grasped, but the coming-into-being of organization? I am suggesting that the infant can experience the *process* of emerging organization as well as the result, and it is this experience of emerging organization that I call the *emergent sense of self.* It is the experience of a process as well as a product.

The emergence of organization is no more than a form of learning. And learning experiences are powerful events in an infant's life. As we have already noted, infants are predesigned to seek out and engage in learning opportunities. All observers of learning, in any form, have been impressed with how strongly motivated (that is, positively reinforcing) is the creation of new mental organizations. It has been proposed that the early learning described by Piaget that results in the consolidation of sensorimotor schemes such as thumb-to-mouth is intrinsically motivated (Sameroff 1984). The experience of forming organization involves both the motivated process and the reinforcing product; I will focus here more on the process.[3]

But first, can infants also experience non-organization? No! The "state" of undifferentiation is an excellent example of non-organization. Only an observer who has enough perspective to know the future course of things can even imagine an undifferentiated state. Infants cannot know *what* they do not know, nor *that* they do not know. The traditional notions of clinical theorists have taken the observer's knowledge of infants—that is, relative undifferentiation compared with the differentiated view of older children—reified it, and given it back, or attributed it, to infants as their own dominant subjective sense of things. If, on the other hand, one does not reify undifferentiation as an attribute of the infant's subjective experience, the picture looks quite different. Many separate experiences exist, with what for the infant may be exquisite clarity and vividness. The lack of relatedness between these experiences is not noticed.

When the diverse experiences are in some way yoked (associated, assimilated, or connected in some other way), the infant experiences the emergence of organization. In order for the infant to have any formed sense of self, there must ultimately be some organization that is sensed as a reference point. The first such organization concerns the body: its coherence, its actions, its inner feeling states, and the memory of all these. That is the experiential organization with which the sense of a core self is concerned. Immediately prior to that, however, the reference organization for a sense of self is still forming; in other words, it is emergent. The sense of an emergent self thus concerns the process and product of forming organization. It concerns the learning about the relations between the infant's sensory experiences. But that is essentially what all learning is about.

3. The self-organizing tendencies of many systems have been noted, and Stechler and Kaplan (1980) have applied these notions to the self in development. The concern here is, however, with the subjective experience of forming organization.

Learning is certainly not designed for the exclusive purpose of forming a sense of self, but a sense of self will be one of the many vital byproducts of the general learning capacity.

The sense of an emergent self thus includes two components, the products of forming relations between isolated experiences and the process. The products will be discussed in greater detail in the next chapter, on the sense of a core self, which describes which products come together to form the first encompassing perspective of the self. In this chapter I will focus more sharply on the process, or the experience of organization-coming-into-being. To do so, I will examine the various processes available to the young infant for creating relational organization and the kinds of subjective experiences that might evolve from engaging in these processes.

Processes Involved in Forming the Sense of an Emergent Self and Other

AMODAL PERCEPTION

In the late 1970s, the findings of several experiments raised profound doubts about how infants learn about the world, that is, how they connect experiences. What was at stake was the long-standing philosophical and psychological problem of perceptual unity—how we come to know that something seen, heard, and touched may in fact be the same thing. How do we coordinate information that comes from several different perceptual modalities but emanates from a single external source? These experiments drew widespread attention to the infant's capacity to transfer perceptual experience from one sensory modality to another and did so in an experimental format open to replication.

Meltzoff and Borton's experiment (1979) lays out the problem and issue clearly. They blindfolded three-week-old infants and gave them one of two different pacifiers to suck on. One pacifier had a spherical-shaped nipple and the other was a nipple with nubs protruding from various points around its surface. After the baby had had some experience feeling (touching) the nipple with only the mouth, the nipple was removed and placed side by side with the other kind of nipple. The blindfold was taken off. After a quick visual comparison, infants looked more at the nipple they had just sucked.

These findings seemed to run counter to current accounts of infant learning and world knowledge. On theoretical grounds, infants should not have been able to do this task. A Piagetian account would have required that they first form a schema of what the nipple felt like (a haptic schema) and a schema of what the nipple looked like (a visual schema); then these two schemas would have to have some traffic or interaction (reciprocal assimilation), so that a coordinated visual-haptic schema would result (Piaget 1952). Only then could the infants accomplish the task. Clearly, the infants did not in fact have to go through these steps of construction. They immediately "knew" that the one they now saw was the one they had just felt. Similarly, a strict learning theory or associationist account of these findings would be at a total loss to explain them, since the infants had had no prior experience to form the required associations between what was felt and what was seen. (For fuller accounts of the problem in its theoretical context, see Bower 1972, 1974, 1976; Moore and Meltzoff 1978; Moes 1980; Spelke 1980; Meltzoff and Moore 1983.) While this haptic-visual transfer of information appears to improve and get faster as infants get older (Rose et al. 1972), it is clear that the capacity is present in the first weeks of life. Infants are predesigned to be able to perform a cross-modal transfer of information that permits them to recognize a correspondence across touch and vision. In this case the yoking of the tactile and visual experiences is brought about by way of the innate design of the perceptual system not by way of repeated world experience. No learning is needed initially, and subsequent learning about relations across modalities can be built upon this innate base.

The correspondence just described occurred between touch and vision, and it concerned shape. What about other modalities, and what about other qualities of perception, such as intensity and time? Are infants equally gifted in recognizing these cross-modal equivalences? Using heart rate as an outcome measure in a habituation paradigm, Lewcowicz and Turkewitz (1980) "asked" three-week-old infants which levels of light intensity (luminescence of white light) corresponded best with certain levels of sound intensity (decibels of white noise). The infant was habituated to one level of sound, and attempts at dishabituation were then made with various levels of light, and vice versa. In essence, the results revealed that these young infants did find that certain absolute levels of sound intensity corresponded with specific absolute levels of light intensity. Furthermore, the matches of intensity level across modes that the three-week-olds found to be most correspondent were the same matches that adults chose. Thus, the ability to perform audio-visual cross-modal matching of the absolute level of intensity appears to be well within infants' capacity by three weeks of age.

How about time? At present, few experiments bear directly on the question of whether an infant can translate temporal information across perceptual modalities (see Allen et al. 1977; Demany et al. 1977; Humphrey et al. 1979; Wagner and Sakowitz 1983; Lewcowicz, in press; and Morrongiello 1984). Using heart rate and behavior as the respondent measures, these investigators show that infants recognize that an auditory temporal pattern is correspondent with a similar visually presented temporal pattern. It is almost certain that in the near future there will be many more such experiments demonstrating infants' capacities to transfer, intermodally, the properties of duration, beat, and rhythm, as specifically defined. These temporal properties are readily perceived in all modalities and are excellent candidates as properties of experience that can be transferred cross-modally, because it is becoming clearer that the infant from early in life is exquisitely sensible of and sensitive to the temporal features of the environment (Stern and Gibbon 1978; DeCasper 1980; Miller and Byrne 1984).

Of all these transfers of properties between modes, the hardest to imagine is how an infant might be able to transfer information about shape between the visual and auditory modes. Shape is not usually conceived of as an acoustic event; the shape transfer is easier to imagine across the tactile and visual modes. But speech itself, in a natural situation, is a visual as well as an acoustic configuration, because the lips move. Intelligibility goes up considerably when the lips are in view. By six weeks, babies tend to look more closely at faces that speak (Haith 1980). Moreover, when the actual sound produced is in conflict with the lip movements seen, the visual information unexpectedly predominates over the auditory. In other words, we hear what we *see,* not what is *said* (McGurk and MacDonald 1976).[4]

The question then seems irresistible: can infants recognize the correspondence between auditorily and visually presented speech sounds? That is, can they detect the correspondence between the configuration of a sound as heard and the configuration of the articulatory movements of the mouth that produce the sound as seen? Two separate laboratories working simultaneously on this problem came up with a positive answer (MacKain et al. 1981, 1983; Kuhl and Meltzoff 1982). The two experiments used a similar paradigm but different stimuli. They both presented the infant with two faces seen simultaneously. One face articulated one sound and the second face articulated a different sound, but only one of the two sounds was actually produced for the infant to hear. The question was whether the infant looked longer at the "right" face. MacKain et al. used a variety of disyllables as stimuli (mama, lulu, baby, zuzu), while Kuhl and Meltzoff used single vowels "ah" and "ee." Both experiments found that the infants did recognize the audio-visual correspondences.[5] The concordant results of the two experiments greatly strengthen the finding.

How about the sensation of one's own movement or position, that is, the modality of proprioception? In 1977, it was shown that three-week-old infants would imitate an adult model in sticking out their tongues and opening their mouths (Meltzoff and Moore 1977). While the ability to perform these early imitations had been observed previously and commented upon (Maratos 1973; Uzgiris 1974; Trevarthan 1977), the strongest possible inferences had not been made—namely, that there was an innate correspondence between what infants saw and what they did. Subsequent experiments showed that even the protrusion of a pencil or the like could also produce infant tongue protrusion.

Later, the issue was removed to the sphere of affect expression. Field et al. (1982) reported that newborn infants, age two days, would reliably imitate an adult model who either smiled, frowned,

4. For instance, if one views a mouth articulating (silently) the sound "da" and hears a voice-over with the sound "ba," one will experience "da" or sometimes an intermediate sound "ga."

5. MacKain et al. found that this particular audio-visual matching task was facilitated by left hemispheric activation, but discussion of that finding is beyond the scope of this book.

or showed a surprise face. The problems presented by these findings are manifold. How do babies "know" that they have a face or facial features? How do they "know" that the face they see is anything like the face they have? How do they "know" that specific configurations of that other face, as only seen, correspond to the same specific configurations in their own face as only felt, proprioceptively, and never seen? The amount of cross-modal fluency in terms of predesign is extraordinary. This is a special case, however, because one does not know whether the infant's response is imitative or reflex-like. Does the sight of a specific visual configuration of the other's face correspond to a proprioceptive configuration in the infant's own face? In this case one can talk about cross-modal correspondence (vision-proprioception). Or does the specific configuration on the other's face trigger a specific motor program to perform the same act? In that case one is talking about a specific innate social releasing stimulus. At present, it is not possible to make a definitive choice (see Burd and Milewski 1981).

Infants thus appear to have an innate general capacity, which can be called *amodal perception,* to take information received in one sensory modality and somehow translate it into another sensory modality. We do not know how they accomplish this task. The information is probably not experienced as belonging to any one particular sensory mode. More likely it transcends mode or channel and exists in some unknown supra-modal form. It is not, then, a simple issue of a direct translation across modalities. Rather, it involves an encoding into a still mysterious amodal *representation,* which can then be recognized in any of the sensory modes.

Infants appear to experience a world of perceptual unity, in which they can perceive amodal qualities in any modality from any form of human expressive behavior, represent these qualities abstractly, and then transpose them to other modalities. This position has been strongly put forth by developmentalists such as Bower (1974), Moore and Meltzoff (1978), and Meltzoff (1981), who posit that the infant, from the earliest days of life, forms and acts upon abstract representations of qualities of perception. These abstract representations that the infant experiences are not sights and sounds and touches and nameable objects, but rather shapes, intensities, and temporal patterns—the more "global" qualities of experience. And the need and ability to form abstract representations of primary qualities of perception and act upon them starts at the beginning of mental life; it is not the culmination or a developmental landmark reached in the second year of life.

How might amodal perception contribute to a sense of an emergent self or a sense of an emergent other? Take the infant's experience of the mother's breast as an example. Does the baby initially experience two unrelated "breasts," the "sucked breast" and the "seen breast"? A Piagetian account would have said yes, as would most psychoanalytic accounts, since they have adopted Piagetian or associationist assumptions. The present account would say no. The breast would emerge as an already integrated experience of (a part of) the other, from the unlearned yoking of visual and tactile sensations. The same is true for the infant's finger or fist, as seen and sucked, as well as for many other common experiences of self and other. Infants do not need repeated experience to begin to form some of the pieces of an emergent self and other. They are predesigned to forge certain integrations.

While amodal perceptions will help the infant integrate potentially diverse experiences of self and other, a sense of an emergent self is concerned not only with the product but with the process of integration, as we saw earlier. Ultimately, the breast as seen and the breast as sucked will become related, whether by amodal perception, by assimilation of schemas, or by repeated association. What might the particular experience of amodally derived integration be like as an emergent experience, compared with an integration brought about by assimilation or association? Each process of relating diverse events may constitute a different and characteristic emergent experience.

For instance, the actual experience of looking for the first time at something that, on the basis of how it felt to the touch, should look a certain way and having it, indeed, look that way is something like a déjà vu experience. The infant presumably does not anticipate how an object should look and therefore has no experience of cognitive confirmation. Many would suggest that such an experience would go totally unnoticed, or that at most it would be registered nonspecifically as "all-rightness" with smooth functioning. They would further suggest that the experience would take on specific qualities only if sight happened to disconfirm the tactile information—again a cognitive perspective on the matter. I suggest that at a preverbal level (outside of awareness) the experience of finding a cross-modal match (especially the first time) would feel like a correspondence or imbuing of present experience with something prior or familiar. Present experience would feel related in some way to experience from elsewhere. This primitive form of a déjà vu event is quite different from the process of making associational linkages, which may have more the quality of a discovery—that two things already apprehended belong together. It is likely that in this domain of emergent experience there is also the experience of premonition of a hidden future in the process of revealing a structure that can only be sensed opaquely. A typology of such events at the experiential level rather than at a conceptual level is greatly needed.

"PHYSIOGNOMIC" PERCEPTION

Heinz Werner (1948) proposed a different kind of amodal perception in the young infant, which he called "physiognomic" perception. In Werner's view, the amodal qualities that are directly experienced by the infant are categorical affects rather than perceptual qualities such as shape, intensity, and number. For instance, a simple two-dimensional line or a color or a sound is perceived to be happy ( ), sad (), or angry (). Affect acts as the supra-modal currency into which stimulation in any modality can be translated. This is a kind of amodal perception too, since an affect experience is not bound to any one modality of perception. All of us engage in "feeling perception"—but is it frequent, continuous, or otherwise? It is likely to be a component (though usually unconscious) of every act of perception. Its mechanism, however, remains a mystery, as does the mechanism of amodal perception in general. Werner suggested that it arose from experience with the human face in all its emotional displays, hence the name "physiognomic" perception. To date there is no empirical evidence, only speculation, about its existence or nature in young infants.

"VITALITY AFFECTS"

We have so far considered two ways in which the infant experiences the world about him. The experiments on cross-modal capacities suggest that some properties of people and things, such as shape, intensity level, motion, number, and rhythm, are experienced directly as global, amodal perceptual qualities. And Werner suggests that some aspects of people and things will be experienced directly as categorical affects (angry, sad, happy, and so on).

There is a third quality of experience that can arise directly from encounters with people, a quality that involves vitality affects. What do we mean by this, and why is it necessary to add a new term for certain forms of human experience? It is necessary because many qualities of feeling that occur do not fit into our existing lexicon or taxonomy of affects. These elusive qualities are better captured by dynamic, kinetic terms, such as "surging," "fading away," "fleeting," "explosive," "crescendo," "decrescendo," "bursting," "drawn out," and so on. These qualities of experience are most certainly sensible to infants and of great daily, even momentary, importance. It is these feelings that will be elicited by changes in motivational states, appetites, and tensions. The philosopher Suzanne Langer (1967) insisted that in any experience-near psychology, close attention must be paid to the many "forms of feeling" inextricably involved with all the vital processes of life, such as breathing, getting hungry, eliminating, falling asleep and emerging out of sleep, or feeling the coming and going of emotions and thoughts. The different forms of feeling elicited by these vital processes impinge on the organism most of the time. We are never without their presence, whether or not we are conscious of them, while "regular" affects come and go.

The infant experiences these qualities from within, as well as in the behavior of other persons. Different feelings of vitality can be expressed in a multitude of parental acts that do not qualify as "regular" affective acts: how the mother picks up baby, folds the diapers, grooms her hair or the baby's hair, reaches for a bottle, unbuttons her blouse. The infant is immersed in these "feelings of vitality." Examining them further will let us enrich the concepts and vocabulary, too impoverished for present purposes, that we apply to nonverbal experiences.

A first question is, why do these important experiences not fit into the terms and concepts of already existing affect theories? Usually one thinks of affective experience in terms of discrete categories of affect—happiness, sadness, fear, anger, disgust, surprise, interest, and perhaps shame, and their combinations. It was Darwin's great contribution (1892) to postulate that each of these had an innate discrete facial display and a distinct quality of feeling and that these innate patterns evolved as social signals "understood" by all members to enhance species survival.[6] Each discrete category of affect is also generally thought to be experienced along at least two commonly agreed upon dimensions: *activation* and *hedonic tone.* Activation refers to the amount of intensity or urgency of the feeling quality, while hedonic tone refers to the degree to which the feeling quality is pleasurable or unpleasurable.[7]

Vitality affects do not comfortably fit into these current theories of affect, and for that reason they require a separate name. Yet they are definitely feelings and belong within the domain of affective experience. They will be tentatively called *vitality affects,* to distinguish them from the traditional or Darwinian *categorical affects* of anger, joy, sadness, and so on.

Vitality affects occur both in the presence of and in the absence of categorical affects. For example, a "rush" of anger or of joy, a perceived flooding of light, an accelerating sequence of thoughts, an unmeasurable wave of feeling evoked by music, and a shot of narcotics can all feel like "rushes." They all share similar envelopes of neural firings, although in different parts of the nervous system.

6. These seven or eight discrete expressions, taken alone or in combinatory blends, account for the entire emotional repertoire of facial expressiveness in man. This has come to be known as the "discrete affect hypothesis." And this hypothesis has proven very robust for over one hundred years. Well-known cross-cultural studies indicate fairly convincingly that photographs of the basic facial expressions will be similarly recognized and identified in all cultures tested (Ekman 1971; Izard 1971). Universality in the face of wide socio-cultural differences argues for innateness. Similarly, it is now well known that a child born blind shows the normally expected repertoire of facial expressions until about three to four months (Freedman 1964; Fraiberg 1971), strongly suggesting that these discrete display patterns are innate, emerging without the need of learning provided by the feedback of vision. However, when we inquire about the subjective quality of feeling associated with any facial expression, the cross-cultural fit appears to be present but less tight. The *central* sensation of sadness can have its own distinctive qualities as verbally expressed by one people compared with another people (Lutz 1982). We share the same finite set of affect expressions, but not necessarily the same set of feeling qualities.

7. Some affect categories such as happiness or sadness are always pleasurable or unpleasurable, but to varying degrees others, like surprise, are not. Generally, activation and hedonic tone are seen as dimensions along which categories of affects are experienced. For example, exuberant joy is the happiness category of affect experienced at the high end of the activation dimension, in contrast to, say, contemplative bliss, which is also in the happiness category but experienced at the low end of activation. Both feelings, however, could be judged to be equally pleasurable in hedonic tone. Conversely, pleasant surprise and unpleasant surprise fall at different ends of the hedonic tone dimension but could be at the same level on the activation dimension. There are other dimensions along which affect categories are thought to fall (see Arnold 1970; Dahl and Stengel 1978; Plutchik 1980).

The felt quality of any of these similar changes is what I call the vitality affect of a "rush."

Expressiveness of this kind is not limited to categorical affect signals. It is inherent in all behavior. Various activation contours or vitality affects can be experienced not only during the performance of a categorical signal, such as an "explosive" smile, but also in a behavior that has no inherent categorical affect signal value; for example, one can see someone get out of a chair "explosively." One does not know whether the explosiveness in arising was due to anger, surprise, joy, or fright. The explosiveness could be linked to any of those Darwinian feeling qualities, or to none. The person could have gotten out of the chair with no specific category of affect but with a burst of determination. There are a thousand smiles, a thousand getting-out-of-chairs, a thousand variations of performance of any and all behaviors, and each one presents a different vitality affect.

The expressiveness of vitality affects can be likened to that of a puppet show. The puppets have little or no capacity to express categories of affect by way of facial signals, and their repertoire of conventionalized gestural or postural affect signals is usually impoverished. It is from the way they move in general that we infer the different vitality affects from the activation contours they trace. Most often, the characters of different puppets are largely defined in terms of particular vitality affects; one may be lethargic, with drooping limbs and hanging head, another forceful, and still another jaunty.

Abstract dance and music are examples par excellence of the expressiveness of vitality affects. Dance reveals to the viewer-listener multiple vitality affects and their variations, without resorting to plot or categorical affect signals from which the vitality affects can be derived. The choreographer is most often trying to express a way of feeling, not a specific content of feeling. This example is particularly instructive because the infant, when viewing parental behavior that has no intrinsic expressiveness (that is, no Darwinian affect signal), may be in the same position as the viewer of an abstract dance or the listener to music. The manner of performance of a parent's act expresses a vitality affect, whether or not the act is (or is partially colored with) some categorical affect.

One can readily imagine, in fact, that the infant does not initially perceive overt acts as such, as do adults. (This act is a reach for the bottle. That act is the unfolding of a diaper.) Rather, the infant is far more likely to perceive directly and begin to categorize acts in terms of the vitality affects they express. Like dance for the adult, the social world experienced by the infant is primarily one of vitality affects before it is a world of formal acts. It is also analogous to the physical world of amodal perception, which is primarily one of abstractable qualities of shape, number, intensity level, and so on, not a world of things seen, heard, or touched.

Another reason for separating vitality affects from categorical affects is that they cannot be adequately explained by the concept of level of activation. In most accounts of affects and their dimensions, what are here called vitality affects might be subsumed under the all-purpose, unswerving dimension of level of activation or arousal. Activation and arousal certainly occur, but they are not experienced simply as feelings somewhere along, or at some point on, this dimension. They are experienced as dynamic shifts or patterned changes within ourselves. We can use the dimension of arousal-activation only as a general index of level of arousal-activation. We need to add an entirely new categorization of this aspect of experience, namely, vitality affects that correspond to characteristic patterned changes. These patterned changes over time, or activation contours, underlie the separate vitality affects.[8]

Because activation contours (such as "rushes" of thought, feeling, or action) can apply to any kind of behavior or sentience, an activation contour can be abstracted from one kind of behavior and can exist in some amodal form so that it can apply to another kind

8. All the different activation contours can be described in terms of intensity of sensation as a function of time. Changes in intensity over time are adequate to explain "explodings," "fadings," "rushes," and so on, no matter what actual behavior or neural system is the source of these changes. That is why vitality affects have been hidden within the dimension of activation-arousal. However, the activation-arousal dimension needs to be broken apart and viewed not only as a single dimension but also as more momentary patterned changes of activation in time—that is, activation contours that exist in some amodal form. These contours of activation give rise to vitality affects at the level of feeling.

This account of vitality affects is greatly indebted to the work of Schneirla (1959, 1965) and particularly of Tompkins (1962, 1963, 1981). However, Tompkins concluded that discrete patterns of neural firing (density × time)—what are here called activation contours—result in discrete Darwinian affects, while I conclude that they result in a distinct form of affective experience, or vitality affects. Nonetheless, Tompkins's work is the basis for the present account.

of overt behavior or mental process.[9] These abstract representations may then permit intermodal correspondences to be made between similar activation contours expressed in diverse behavioral manifestations. Extremely diverse events may thus be yoked, so long as they share the quality of feeling that is being called a vitality affect. An example of such a correspondence may be the basis for a metaphor as seen in Defoe's novel *Moll Flanders.* When the heroine is finally caught and imprisoned after a life of crime, she says, "I had . . . no thought of heaven or hell, at least that went any farther than a bare flying touch. . . ." ([New York: Signet Classics, 1964], p. 247). The activation contour of her ideation reminds her of the activation contour of a particular physical sensation, a fleeting touch. And they evoke the same vitality affect.

If young infants experience vitality affects, as is being suggested, they will often be in a situation analogous to that of Moll Flanders, in which a variety of diverse sensory experiences with similar activation contours can be yoked—that is, they can be experienced as correspondent and thereby as creating organization. For instance, in trying to soothe the infant, the parent could say, "There, there, there . . . ," giving more stress and amplitude on the first part of the word and trailing off towards the end of the word. Alternatively, the parent could silently stroke the baby's back or head with a stroke analogous to the "There, there" sequence, applying more pressure at the onset of the stroke and lightening or trailing it off toward the end. If the duration of the contoured stroke and the pauses between strokes were of the same absolute and relative durations as the vocalization-pause pattern, the infant would experience similar activation contours no matter which soothing technique was performed. The two soothings would feel the same (beyond their sensory specificity) and would result in the same vitality affect experience.

If this were so, the infant would be a step up in the process of experiencing an emergent other. Instead of one distinct stroking-mother and a second and separate "There, there"-mother, the infant would experience only a single vitality affect in soothing activities—

9. All of this assumes that infants are early endowed with pattern- or sweep-detectors that can identify such contours. Suggestive evidence exists that they are. Fernald (1984), for example, showed that infants can readily discriminate a rising pitch contour from a falling one, even though the two are the same voice making the same vowel sound with the same pitch range and amplitude and differing only in temporal pattern. New research in this area is crucial.

a "soothing vitality affective mother." In this fashion the amodal experience of vitality affects as well as the capacities for cross-modal matching of perceived forms would greatly enhance the infant's progress toward the experience of an emergent other.[10]

The notion of activation contours (as the underlying feature of vitality affects) suggests a possible answer to the mysterious question of what form the amodal representation resides in when it is held abstracted from any particular way of perceiving it. The amodal representation could consist of a temporal pattern of changes in density of neural firing. No matter whether an object was encountered with the eye or the touch, and perhaps even the ear, it would produce the same overall pattern or activation contour.

The notion of vitality affects may prove helpful in imagining some of the infant's experiences of forming organization in yet another way. The consolidation of a sensorimotor schema provides an illustration. The thumb-to-mouth schema is a good one, since it occurs quite early. Following the suggestion of Sameroff (1984), we can describe the initial consolidation of the thumb-to-mouth schema as something like this. The infant initially moves his hand toward the mouth in a poorly coordinated, loosely directed, jerky manner. The entire pattern—thumb-to-mouth—is an intrinsically motivated, species-specific behavioral pattern that tends to completion and smooth functioning as the goals. During the initial part of a successful trial, while the thumb is getting closer but is not yet in the mouth, the pattern is incomplete and there is increased arousal. When the thumb finally finds its way into the mouth, there is a falloff in arousal, because the pattern is consummated and "smooth functioning" of sucking (an already consolidated schema) takes over. Along with the decrease in arousal there is a relative shift toward positive hedonic tone upon the resumption of smooth functioning. This thumb-finding-the-mouth and mouth-finding-the-thumb occurs over and over until it is smoothly functioning, that is, until adaptation of the pattern is accomplished through assimilation/accommodation of the sensorimotor schema. When this happens and the scheme is fully

10. There are infinite possible activation contours. One can only assume that they organize into recognizable groupings, so that we can recognize families of contours for which relatively discrete vitality affects are the felt component and can even designate words—"surgings," "fadings," "resolutions," and so on to some of these families. The differentiation into a greater number of more discrete families is an empirical developmental issue.

consolidated, the thumb-to-mouth behavior is no longer accompanied by arousal and hedonic shifts. It then goes unnoticed as "smooth functioning." But during the initial trials, when the schema is still being consolidated, the infant experiences, for each precariously successful attempt, a specific contour of arousal buildup as the hand is uncertainly finding its way to the mouth and then a falloff in arousal and a shift in hedonic tone when the mouth is found and secured. In other words, each consolidating trial is accompanied by a characteristic vitality affect associated with sensations from the arm, hand, thumb, and mouth—all leading to consummation.

The product of this development—a smoothly functioning thumb-to-mouth schema—may go unnoticed once formed. But the process of formation, itself, will be quite salient and the focus of heightened attention. This is an experience of organization in formation. This example is not different in principle from the more familiar case of the buildup of hunger (tension, arousal), consummation in the act of feeding (arousal reduction and hedonic shift), and sensations and perceptions about self and others. However, the thumb-in-mouth case is different in that it concerns a sensorimotor schema, not a physiological need state, that its motivation is conceptualized somewhat differently, and most important for our purposes, that it gives rise to a different vitality affect associated with different body parts and different contexts.

There are many different sensorimotor schemas that need to be adapted, and the consolidation process for each of them involves a subjective experience of somewhat different vitality affects associated with different body parts and sensations in different contexts. It is these subjective experiences of various organizations in formation that I am calling the sense of an emergent self. The particular experiences of the consolidation of a sensorimotor schema may have more of a quality of tension resolution than of déjà vu or of discovery as already described for some of the other senses of an emergent self.

We have now examined three processes involved in forming a sense of an emergent self and other: amodal perception, physiognomic perception, and the perception of corresponding vitality affects. All three are forms of direct, "global" perception, in which the yoking of diverse experiences is accompanied by distinctive subjective experiences. However, that is not the only way the world of related experiences comes into being. There are also constructionist processes that provide the infant with different ways to experience an emergent self and other. These processes are associated with a different approach to infant experience, but one that is complementary to the approach just discussed.

CONSTRUCTIONIST APPROACHES TO RELATING SOCIAL EXPERIENCES

The constructionist view assumes that the infant perceives the human form initially as one of many arrays of physical stimuli, not essentially different from various other arrays, such as windows, cribs, and mobiles. It further assumes that the infant first detects separate featural elements of persons: size, motion, or vertical lines. These featural elements, which could by themselves belong to any stimulus array, are then progressively integrated until a configuration, a whole form, is synthesized into a larger constructed entity—first, a face, and gradually a human form.

The processes that form the constructionist view are assimilation, accommodation, identifying invariants, and associational learning. The emergence of the sense of self is therefore described more in terms of discoveries about the relations between peviously known disparate experiences than in terms of the process itself. While learning in one form or another, is the underlying process of a constructionist approach, what can and will be learned is channeled by innate predilections common to the species. Humans are born with preferences or tendencies to be attentive to specific features within a stimulus array. This is true for stimulation in any sensory modality. There is a developmental sequence in which the infant detects or finds most salient different features at different ages. This progression is best studied in vision. From birth to two months, infants have a tendency to seek out the stimulus features of movement (Haith 1966), size, and contour density, the number of contour elements per unit area (Kessen et al. 1970; Karmel, Hoffman, and Fegy 1974; Salapatek 1975). After two months of age, curvature, symmetry, complexity, novelty, aperiodicity, and ultimately configurations (form) become more salient stimulus features (See Hainline 1978; Haith 1980; Sherrod 1981; Bronson 1982).

Infants also come into the world with attentional (potential information-gathering) strategies that have their own maturational unfolding. Again, these have been best studied in vision. Up to two months of age, infants predominantly scan the periphery or edges of objects. After that age, they begin to shift their gaze to look at the internal features (Salapatek 1975; Haith et al. 1977; Hainline 1978). When the object is a face, there are two important exceptions to this general progression of attentional strategy. When some auditory stimulation such as speaking is added, even infants younger than two months tend to shift their gaze from the periphery to the internal features of the face (Haith et al. 1977). The same tendency has been observed when there is movement of the facial features (Donee 1973).

Using this information to predict how the human face will be experienced in constructionist terms, we could predict roughly the following progression. During the first two months, infants should find the face no different from other objects that move, that are roughly the same size, and that have similar contour density. Infants would acquire much familiarity with the features that make up the border areas, such as the hairline, but little familiarity with the internal features of the face: the eyes, nose, mouth—in short, all the features that taken together make up its configuration or "faceness." After the age of about two months, when attentional strategy shifts to internal scanning, infants would first pay attention to those features with more of the stimulus properties they preferred: curvature, contrast, vertical symmetry, angles, complexity, and so on. These preferences would lead them to be attentive first to the eyes, then to the mouth, and last to the nose. After considerable experience with these features and their invariant spatial relationships, they would have constructed a schema or identified the invariants of the configuration that designates "faceness."

Indeed, it is readily demonstrable that by the age of five to seven months infants can remember for over a week the picture of a particular face that has been seen only once and for less than a minute (Fagan 1973, 1976). This feat of long-term recognition memory requires a representation of the unique form of a particular face. It is unlikely that it is done on the basis of feature recognition. The fact that faces make sounds and that their internal parts move in talking and expressing should push the constructionist timetable somewhat earlier, but it does not change the sequence in which the construction of form perception progresses.

This constructionist approach could be applied equally well to audition, touch, and the other modalities of human stimulation. If one accepts the constructionist picture and timetable for the earliest perceptual encounter with human stimuli, one must conclude that the infant is not related in any distinctive or unique way to other persons. Interpersonal relatedness does not yet exist as distinct from relatedness to things. The infant is asocial, but by virtue of being indiscriminate, not by virtue of being unresponsive, as suggested by psychoanalytic formulations of a stimulus barrier that protects the infant for the first few months of life. One can entertain a notion of relatedness to isolated stimulus features or properties, but that is a weak notion indeed. The idea of relatedness to circles or spheres (or to "part objects," in psychoanalytic terms) does not seem to carry one far into the domain of the interpersonal.

The problem is, then, how and when do these constructions become related to human subjectivity, so that selves and others emerge? Before dealing with that problem, we should note that some evidence suggests that infants never experience any salient human form (face, voice, breast) as nothing more than a particular physical stimulus array among others, but rather that they experience persons as unique forms from the start. The evidence is of several kinds: (1) By the age of one month, infants do show appreciation of more global (nonfeatural) aspects of the human face such as animation, complexity, and even configuration (Sherrod 1981). (2) Infants gaze differently when scanning live faces than when viewing geometric forms. They are less captured by single featural elements and scan more fluidly during these first months (Donee 1973). (3) When scanning live faces, newborns act differently than when scanning inanimate patterns. They move their arms and legs and open and close their hands and feet in smoother, more regulated, less jerky cycles of movement. They also emit more vocalizations (Brazelton et al. 1974, 1980). (4) The recent finding of Field et al. (1982), that two- to three-day-old infants can discriminate and imitate smiles, frowns, and surprise expressions seen on the face of a live interactant, clearly indicates that the infant not only is perceiving internal facial features but appears to be discriminating some of their different configurations.[11] (5) The recognition of a specific individual's face or voice is supportive evidence for some kind of specialness attached to

11. It can, however, be argued that the discrimination of expressive configurations is based on the detection of a single feature necessary and sufficient for each configuration.

that person's stimuli. The evidence is convincing that the neonate can discriminate the mother's voice from another woman's voice reading the exact same material (DeCasper and Fifer, 1980).[12] The evidence for recognition of individual faces prior to two months is less secure. Many researchers continue to find it, but a larger number do not (see Sherrod 1981). Despite these qualifications of the constructionist view, there is little question that infants do construct relationships as well as perceive them directly.

Approaches to an Understanding of the Infant's Subjective Experience

Amodal perception (based on abstract qualities of experience, including discrete affects and vitality affects) and constructionistic efforts (based on assimilation, accommodation, association, and the identification of invariants) are thus the processes by which the infant experiences organization. While these processes have been most studied in perception, they apply equally well to the formation of organization in all domains of experience: motor activity, affectivity, and states of consciousness. They also apply to the yoking of experiences across different domains (sensory with motor, or perceptual with affective, and so on).

One of the most pervasive problems in understanding infants continues to be the difficulty in finding unifying concepts and language that will include the formation of organization as it occurs in the various domains of experience. For instance, when speaking about the yoking of diverse perceptions to form higher-order perceptions, we can talk in cognitive terms. When speaking about the yoking of sensory experience and motor experience, we can adopt Piaget's conceptual system and talk in terms of sensorimotor schemas. When speaking about the yoking of perceptual and affective experience, we are thrown back on more experiential concepts that are less systematized, such as those employed in psychoanalysis. All of these

12. The pitch range and general stress patterns do not appear to be the distinctive features that permit the infant to make this discrimination. Voice quality may be the best bet (Fifer, personal communication, 1984).

yokings must draw upon the same basic processes that we have discussed, yet we tend to act as if the formation of organization follows its own unique laws in each domain of experience. And to some extent it may. But the commonalities are likely to be far greater than the differences.

There is no reason to give any one domain of experience primacy and make it the point of departure to approach the infant's organization of experience. Several approaches can be described, all of them valid, all of them necessary, and all of them equally "primary."[13]

The infant's actions. This is the route implied in Piaget's work. Self-generated action and sensations are the primary experiences. The emergent property of things, in the beginning, is an action-sensation amalgam in which the object is first constructed in the mind by way of the actions performed on it; for example, there are things that can be grasped and things that can be sucked. While learning about the world, the infant necessarily identifies many invariants of subjective experience of self-generated actions and self-sensations—in other words, of emergent self experiences.

Pleasure and unpleasure (hedonic tone). This is the route that Freud initially explored. He stated that the most salient and unique aspect of human experience is the subjective experience of pleasure (tension reduction) and unpleasure (tension or excitation buildup). This is the basic assumption of the pleasure principle. He assumed that visual perceptions of the environment such as the breast or face or tactile sensations or smells associated with pleasures (such as feeding) or unpleasure (such as hunger) become affect-imbued. It is in this way that affective and perceptual experiences are yoked. On the surface it is an associationist's view, but Freud's version of this view was slightly different. Affects not only make perceptions relevant by way of association; they also provide the ticket of admission for perceptions even to get into the mind. Without the experience of hedonic tone, no perceptions would be registered at all. Hedonic tone did for Freud what self-generated action did for Piaget. They both "created" perceptions as mental phenomena and yoked these perceptions to primary experiences.

Do infants experience hedonic tone in the first months of life? When watching an infant in distress or contentment, one finds it very hard not to believe so. Emde (1980a, 1980b) has postulated that hedonic tone is the first experience of affect. Biologists have generally assumed that from an evolutionary standpoint, pain and pleasure or approach and withdrawal should be the primary affective experiences, for their value to survival.

13. One could argue that some experiences are more crucial for survival then others, but that is outside of considerations of subjective experience.

Further, evolution built the experience of categories of affect upon the foundation of hedonic tone (Schneirla 1965; Mandler 1975; Zajonc 1980). Emde et al. (1978) suggests that ontogeny may recapitulate phylogeny in the progression of affective experience. In this light it is interesting that Emde et al. report that in interpreting the facial expressions of the youngest infants, mothers feel most confident about their attribution of hedonic tone, somewhat less confident about level of activation, and least confident about the discrete category of affect seen on the infant's face.

Discrete categories of affect. Even if hedonic tone emerges earlier or faster as an affective experience, the study of infants' faces also makes clear that they express (whether or not they feel) discrete categories of affect. Using detailed film analysis, Izard (1978) observed that newborns show interest, joy, distress, disgust, and surprise. Facial displays of fear appear at about six months (Cicchetti and Sroufe 1978), and shame appears much later. Affect is expressed not only in the face, in the beginning. Lipsitt (1976) has described how newborns express anger by moving the face, arms, and whole body in concert when they experience lack of air from nasal occlusion at the breast. In a similar vein, Bennett (1971) has described how the infant's entire body expresses pleasure; there are quiverings of pleasure as well as smiles.

We simply do not know if infants are actually feeling what their faces, voices, and bodies so powerfully express to us, but it is very hard to witness such expressions and not to make that inference. It is equally hard theoretically to imagine that infants would be provided initially with an empty but convincing signal, when they need the feelings they express to regulate themselves, to define their very selves, and to learn with.[14]

Infant states of consciousness. In the first months of life, the infant cycles dramatically through the sequence of states first described by Wolff (1966): drowsiness, alert inactivity, alert activity, fuss-cry, regular sleep, and paradoxical sleep. It has been suggested that the different waking states of consciousness may also serve the role of an organizing focus for all other experiences, and accordingly they provide a primary approach for describing early infant subjective experience (Stechler and Carpenter 1967; Sander 1983a, 1983b).

Perceptions and cognitions. This is the route most often taken by experimentalists. It results in a view of the infant's social experience as a

14. During the last decade, developmental psychologists have tended to stress the cognitive capacities required for an infant to have an affective experience (Lewis and Rosenblum 1978). The result has been an overemphasis on the linkage between the development of cognitive structure and affect. The realization is now occurring that not all affective life is the handmaiden to cognition, either for infants or for adults, and that infants' *feelings,* especially in the beginning, can and must be considered irrespective of what they *know.* (See Demos [1982a, 1982b]; Fogel et al. [1981]; and Thoman and Acebo [1983] for a discussion of this issue in relation to infants, and Zajonc [1980] and Tompkins [1981] in relation to adults.)

subset of perception and cognition in general. Social perception and social cognition follow the same rules applicable to all other objects.

The problem with each of these approaches is that infants do not see the world in these terms (that is, in terms of our academic subdisciplines). Infant experience is more unified and global. Infants do not attend to what domain their experience is occurring in. They take sensations, perceptions, actions, cognitions, internal states of motivation, and states of consciousness and experience them directly in terms of intensities, shapes, temporal patterns, vitality affects, categorical affects, and hedonic tones. These are the basic elements of early subjective experience. Cognitions, actions, and perceptions, as such, do not exist. All experiences become recast as patterned constellations of all the infant's basic subjective elements combined.

This is what Spitz (1959), Werner (1948), and others had in mind when they spoke of global and coenesthetic experience. What was not recognized at the time of their formulations was the extent of the infant's formidable capacities to distill and organize the abstract, global qualities of experience. Infants are not lost at sea in a wash of abstractable qualities of experience. They are gradually and systematically ordering these elements of experience to identify self-invariant and other-invariant constellations. And whenever any constellation is formed, the infant experiences the emergence of organization. The elements that make up these emergent organizations are simply different subjective units from those of adults who, most of the time, believe that they subjectively experience units such as thoughts, perceptions, actions, and so on, because they must translate experience into these terms in order to encode it verbally.

This global subjective world of emerging organization is and remains the fundamental domain of human subjectivity. It operates out of awareness as the experiential matrix from which thoughts and perceived forms and identifiable acts and verbalized feelings will later arise. It also acts as the source for ongoing affective appraisals of events. Finally, it is the ultimate reservoir that can be dipped into for all creative experience.

All learning and all creative acts begin in the domain of emergent relatedness. That domain alone is concerned with the coming-into-being of organization that is at the heart of creating and learning. This domain of experience remains active during the formative period of each of the subsequent domains of sense of self. The later senses of self to emerge are products of the organizing process. They are true, encompassing perspectives about the self—about the physical, actional self, about the subjective self, about the verbal self. The process of forming each of these perspectives, the creative act concerning the nature of self and others, is the process that gives rise to the sense of an emergent self, which will be experienced in the process of forming each of the other senses of the self, to which we can now turn.

Chapter 4

The Sense of a Core Self: I. Self versus Other

AT THE AGE of two to three months, infants begin to give the impression of being quite different persons. When engaged in social interaction, they appear to be more wholly integrated. It is as if their actions, plans, affects, perceptions, and cognitions can now all be brought into play and focused, for a while, on an interpersonal situation. They are not simply more social, or more regulated, or more attentive, or smarter. They seem to approach interpersonal relatedness with an organizing perspective that makes it feel as if there is now an integrated sense of themselves as distinct and coherent bodies, with control over their own actions, ownership of their own affectivity, a sense of continuity, and a sense of other people as distinct and separate interactants. And the world now begins to treat them as if they are complete persons and do possess an integrated sense of themselves.

In spite of this very distinctive impression, the prevailing views of clinical developmental theory do not reflect the image of an infant with an integrated sense of self. Instead, it is widely held that infants go through an extended period of self/other undifferentiation and that only very slowly, sometime towards the end of the first year of life, do they differentiate a sense of self and other. Some psychoanalytic developmental theories, of which Mahler provides the most influential example, propose that during the undifferentiated phase infants experience a state of fusion or "dual-unity" with mother. This is the phase of "normal symbiosis," lasting roughly from the second to the seventh or ninth month. This state of dual-unity is proposed as the background from which the infant gradually separates and individuates to arrive at a sense of self and of other. Academic theories have not differed basically from the psychoanalytic theories in the sense that both propose a slow emergence of self after a long period of undifferentiation.

Recent findings about infants challenge these generally accepted timetables and sequences and are more in accord with the impression of a changed infant, capable of having—in fact, likely to have—an integrated sense of self and of others. These new findings support the view that the infant's first order of business, in creating an interpersonal world, is to form the sense of a core self and core others. The evidence also supports the notion that this task is largely accomplished during the period between two and seven months. Further, it suggests that the capacity to have merger- or fusion-like experiences as described in psychoanalysis is secondary to and dependent upon an already existing sense of self and other. The newly suggested timetable pushes the emergence of the self earlier in time dramatically and reverses the sequencing of developmental tasks. First comes the formation of self and other, and only then is the sense of merger-like experiences possible.

Before examining the new evidence, we must ask, what kind of a sense of self is the infant likely to discover or create, beyond the sense of an emergent self that appeared in the first two months?

The Nature of an Organized Sense of Self

The first organizing subjective perspective about the self must be at a fairly basic level.[1] A tentative list of the experiences available to the infant, and needed to form an organized sense of a core self

1. This discussion will generally concern sense of self. The sense of other is most often the opposite side of the same coin and is implied.

includes (1) *self-agency,* in the sense of authorship of one's own actions and nonauthorship of the actions of others: having volition, having control over self-generated action (your arm moves when you want it to), and expecting consequences of one's actions (when you shut your eyes it gets dark); (2) *self-coherence,* having a sense of being a nonfragmented, physical whole with boundaries and a locus of integrated action, both while moving (behaving) and when still; (3) *self-affectivity,* experiencing patterned inner qualities of feeling (affects) that belong with other experiences of self; and (4) *self-history,* having the sense of enduring, of a continuity with one's own past so that one "goes on being" and can even change while remaining the same. The infant notes regularities in the flow of events.

These four self-experiences, taken together, constitute a sense of a core self. This sense of a core self is thus an experiential sense of events. It is normally taken completely for granted and operates outside of awareness. A crucial term here is "sense of," as distinct from "concept of" or "knowledge of" or "awareness of" a self or other. The emphasis is on the palpable experiential realities of substance, action, sensation, affect, and time. Sense of self is not a cognitive construct. It is an experiential integration. This sense of a core self will be the foundation for all the more elaborate senses of the self to be added later.[2]

These four basic self-experiences seem to be reasonable choices from a clinical point of view as well as from a developmental point of view, in that they are necessary for adult psychological health. It is only in major psychosis that we see a significant absence of any of these four self-experiences. Absence of agency can be manifest in catatonia, hysterical paralysis, derealization, and some paranoid states in which authorship of action is taken over. Absence of coherence can be manifest in depersonalization, fragmentation, and psychotic experiences of merger or fusion. Absence of affectivity can be seen in the anhedonia of some schizophrenias, and absence of continuity can be seen in fugue and other disassociative states.

A sense of a core self results from the integration of these four basic self-experiences into a social subjective perspective. Each of these self-experiences can be seen as self-invariant. An invariant is that which does not change in the face of all the things that do

2. It is reasonable to believe that many higher nonhuman animals form such a sense of a core self. That in no way diminishes this achievement.

change. To be persuaded that a sense of a core self is likely to form during the first half year of life as a primary social task, one would want to be assured that the infant has the appropriate opportunities to find the necessary self-invariants (agency, coherence, and so on) in daily social life, the capacities to identify these self-invariants, and the ability to integrate all of these self-invariants into a single subjective perspective. Let us begin with the opportunities.

The Natural Opportunities for Identifying Self-Invariants

The period roughly from two to six months is perhaps the most exclusively social period of life. By two or three months the social smile is in place, vocalizations directed at others have come in, mutual gaze is sought more avidly, predesigned preferences for the human face and voice are operating fully, and the infant undergoes that biobehavioral transformation resulting in a highly social partner (Spitz 1965; Emde et al. 1976). Before these changes at two months, the infant is relatively more engaged with social behaviors directly bearing on the regulation of physiological needs—sleep and hunger. And after six months the infant changes again and becomes fascinated by, and proficient in, manipulating external objects; coordination of limbs and hand-to-eye have improved rapidly, and an interest in inanimate objects sweeps the field. When in physiological and affective equilibrium, the infant becomes relatively more engaged with things than with people. So it is in between these two shifts at two and six months of age that the infant is relatively more socially oriented. This short period of intense and almost exclusive sociability results both from default and design.

Given this honeymoon period of intense sociability, how are the interpersonal interactions mutually constructed so that the infant is in a position to identify the invariants ("islands of consistency") that will come to specify a core self and a core other? This has been discussed in greater detail elsewhere (Stern 1977), but the highlights for our purposes are as follows:

First, the caregivers' social behaviors elicited by the infant are generally exaggerated and moderately stereotypic. "Baby talk," the example par excellence, is marked by raised pitch, simplified syntax, reduced rate, and exaggerated pitch contours (Ferguson 1964; Snow 1972; Fernald 1982; Stern, Spieker, and MacKain 1983). "Baby faces" (the often odd but effective faces made automatically by adults towards infants) are marked by exaggeration in fullness of display, longer duration, and slower composition and decomposition of the display (Stern 1977). Similarly, gaze behaviors are exaggerated, and adults tend to "work in closer" to proximate positions best suited for the infant to focus on and attend exclusively to the adult's behavior. The social presence of an infant elicits variations in adult behavior that are best suited to the infant's innate perceptual biases; for example, infants prefer sounds of a higher pitch, such as are achieved in "baby talk." The result is that the adult's behavior is maximally attended by the infant.

Ultimately, it is these same caregiver behaviors that are the stimuli from which the infant must pick out the many invariants that specify an other. The matching of caregiver behavioral variations and infant predelictions gives the infant the optimal opportunity to perceive those behavioral invariants that identify self or other.

Caregivers typically perform these exaggerated behaviors in a theme and variation format. An example of this format in verbal behavior might go something like this:

> Hey, *honey* . . . Yeah, *honey* . . . Hi, *honey* . . . Watcha doing, *honey?* . . . Yeah, what*cha doing?* . . . what are *ya doing?* . . . what are *ya doing* there? . . . *ya doing* nothing?

There are two themes, "honey" and "ya doing." Each theme is restated several times, with minor variations in language or paralanguage.

The same kind of theme and variations format is also the rule for repetitious facial displays or body-touching games. For example, the general game "I'm going to get you," when played in the tickle form of "walking fingers," consists of repeated finger marches up the infant's legs and torso, ending up with a neck or chin tickle as the punch line. It is played over and over, but each finger march is distinctly different from the previous one in speed, in suspense, in vocal accompaniment, or in some other way. The longer the caregiver can introduce an optimal amount of novelty into the performance of each successive round, the longer the infant will stay entranced.

There are two reasons why caregivers engage in this kind of varied repetitiveness (though they generally are not conscious of their reasons). First, if the caregiver did the exact same thing at each repeat, the infant would habituate and loose interest. Infants rapidly determine if a stimulus is the same as those seen or heard immediately before; if it is, they soon stop responding to it. So the caregiver who wishes to maintain a steady high level of interest must constantly change the stimulus presentation a little bit to prevent the baby from habituating. The caregiver's behavior must keep changing, to keep the baby in the same place; it cannot be exact repeats. But then why not do something completely different each time? Why use variations on a theme? This leads to the second reason, the importance of order and repetitiveness.

One of the central tendencies of mind that infants readily display is the tendency to order the world by seeking invariants. A format in which each successive variation is both familiar (the part that is repeated) and novel (the part that is new) is ideally suited to teach infants to identify interpersonal invariants. They get to see a complex behavior and observe which parts of it, so to speak, can be deleted and which parts must remain for it to be the same. They are getting lessons in identifying the invariant features of interpersonal behavior.

The use of exaggerated infant-elicited behaviors and their organization into a theme-and-variation format are not done by caregivers to teach the infant about interpersonal invariants. That is a by-product. They are done to help regulate the infant's level of arousal and excitation within a tolerable range (and to keep the parents from getting bored).

Each infant has an optimal level of excitation that is pleasurable. Beyond that level of excitation the experience becomes unpleasurable, and below a certain level the experience becomes uninteresting and stops being pleasurable. The optimal level is actually a range. Both partners adjust to keep the infant within it. On the one side, the caregiver regulates the level of activity in facial and vocal expressions, gestures, and body movements—the stimulus events that determine the infant's level of excitation. Corresponding to each infant's optimal range of excitation is an optimal range of stimulation. By sensitively gearing the level of such behaviors as the extent of exaggeration and the amount of variation to the infant's current level of excitation and the direction of its predictable drift, the caregiver achieves the optimal range of stimulation.

On the other side, the infant also regulates the level of excitation, using gaze aversion to cut out stimulation that has risen above the optimal range and gaze and facial behaviors to seek out and invite new or higher levels of stimulation when the level of excitation has fallen too low (Brazelton et al. 1974; Stern 1974a, 1975; Fogel 1982). When one watches infants play their role in these mutual regulations, it is difficult not to conclude that they sense the presence of a separate other and sense their capacity to alter the behavior of the other as well as their own experience.

With this kind of mutual regulation, infants in effect get extensive experience with self-regulation of their own level of excitation and with regulation, through signals, of a responsive caregiver's level of stimulation. This amounts to an early coping function. Infants also get extensive experience with the caregiver as a regulator of their levels of excitation, that is, of being with an other who helps them self-regulate. All this can be best observed in the fairly stereotypic parent-infant games of this life period (Call and Marschak 1976; Fogel 1977; Schaffer 1977; Stern et al. 1977; Tronick et al. 1977; Field 1978; Kaye 1982).

It is important to note that during this period of life, these social interactions are in no way purely cognitive events. They mainly involve the regulation of affect and excitation. Perceptual, cognitive, and memorial events play a considerable role in these regulatory events, but they are all about affect and excitement. It must also be recalled that during this period, when face-to-face social interactions are one of the main forms of interpersonal engagement, the major emotional peaks and valleys of social life now occur during these encounters and not during activities such as feeding, when physiological regulation is uppermost. These social matters concern both the infant's cognitive and affective experience.

But how about the extreme affective states related to physiological and bodily needs—distress and crying because of hunger or discomfort, and contentment due to satiation? Do these present an entirely different social situation for the infant insofar as discovery of self and other are concerned? No. Parental behavior in these situations follows the same general rules that it does during social play. Behaviors are exaggerated, repeated with appropriate variation, and stereotypic. Imagine an attempt to soothe a distressed baby. The facial, vocal, and tactile behaviors are greatly exaggerated and repeated with constant variations until success is achieved. Soothing, comforting, putting to sleep, and so on are rituals that follow a narrowly prescribed repertoire of themes and variations. (Unsuccessful soothing consists of a series of uncompleted, broken up, ineffective rituals, but it is ritual nonetheless.) And during these events the infant is of course experiencing affective changes that vary along with the parents' behavioral themes and variations.

These, then, are the daily life events that offer up the opportunities from which the infant must identify the invariants that specify a core self and, complementarily, those that specify a core other. We can now turn to the capacities the infant would need in order to be able to discover the basic invariants that will specify a core self and other.

The Identification of Self-Invariants

First of all, the intrinsic motivation to order one's universe is an imperative of mental life. And the infant has the overall capacity to do so, in large part by identifying the invariants (the islands of consistency) that gradually provide organization to experience. In addition to this general motivation and capacity, the infant needs specific capacities to identify the invariants that seem most crucial in specifying a sense of a core self. Let us look closely at the four crucial invariants.

AGENCY

Agency, or authorship of action, can be broken down into three possible invariants of experience: (1) the sense of volition that precedes a motor act, (2) the proprioceptive feedback that does or does not occur during the act, and (3) the predictability of consequences that follow the act. What capacities does the infant have for identifying these features of agency?

The invariant of volition may be the most fundamental invariant of core self-experience. All movements of voluntary (striated) muscles that are organized at a level higher than the reflex are preceded by the elaboration of a motor plan, which is then executed by the muscle groups (Lashley 1951). Exactly how these motor plans are registered in sentience is not clear, but it is commonly accepted that there is some mental registration (usually out of awareness) of the existence of a motor plan prior to action. The existence of the plan can reach awareness quite readily when its execution is inhibited or when for some reason the motor execution misfires and fails to match the original plan (the thumb hits the cheek instead of going into the mouth, for example). We expect our eyes and hands and legs to do what we have planned for them. The presence of the motor plan as it exists in mind allows for the sense of volition or will. Even when we are unaware of the motor plan, the sense of volition makes our actions seem to belong to us and to be self-acts. Without it, an infant would feel what a puppet would "feel" like, as the nonauthor of its own immediate behavior.

One expects to find motor plans from the very beginning of life, at least as soon as voluntary motor skills become evident. And this, of course, occurs in the first month of life, with hand-to-mouth skills, gazing skills, and sucking skills. Later, a four-month-old reaching for an object of a certain size will begin to shape finger position and degree of hand opening to fit the size of the object to be grasped (Bower et al. 1970). These hand adjustments are made en route to the object; they are accommodations to the size of the object as seen and not yet felt. What must be occurring is that the motor plan for the hand-shaping-during-reach is being formed on the basis of visual information.

One could argue that the achievement of a motor plan such as handshaping is simply a match/mismatch operation with goal-correcting feedback. But such arguments still do not address the initiating mental event that forms the motor plan. That is where volition resides. The execution of match/mismatch operations determines only the liklihood of the original plan being successful or not, or brought to awareness or not.

The reality and importance of motor plans as mental phenomena, particularly as these apply to skilled actions such as talking or playing the piano, were beautifully argued by Lashley. Recently, another illustration of this phenomenon was pointed out to me (Hadiks, personal communication, 1983). If subjects are asked to write their signatures twice, first very small on a piece of paper and then in very large script on a blackboard, the two signatures will be remarkably alike when adjusted for size. What is interesting about this example is that entirely different muscle groups are used to render the two signatures. In the first signing, on paper, the elbow and shoulder are fixed and all action occurs in the fingers and wrist. In the second signing, on the blackboard, the fingers and wrist are fixed and all action occurs in the movements at the elbow and shoulder. The motor program for the signature thus in no way resides in the muscles required for the signing. It resides in the mind and is transferable from one set of muscles to a completely different set of muscles for its execution. Volition in the form of motor plans exists as a mental phenomenon that can be combined with a variety of different muscle groups for execution. This is what Piaget had in mind when he spoke of sensorimotor schemas and the ability of the infant to marshal different means to accomplish the same ends. These considerations lead to a clinical vignette.

Several years ago a pair of "Siamese twins" (Xiphophagus conjoint twins) were born at a hospital near the university where I teach. These were only the sixth set of twins of their kind reported in the world literature. They were connected on the ventral surface between the umbilicus and the bottom of the sternum, so that they always faced one another. They shared no organs, had separate nervous systems, and shared essentially no blood supply (Harper et al. 1980). It was noticed that very frequently one would end up sucking on the other's fingers and vice versa, and neither seemed to mind. About one week before they were to be surgically separated at four months of age (corrected for prematurity), Rita Harper, Director of the Neonatal Nursery, called me because of the potential psychological interest of this pair. Susan Baker, Roanne Barnett, and I had an opportunity to do a number of experiments before surgical separation. One experiment bears on volitional motor plans and the self. When twin A (Alice) was sucking on her *own* fingers, one of us placed one hand on her head and the other hand on the arm that she was sucking. We gently pulled the sucking arm away from her mouth and registered (in our own hands) whether her arm put up resistance to being moved from her mouth and/or whether her head strained forward to go after the retreating hand. In this situation, Alice's arm resisted the interruption of sucking, but she did not give evidence of straining forward with her head. The same procedure was followed when Alice was sucking on her sister Betty's fingers rather than her own. When Betty's hand was gently pulled from Alice's mouth, Alice's arms showed no resistance or movement, and Betty's arm showed no resistance, but Alice's head did strain forward. Thus when her own hand was removed, the plan to maintain sucking was put into execution by the attempt to bring her arm back to the mouth, while when another person's hand was removed the plan to maintain sucking was put into execution with the movement of her head forward. Alice seemed, in this case, to have no confusion as to whose fingers belonged to whom and which motor plan would best reestablish sucking.

We were fortunate to come upon several occasions when Alice was sucking on Betty's fingers while Betty was sucking on Alice's fingers. The same interruption of sucking manipulation was performed, except doubly and simultaneously. The results indicated that each twin "knew" that one's own mouth sucking a finger and one's own finger being sucked do not make a coherent self. Two invariants are missing, volition (of the arm) as we have been talking about it, although this cannot be proved, and predictable consequences, which we shall address below.[3]

This aspect of agency, the sense of volition, must occur very early during the newborn period, since the infant's repertoire of action is not all reflexive even at birth. To the extent that the newborn's behaviors are to a considerable extent reflexive, the sense of volition will not be an invariant of movement. Sometimes it will be there, seen in such voluntary movements as some head-turns, some sucking, most gazing behaviors, and some kickings. Sometimes it will not be there, when a behavior is fired off reflexively; such behaviors include many arm movements (tonic neck reflexes), head movements (rooting), and so on. Until the proportion of all self-action that is reflexive becomes quite small, the sense of volition will be an "almost invariant" of self-action. By the second month of life, when core-relatedness begins, this is certainly the case.

The second invariant property specifying agency is proprioceptive feedback. This is a pervasive reality of self-action whether the action

3. This example is in part an unusual case of "single touch" versus "double touch." Double touch is when you touch yourself and the touched part in turn touches the touching part.

is initiated by self or passively manipulated by another. It is clear that infant motor acts are guided by proprioceptive feedback from the earliest days, and we have very reason to assume that proprioception is developmentally a constant invariant of self-agency, even when the infant is not acting but is holding any antigravity posture. The Papoušeks (1979) have commented on this point, which was also central for Spitz (1957).

Given just these two invariants, volition and proprioception, it becomes clearer how the infant could sense three different combinations of these two invariants: self-willed action of self, (bringing thumb up towards own mouth), in which both volition and proprioception are experienced; other-willed action of other (mother bringing pacifier up towards infant's mouth), in which neither volition nor proprioception are experienced; or other-willed action on self (mother holds baby's wrists and plays "clap hands" or "pat-a-cake," at a point when the child does not yet know the game), in which proprioception but not volition will be experienced. It is in this way that the infant is in a position to identify those invariants that specify a core self, core other, and the various amalgams of these invariants that specify self-with-other. As we add more invariant interpersonal properties, the possibilities expand greatly.

The third invariant that potentially can specify agency is consequence of action. Self events generally have contingent relations very different from events with another. When you suck your finger, your finger gets sucked—and not just generally sucked, but with a sensory synchrony between the tongue and palate sensations and the complementary sensations of the sucked finger. When your eyes close, the world goes dark. When your head turns and eyes move, the visual sights change. And so on.

For virtually all self-initiated actions upon the self, there is a felt consequence. A constant schedule of reinforcement results. Conversely, acts of the self upon the other generally provide less certain consequences and result in a quite variable schedule of reinforcement. The infant's ability to sense contingent relations alone will be of no help in self/other differentiation. What will help, however, will be the infant's ability to tell one schedule of reinforcement from another, since only self-generated acts are constantly reinforced.

Recent experiments show that infants have considerable ability to discriminate different schedules of reinforcement (Watson 1979, 1980). Using a paradigm in which infants must turn their heads against a pressurized pillow to get a mobile to turn, Watson has demonstrated that infants by the age of three months can distinguish between schedules of constant reinforcement (each head-turn is rewarded), a fixed ratio of reinforcement (every third head-turn, say, is reinforced) and a variable schedule (where head-turns are less predictably rewarded). The implications for self/other differentiation are clear. This discrimination provides the needed leverage for the problem at hand. Most classes of action by the self upon the self necessarily have a constant reinforcement schedule. (Arm motions always result in proprioceptive sensations. Vocalization always results in unique resonance phenomena from neck and chest and skull. And so on.)

By contrast, actions of the self upon others are usually variably rewarded. The variable and unpredictable nature of maternal responses to infant actions has been documented often (see Watson 1979). For instance, a three-month-old infant who vocalizes has a 100 percent likelihood of feeling the chest resonance of the sound but the likelihood of mother vocalizing back is only probabilistic (Stern et al. 1974; Strain and Vietze 1975; Schaffer et al. 1977). Similarly, if the three-and-one-half-month-old infant gazes toward mother, it is certain she will come into view, but the odds are only high, not certain, that she will look back (Stern 1974b; Messer and Vietze 1982).

In examining the basis of causal inference in infancy, Watson (1980) suggests that there are three features of causal structure available to the infants by three to four months of age: an appreciation of temporal relations between events; an appreciation of sensory relations, that is, the ability to correlate intensity or duration of a behavior and its effect; and an appreciation of spatial relations, the ability to take into account the spatial laws of a behavior and the laws of its effects. These three dimensions of information about causal structure, which we will examine in more detail in the next section, presumably act additively or interactively in providing the infant with rudimentary knowledge of different occasions or conditions of causality. This knowledge in turn should help to separate the world into self-caused and other-caused effects.

The sense of agency is certainly a major specifier of self versus other. But there is a parallel question of equal magnitude. Must the infant not have a sense of a coherent, dynamic physical entity to which the sense of agency can belong?

SELF-COHERENCE

What are the invariant properties of interpersonal experience that might specify that the self versus the other is a single, coherent, bounded physical entity? And what are the infant's capacities to identify them? Without a sense of self and other as coherent entities unto themselves, a sense of a core self or core other would not be possible, and agency would have no place of residence.

There are several features of experience that could help in establishing self-coherence:

Unity of locus. A coherent entity ought to be in one place at one time, and its various actions should emanate from one locus. It has long been known that infants visually orient to the source of a sound at birth (Worthheimer 1961; Butterworth and Castillo 1976; Mendelson and Haith 1976). Part of the problem of discovering unity of locus is thus already solved by predesign of the nervous system. By the age of three months, infants expect that the sound of a voice should come from the same direction as the visual location of the face.

Because infants' relexes and expectations assure that they will be watching what they are listening to and vice versa (under most natural conditions), infants are in a good position to notice that the behaviors specific to an other occupy a separate locus of origin from the locus occupied by the behaviors specific to themselves. Real life interactions, however, confound this picture, and common locus of origin as an identifiable property of self versus other is often violated. For instance, at the close range of face-to-face interactions, the mother's mouth, face, and voice obey the invariant of common locus of origin, but her hands may be holding or tickling the baby. In that case the mother's hands are as far from her face as is the infant's body. Her hands violate the unity of locus of her facial behaviors just as much as any part of the baby's body might be seen to. Unity of locus certainly plays a role as an interpersonal invariant, but by itself it can take the infant only so far in specifying core self and other. It is very helpful when mother is across the room, but of limited help at close range.

Coherence of motion. Things that move coherently in time belong together. Mother as an object seen moving across the room or against any stationary backdrop will be experienced as having coherence because all of her parts are moving relative to some background (Gibson 1969). Ruff (1980) argues that the continuous optical transformations of a moving object (mother) provide the infant with unique kinds of information to detect structural invariants. Because the mind can extract invariants from dynamic events, Ruff deals with the fact that both the infant and the object may be in motion and puts this fact to use. But the problems with motion as an invariant identifying mother as a core other entity are similar to those encountered for unity of locus. First, when she is quite close, the infant observes that parts of her are moving relatively faster than others. This generally means that parts of her become the background, relatively speaking, for other parts of her. When this occurs, and it occurs often, one arm might appear to be a different entity from the other arm, or from the body. The second problem is that infants experience greater coherence if all parts are moving as if associated by rigid connections (Spelke 1983). This is not often the case with a socially interacting mother. Her hand, head, mouth, and body movements may be far too fluidly related ever to give the impression that they all belong to the same whole.

Coherence of motion alone, then, as an invariant would be of limited value in detecting core entities. Happily, human actions have other properties that can serve as more reliable invariants.

Coherence of temporal structure. Time provides an organizing structure that helps identify different entities. The many behaviors that are invariably performed simultaneously by one person share a common temporal structure. Condon and Ogston (1966) have labeled this self-synchrony, not to be confused with interactional synchrony, which will be discussed later in this section. Self-synchrony refers to the fact that separate parts of the body such as limbs, torso, and face tend to move—in fact, must move—together synchronously to a split second, in the sense that starts, stops, and changes in direction or speed in one muscle group will occur synchronously with starts, stops, and changes in other muscle groups. This does not mean that the two arms must be doing the same thing at the same time, nor that the face and leg, for example, start and stop moving together. It permits each body part to trace its own pattern and to start and stop independently, so long as they all adhere to a basic temporal structure such that changes in one body part occur, if they are going to, only in synchrony with changes in other parts. In addition, these changes in movement occur synchronously with natural speech boundaries at the phonemic level, such that the temporal structure of self-synchronous behavior is like an orchestra, in which the body is the conductor and the voice the music. (Try to pat your head, rub your belly, and count all at the same time. Violating temporal coherence in this activity can be done, but only with great concentration.) In short, all of the stimuli (auditory, visual, tactile, proprioceptive) emanating from the self share a common temporal structure, while all of those emanating from an other share a different temporal structure. Furthermore, Stern (1977) has found that all features of maternal self-synchronous behavior are highlighted or exaggerated, and Beebe and Gerstman (1980) have observed that the "packaging" of maternal behaviors into synchronous bursts or units is especially tight. Both of these observations suggest that mothers act to make the temporal structure of their behavior especially obvious.

There is a potential problem with all of this. Condon and Sander (1974) have suggested that in addition to self-synchrony, there also exists between mother and baby "interactional synchrony," in which the infant's movements are in perfect synchrony with the mother's voice. If this were true, then each partner's behavior would not in fact have a separate and distinct temporal structure, because the timing of the behavior would be largely determined by that of the partner. Since the original publication, however, there have been several unsuccessful attempts to replicate the original demonstration of interactional synchrony. There have also been unsuccessful attempts to demonstrate the same phenomenon using other and more precise methods. In spite of the rapid and wide initial acceptance of the phenomenon of interactional synchrony—its appeal is obvious—it has not stood the test of time, and we do not need to consider it. Self-synchrony does seem to have stood up, and we are left with two persons who, most of the time, have different and distinct temporal patterns common to their individual behavior.

If the infant were equipped with the ability to perceive a common temporal structure in that which is seen and heard, the task of differentiating self from other, and the task of differentiating this other from that other, would be greatly facilitated. Recent evidence strongly suggests that infants do indeed have such a capacity and that it is observable by four months of age, if not earlier.

Spelke (1976, 1979) has reported that infants are responsive to temporal congruity between auditory and visual stimuli, with a tendency to match events that are synchronous in time across sensory modality. She presented four-month-old infants with two animated cartoon films projected side by side, with the sound track appropriate (that is, synchronous) to only one of the films emanating from a speaker placed midway between the two images. The infants could tell which film was synchronous with the sound track and preferred to look at the sound-synchronous film. Through a variety of similar experiments, researchers have found that infants can recognize common temporal structure. It does not matter whether the two synchronous events are in the same modality (both visual) or in mixed modes (one auditory and one visual); infants will spot the two that share the same temporal structure (Spelke 1976; Lyons-Ruth 1977; Lawson 1980). Moreover, infants will notice a discrepancy of 400 milliseconds between a sight and sound that are expected to be paired, such as in lip reading (Dodd 1979).

This work suggests that temporal structure is a valuable invariant in identifying core entities. Infants act as though two events sharing the same temporal structure belong together. Taking the step from experimental stimuli to the stimuli provided by natural human behavior, it seems more than likely that infants should readily perceive that the sounds and sights (voice, movements, and expressions) that share a common temporal structure belong to an entity (self or other) that is distinct by virtue of its unique temporal organization (Spelke and Cortelyou 1981; Sullivan and Horowitz 1983). While there have as yet been no experiments that have extended these findings to the proprioceptive or tactile senses, the weight of evidence is increasing that infants inhabit a sensory world in which they integrate cross-modal experience, recognizing the patterns of sounds, sights, and touches that come from self and those that come from an other as separate phenomena, each with its own singular temporal structure.

If we assume that the infant can identify coherent entities (such as mother's behavior) that have a common temporal structure, will the temporal structure that identifies her be destroyed or interfered with by the infant's own behavior? Will the performance by the infant of an arm movement or a vocalization get mixed up in the mother's temporal structure, or set up a competing temporal structure that obscures it? Can the infant exert selective auditory and visual attention to the temporal structure of the stimuli emanating from one member of the pair, without being distracted or having that structure disorganized by the behavior of the other member?

A recent experiment bears on this question. Walker et al. (1980) demonstrated the ability of four-month-old infants to be selectively inattentive to competing visual events with different time structures. The infants were placed in front of a rear projection screen. Two films of different events were projected on the same area of the screen, one superimposed upon the other. The sound track that was played was synchronous with only one of the films. The images of the two films were then gradually separated, so that they were seen side by side on the screen. After a moment's hesitation, the infants looked at the film that was not synchronous with the sound. They acted as though the film not accompanied by the sound track were a novel event, not noticed before; even though they had been watching it all along during the superimposition. The authors concluded that "perceptual selection is not accomplished through special mechanisms constructed in the course of cognitive development, but is a feature of the art of perceiving early on" (p. 9). The problem of one partner's disrupting the temporal structure of another partner's behavior and thus confusing the discrimination of a core self from a core other may be a theoretical problem for us, but it is not a practical problem for infants in real life.

Coherence of intensity structure. Another invariant identifying the behavior of a separate and distinct person is a common intensity structure. In the separate behaviors that emanate from one person, the modulations in the intensity gradient of one behavior or modality generally match the gradations in the intensity in another behavior. In an angry outburst, for example, the loudness of a vocalization is generally matched by the speed or forcefulness of an accompanying movement, not only absolutely but as the intensity of the behaviors is contoured during their performance. This match of intensity structure is true for the infant's own behavior and the infant's perception of that behavior. For example, as an infant's distress builds and the cry builds in intensity (as an acoustic event), so do the proprioceptive sensations in the chest and vocal cords and the sight and proprioception of a forcefully flailing arm. In short, all the stimuli (auditory, visual, tactile, proprioceptive) emanating from the self (versus other) may share a common intensity structure.

Is it possible that the infant utilizes the perception of levels of intensity to discriminate self and others? Recent experimental work, already mentioned in chapter 3, provides a clue that infants may be able to perceive common intensity level across modalities, just as they can perceive common shape or temporal structure across modalities, and that they can use this information to determine the source (self versus other) of interpersonal events. Lewcowicz and Turkewitz (1980) showed that infants in a laboratory setting can match the intensity of a stimulus experienced in one modality (light) with the intensity of a stimulus experienced in another modality (sound). Intensity-matching across modalities (the seeking of cross-modal equivalence of intensity) is thus another way in which infants are aided in distinguishing self from other.[4]

Coherence of form. The form (or configuration) of the other is an obvious property that "belongs" to someone and can serve to identify that person as an enduring and coherent entity. Infants of two to three months of age have no trouble recognizing the particular facial configuration that belongs to still photographs of their own mothers. Two questions arise. What happens when a face changes expression? And what happens when a face or head changes its angle or position of presentation? First, how does the infant handle internal changes in form? Whenever a face changes its emotional expression, its configuration changes. Does the infant identify different expressional configurations as many different faces, resulting in a "happy mother," a "sad mother," a "surprised mother," and so on, each a separate and unrelated entity? Spieker has results suggesting that infants "know" that the same face showing happiness, surprise, or fear is

4. Several authors have recently stressed that gradient or dimensional information, as opposed to categorical information (brightness vs. pattern, or loudness vs. phonemic structure), has greater importance for the infant than for the adult (Emde 1980a; Stern et al. 1983). Given that young infants may be particularly attentive to the quantitative variations in stimulation, especially variations in intensity, in preference to qualitative variation, the ability to match intensities across modalities will be most helpful in dscriminating whether a particular stimulus (such as the loudness of a vocalization or the speed of forcefulness of a movement) belongs to one or the other member of the dyad in which the infant is participating.

still the same face (1982). They conserve the identity of a particular face across the various transformations of that face in different facial expressions.[5]

The second question is, how do infants handle external changes in form? The boundary form of the face changes as the head is turned, so that the face is seen full on, in a three-quarter presentation, and in profile. Similarly, as a person comes forward or goes away, the size of the face changes, even though the configuration is not transformed. Is a "new" entity revealed to the infant with each of these changes? Are there small mothers, large mothers, full-faced mothers, profile mothers?

The infant's perceptual system (given some experience with the world) seems able to keep track of the identity of an object in spite of changes in its size or distance, its orientation or position of presentation, its degree of shading, and so on. While different theories abound as to how the infant can maintain the identity of inanimate objects across these kinds of changes (see, for example, Gibson 1969; Cohen and Salapatek 1975; Ruff 1980; and Bronson 1982). All agree that the infant can do it. These abilities certainly apply to human stimuli as well as inanimate ones. For example, Fagan finds that five- to seven-month-old infants can recognize the never-before-seen profile of a face after a short familiarization with the full face, or even better with the three-quarter view of the face (Fagan 1976, 1977).[6]

Sometimes these abilities may be enhanced by cues provided by the infant's abilities at cross-modal matching. Walker-Andrews and Lennon (1984) showed that when five-month-old infants were shown two movies side by side, one of a Volkswagen approaching and one of the same car receding, they would look at the approaching car if at the same time they heard the sound of a car getting

5. Spieker also found that when looking at strange faces an infant also conserves the identity of a given expression across different faces displaying that expression. While the infants could conserve both identity and expression, when dealing with strangers they acted as though the facial expression rather than the facial identity was more salient: "If you don't know them, you'd better know what their affect is, rather than who they are." When dealing with a very familiar face, we assume the reverse is the case: "It is still that person, but wearing a different expression."

6. Fagan found that infants extracted the most information about the invariants of configuration from a three-quarter face presentation, compared with a full or profile presentation. So do adults, according to police department experts in criminal identification.

progressively louder, and they would look at the receding car if the sound got progressively softer. The comings and goings of parents must provide innumerable similar examples.

The evidence thus suggests that distance and positional and expressional (internal) changes, which normally accompany the interactive behavior of an other, need not be seen as problematic for the infant. The infant recognizes that form survives these changes, and early in the infant's life, the invariant of form provides yet another means of discriminating one other from all others.

So far, we have discussed five different potential invariant properties that specify a coherent self entity. Many of these invariants are not truly invariant—that is, always nonvarying—but it is likely that their effect is cumulative in the task of discovering the separate organizations that constitute a core self and a core other. A remaining problem concerns whose organization belongs to whom. How, for instance, does the infant sense that a particular coherent organization of behaviors actually is his or her own, and not an other's? The most ready answer is to assume that only the infant's own organization is accompanied by the invariants of agency, especially volition and proprioception.

SELF-AFFECTIVITY

By the age of two months or so, the infant has had innumerable experiences with many of the affects—joy, interest, and distress and perhaps surprise and anger. For each separate emotion, the infant comes to recognize and expect a characteristic constellation of things happening (invariant self-events): (1) the proprioceptive feedback from particular motor outflow patterns, to the face, respiration, and vocal apparatus; (2) internally patterned sensations of arousal or activation; and (3) emotion-specific qualities of feeling. These three self-invariants, taken together, become a higher-order invariant, a constellation of invariants belonging to the self and specifying one category of emotion.

Affects are excellent higher-order self-invariants because of their relative fixity: the organization and manifestation of each emotion is well fixed by innate design and changes little over development (Izard 1977). The facial display (and therefore the proprioceptive feedback from the facial muscles) is invariant in configuration for each discrete affect. If the preliminary evidence of Ekman et al. (1983) is confirmed, each discrete affect also has a specific profile of autonomic firing with its concomitant discrete constellation of internal feelings, at least in adults. And finally, the quality of subjective feeling is specific to each emotion. Therefore, with each separate emotion there occurs the invariant coordination of three discrete self-invariant events.

The self-invariant constellation belonging to each discrete emotion occurs, for any infant, in a number of contexts and usually with different persons. Mother's making faces, grandmother's tickling, father's throwing the infant in the air, the babysitter's making sounds, and uncle's making the puppet talk may all be experiences of joy. What is common to all five "joys" is the constellation of three kinds of feedback: from the infant's face, from the activation profile, and from the quality of subjective feeling. It is that constellation that remains invariant across the various contexts and interacting others. Affects belong to the self, not to the person who may elicit them.

While we have been concerned so far in this discussion only with the categorical affects, a similar case can be made for the vitality affects. The infant experiences a multitude of crescendos, for example, in diverse actions, perceptions, and affects. All of them trace a similar family of activation contours that create a familiar internal state despite the variety of eliciting events. The subjective quality of feeling remains as the self-invariant experience.

SELF-HISTORY (MEMORY)

A sense of a core self would be ephemeral if there were no continuity of experience. Continuity or historicity is the crucial ingredient that distinguishes an interaction from a relationship, with self as well as with an other (Hinde 1979). It is the ingredient that accounts for Winnicott's sense of "going on being" (1958). The infant capacity necessary for this form of continuity is memory. Is the infant's memory up to the task of maintaining a core self-history—a self continuous in time? Is the infant capable of remembering the three different kinds of experience that make up the other main core self-invariants—agency, coherence, and affect? Does an infant of the age of two to seven months have a "motor memory" for experiences of agency, a "perceptual memory" for the experiences of coherence, and an "affect memory" for the affective experiences?[7]

The issues of agency mainly involve motor plans and acts and their consequences. It has long been assumed that infants must have excellent motor memories. Bruner (1969) has called such memory "memory without words." It refers to memories that reside in voluntary muscular patterns and their coordinations: how to ride a bicycle, throw a ball, suck your thumb. Motor memory is one of the more obvious features of infant maturation. Learning to sit, to perform hand-eye coordinations, and so on require some component of motor memory. Piaget implied exactly this (and more) in his concept of a sensorimotor schema.

It is now clear that there are recall memory "systems" that are not language-based and that operate very early (see Olson and Strauss 1984). Motor memory is one of them. Rovee-Collier and Fagen, and their colleagues have demonstrated long-term cued recall for motor memories in three-month-olds (Rovee-Collier et al. 1980; Rovee-Collier and Fagen 1981; Rovee-Collier and Lipsitt 1981). The infants were placed in a crib with an attractive overhead mobile. A string was tied connecting the infant's foot to the mobile, so that each time the infant kicked, the mobile would move. The infants quickly learned to kick to make the mobile move. Several days after the training session, the infants were placed in the same crib with an overhead mobile but without the attaching string. The context of room, personnel, crib, mobile, and so on recalled the motor act, and the infants began to kick at a high rate, even though there was no string and therefore no movement of the mobile. If a different mobile was used during the memory test session, the infant kicked less than with the original mobile; that is, it was a poorer cue for retrieving or recalling the motor act. Similarly, a change in the design of the crib guard, a peripheral visual attribute of the whole episode, altered

7. For the moment, the distinction between recognition memory (in the presence of the object to be remembered) and recall or evocative memory (in the absence of the object) will be overlooked. The dichotomy between recall and recognition memory has been overdrawn. There is probably no such thing as a memory that is spontaneously evoked (pure recall). Some association or cue, regardless of how farflung, must have triggered it. There is a continuum of recall cues, from farflung and slight, as occurs in some free association, to something fairly close to but not identical with the original, to the reappearance of the original itself, which brings us back to recognition memory (see also Nelson and Greundel 1981). The sharp distinction was partially due to the older assumption that recall memory systems had to be language- or symbol-based (Fraiberg 1969).

the infant's cued recall (Rovee-Collier, personal communication, 1984).

One can argue that cued recall is neither truly evocative memory nor recognition memory. The cue is not the same as the original, nor is the memory spontaneously recalled in vacuo. But that is immaterial. The point is that cued recall for motor experiences can be experimentally demonstrated, as well as inferred from natural behavior, and that these motor memories assure self-continuity in time. They thus constitute another set of self-invariants, part of the "motor self."

The issue of coherence mainly involves the infant's perceptions and sensations. What evidence exists for the infant's capacity for remembering perceptions? It is well established that infants by five to seven months have extraordinary long-term recognition memory for visual perceptions. Fagan (1973) has shown that an infant who is shown the picture of a strange person's face for less than one minute will be able to recognize the same face more than one week later. How early does this perceptual memory begin? Perhaps in the womb. DeCasper and Fifer (1980) asked mothers to talk to their fetuses, that is, to direct speech to their pregnant bellies during the last trimester of pregnancy. He gave each a particular script to speak many times each day. The scripts used (for example, passages from stories by Dr. Seuss) had distinctive rhythmic and stress patterns. Shortly after birth the infants were "asked" (using sucking as the response) whether the passage they had heard in utero was more familiar than a control passage. The infants treated the passage they had been exposed to as familiar. In a similar vein, Lipsitt (personal communication, 1984) presented pure tones to fetuses just prior to a caesarian delivery. The tones were treated as familiar by the newly born infants. Thus, for some events, recognition memory appears to operate across the birth gap.

The recognition memory for the smell of the mother's milk and for the mother's face and voice has already been mentioned. It is clear that the infant has an enormous capacity for registering perceptual events in memory. Furthermore, whenever recognition memory of external events occurs, it is not only continuity of the external world that is affirmed, but also continuity of the mental percepts or schemas that permit recognition to begin with. The likelihood that recognition memory is experienced as self-affirming, as well as world-affirming, is suggested by the well-known "smile of recognition," which may be more than pleasure at successful effortful assimilation. ("My mental representation works—that is, it applies to the real world—and that is pleasurable!") In this light, the act of memory itself can be seen as a self-invariant.

Finally, what evidence exists for the infant's capacity to recognize or recall affective experiences? Emde has recently spoken of an affective core to the prerepresentational self (1983). This is exactly what we mean by the continuity of affective experience, in the form of constellations of self-invariants, that contributes to the sense of continuity of self. Affects, as we have seen, are well suited to this task because after two months emotions as displayed and presumably felt change very little from day to day or from year to year. Of all human behavior, affects perhaps change the least over the life span. The muscles that the two-month-old uses to smile or cry are the exact same ones that the adult uses. Accordingly, the proprioceptive feedback from smiling or crying remains the same from birth to death. For this reason, "our affective core guarantees our continuity of experience across development in spite of the many ways we change" (Emde 1983, p. 1). But this does not answer the question of whether the specific conditions that elicit particular affective experiences can be remembered at these ages.

To answer this question experimentally, Nachman (1982) and Nachman and Stern (1983) made six- to seven-month-old infants laugh with a hand puppet that moved, "spoke," and played peek-a-boo, disappearing and reappearing. When the infants were shown the puppet a week later, the sight of it made them smile.[8] This response is considered cued recall because the sight alone of the unmoving, silent puppet made them smile; in other words, it activated an affective experience. Moreover, they smiled at the puppet only after they had had the game experience. Cued recall memory for affective experience as well as motor experience thus seems not to have to await the development of linguistic encoding vehicles. A different form of encoding is involved. This should hardly be surprising to most psychoanalytic theorists, who have always assumed

8. This was not a smile of recognition, because another group of infants were shown unmoving puppets that did not make them smile. When this group returned one week later they recognized the test puppet in a paired comparison procedure, but they never smiled at it in spite of their recognition.

that affect memories were laid down from the first moments, or at least weeks, of life and have in fact described the first year of this process (McDevitt 1979).

Gunther describes an example of cued recall memory for an affective experience in the first days of life (1967). A newborn whose breathing is accidentally occluded by the breast during a feeding will be "breast shy" for the next several feedings. Clearly, the infant has the memorial capacities to register, recognize, and recall affective experiences so that continuity of the affective self is assured.

In short, the infant has the abilities to maintain an updated history for his "motor," "perceptual," and "affective" selves—that is, for his agency, coherence and affectivity.

Integrating the Self-Invariants

How do agency, coherence, affectivity, and continuity all become integrated into one organizing subjective perspective? Memory may provide the answer to the extent that it is a system or process for integrating the diverse features of a lived experience. An experience as lived in real time does not have a completed structure until it is over. Its structure is then immediately reconstituted in memory. It is in this sense that the structure of experience as it is lived and as it is remembered may not be so different, and a closer look at what is called *episodic memory* is now crucial for understanding how the different self-invariants embedded in lived experience are integrated.

Episodic memory, as described by Tulving (1972), refers to the memory for real-life experiences occurring in real time. These episodes of lived experience range from the trivial—what happened at breakfast this morning, what I ate, in what order, where I was sitting—to the more psychologically meaningful—what I experienced when they told me my father had had a stroke. Episodic memory has the great advantage, for our purposes, of being able to include actions, perceptions, and affects as the main ingredients or attributes of a remembered episode. It is therefore the view on memory that is most relevant to our inquiry about infant experience. It attempts to render the daily personal events of a life in memorial and representational terms (Nelson 1973, 1978; Shank and Abelson 1975, 1977; Nelson and Greundel 1979, 1981; Nelson and Ross 1980; Shank 1982).

The basic memorial unit is the episode, a small but coherent chunk of lived experiences. The exact dimensions of an episode cannot be specified here; they represent an ongoing problem in the field. There is agreement, however, that an episode is made of smaller elements or attributes. These attributes are sensations, perceptions, actions, thoughts, affects, and goals, which occur in some temporal, physical, and causal relationship so that they constitute a coherent episode of experience. Depending on how one defines episodes, there are no lived experiences that do not clump to form episodes, because there are rarely, if ever, perceptions or sensations without accompanying affects and cognitions and/or actions. There are never emotions without a perceptual context. There are never cognitions without some affect fluctuations, even if only of interest. An episode occurs within one single physical, motivational setting; events are processed in time and causality is inferred, or at least expectations are set up.

An episode appears to enter into memory as an indivisable unit. The different pieces, the attributes of experience that make up an episode, such as perceptions, affects, and actions, can be isolated from the entire episode of which they are attributes. But in general the episode stands as a whole.

Let us say that an infant has experienced a specific episode once, an episode with the following attributes: being hungry, being positioned at the breast (with accompanying tactile, olfactory, and visual sensations and perceptions), rooting, opening mouth, beginning to suck, getting milk. Let us call that a "breast-milk" episode. The next time a similar "breast-milk" episode occurs, if the infant can recognize that most of the important attributes of the current "breast-milk" episode are similar to the past "breast-milk" episode, two *specific* "breast-milk" episodes will have occurred. Two may be enough, but surely if several more occur with detectable similarities and only minor differences, the infant will soon begin to form a *generalized* "breast-milk" episode. This generalized memory is an individualized, personal expectation of how things are likely to proceed on a moment-to-moment basis. The generalized breast-milk episode is not in itself a specific memory any more; it is an abstraction of many specific memories, all inevitably slightly different, that produces one generalized memory structure. It is, so to speak, averaged experience made prototypic. (In this sense it is now potentially part of semantic memory.)

Now, suppose that the next time a specific breast-episode begins, a deviation from the generalized episode happens. For example, at the moment the infant takes the nipple, the infant's nose gets occluded by the breast. The infant cannot breathe, feels distress, flails, averts head from breast, and regains breath. This new specific episode ("breast-occlusion" episode) is similar to, yet importantly and recognizably different from, the anticipated generalized "breast-milk" episode. It becomes a remembered specific episode. Shank (1982) calls the memory of this specific "breast-occlusion" episode the result of a failed expectation. Memory is failure-driven in that the specific episode is only relevant and memorable as a piece of lived experience to the extent that it violates the expectations of the generalized episode.[9] An episode need not be so deviant as this to be memorable as a specific instance of the generalized episode, so long as it is distinctive enough to be discriminated from the prototype.

At this point, one of three things can happen. The "breast-occlusion" experience may never recur, in which case it will persist enshrined as a specific episodic memory. Gunther (1961) has reported that one episode of breast-occlusion appears to influence newborn behavior for several feedings afterwards. The episode then probably becomes part of long-term, cued recall memory. Or the breast-occlusion experience may recur again and again. In that case the specific episodes become generalized to form a new generalized episode, which we can call the generalized "breast-occlusion" episode. Once this has formed, specific instances of these episodes will be memorable as actual episodes only if they are detectably distinctive from the averaged generalized breast-occlusion episode.

Finally, after the first "breast-occlusion" experience, the infant may never again experience an actual specific instance of the generalized "breast-milk" episode. That is to say, there may continue to be feeding trouble, so that the mother has to switch to a bottle. In this case, the original "breast-milk" generalized episode will after a time no longer be a normal, expected part of daily living and may

9. The occlusion episode would be memorable for other reasons, too. But the concern here is mainly with the relations between relative events.

cease to be an active (even retrievable) memory structure.

There are several points to be made about generalized episodes. The generalized episode is not a specific memory. It does not describe an event that actually ever happened exactly that way. It contains multiple specific memories, but as a structure it is closer to an abstract representation, as that term is used clinically. It is a structure about the likely course of events, based on average experiences. Accordingly, it creates expectations of actions, of feelings, of sensations, and so on that can either be met or be violated.

Exactly what events make up these generalized episodes? Nelson and Greundel (1981), in their study of preschoolers, have focused on what might best be called external events (verbally reported as a rule) such as what happens at a birthday party. The actions that make up the episode are: decorate cake, greet guests, open presents, sing "Happy Birthday," blow candles, cut cake, eat cake. These actions occur predictably and in predictable temporal and causal sequence. Children as young as two years construct generalized episodes about these happenings. Nelson and Greundel have called these general schemes (with variable elements but structured wholes) Generalized Event Structures (GERs) and consider them to be basic building blocks of cognitive development as well as of autobiographical memory.

Our concern, in contrast, is with preverbal infants and with different happenings such as what happens when you are hungry and at the breast, or what happens when you and mom play an exciting game. Moreover, our interest concerns not only the actions but also the sensations and affects. What we are concerned with, then, are episodes that involve interpersonal interactions of different types. Further, we are concerned with the interactive experience, not just the interactive events. I am suggesting that these episodes are also averaged and represented preverbally. They are Representations of Interactions that have been Generalized (RIGs).

We do know that infants have some abilities to abstract, average, and represent information preverbally. A recent experiment on the formation of prototypes is instructive in describing the infant's capacities for the kind of process involved. Strauss (1979) showed ten-month-old infants a series of schematic face drawings. Each face was different in length of the nose or placement of the eyes or ears. After the whole series was shown, the infants were asked (in terms of the detection of novelty) which single drawing best "represented" the entire series. They chose a drawing that they had, in fact, never seen. It was a picture that averaged all of the facial feature sizes and placements previously seen, but this "averaged face" was not part of the series and had not been shown before. The conclusion is that infants have a capacity to aggregate experiences and distill (abstract out) an averaged prototype. I suggest that when it comes to more familiar and important matters, such as interactive experiences, the infant's ability to abstract and represent such experiences as RIGs, begins much earlier.

RIGs can thus constitute a basic unit for the representation of the core self. RIGs result from the direct impress of multiple realities as experienced, and they integrate into a whole the various actional, perceptual, and affective attributes of the core self.[10] RIGs can get organized in terms of particular attributes, just as attributes can get organized in terms of RIGs. Any one attribute, such as hedonic feeling tone, will set limits on what kinds of RIGs are likely to occur when that attribute is present.

Somehow, the different invariants of self-experience are integrated: the self who acts, the self who feels, and the self who has unique perceptions about the self's own body and actions all get assembled. Similarly, the mother who plays, the one who soothes, and the ones that are perceived when the infant is happy and distressed all get disentangled and sorted. "Islands of consistency" somehow form and coalesce. And it is the dynamic nature of episodic memory using RIGs as a basic memory unit that makes it happen.

The advantage of an episodic memory system similar to the one that has been briefly described here is that it permits the indexing and reindexing and the organizing and reorganizing of memorial events about self-invariants (or other invariants) in a fluid and dynamic fashion. It allows one to imagine attributes of many different kinds, interrelating in different ways and resulting in a growing and

10. Nelson and Greundel (1981) have argued that the task of forming generalized episodes is of obvious primary importance in infancy and young childhood and that a specific (episodic) memory only forms if it is an unusual example, that is, a partial violation of the generalized episode (Shank's failure-driven memory). She suggests that much of "infantile amnesia" can be explained by the fact that generalized episodes are insufficiently formed or still in formation, so that specific deviations (specific episodic memories) will not get encoded until the generalizing process is further advanced. In other words, there is nothing to remember against. Some of the real problems of reconstruction in treatment may have to do with the fact that specific memories are deviant examplars of a class of events.

integrating network of organized self-experience. (This is what Shank [1982] means by a dynamic memory.)

It is presumably in this way that the different major self-invariants of agency, coherence, and affectivity become sufficiently integrated (with continuity in the form of memory acting as part of the integrating process) that all together they provide the infant with a unified sense of a core self, suggest that during this life period, age two to seven months, the infant gains enough experience with the separate major self-invariants, and the integrating processes reflected in episodic memory advance far enough, that the infant will make a quantum leap and create an organizing subjective perspective that can be called a sense of a core self. (One would assume that a sense of a core other emerges in parallel via complementary processes.) During this period the infant has the capacities to recognize those events that will identify a self and an other. The social interactive situation offers multiple opportunities to capture those events. And the integrative processes are present to organize these subjective events. The combination of capacities, opportunities, and integrative ability, along with the clinical impression of a changed infant as a more complete person, makes it reasonable to conclude that a firm sense of a core self and a core other emerge during this period.

Chapter 5

The Sense of a Core Self: II. Self with Other

SOMETHING of importance is missing from the last chapter. We have discussed the infant's sense of self versus other, but not the sense of self *with* other. There are many ways that being with an other can be experienced, including some of the most widely used clinical concepts, such as merging, fusion, a haven of safety, a security base, the holding environment, symbiotic states, self-objects, transitional phenomena, and cathected objects.

The sense of being with an other with whom we are interacting can be one of the most forceful experiences of social life. Moreover, the sense of being with someone who is not actually present can be equally forceful. Absent persons can be felt as potent and almost palpable presences or as silent abstractions, known only by trace evidence. In the mourning process, as Freud (1917) pointed out, the one who has died almost rematerializes as a presence in many different felt forms. Falling in love provides a different normal example. Lovers are not simply preoccupied with one another. The loved other is often experienced as an almost continual presence, even an aura, that can change almost everything one does—heighten one's perceptions of the world or reshape and refine one's very movements. How can experiences such as these be accounted for in the present framework? How can the ultimately social nature of the infant's and the adult's experience be captured?

In Winnicott's, Mahler's, and many other theoretical renditions, the various important experiences of being with mother are founded on the assumption that the infant cannot adequately differentiate self from other. Self/other fusion is the background state to which the infant constantly returns. This undifferentiated state is the equilibrium condition from which a separate self and other gradually emerge. In one sense, the infant is seen as totally social in this view. Subjectively, the "I" is a "we." The infant achieves total sociability by not differentiating self from other.

In contrast to these views, the present account has stressed the very early formation of a sense of a core self and core other during the life period that other theories allot to prolonged self/other undifferentiation. Further, in the present view, experiences of being with an other are seen as active acts of integration, rather than as passive failures of differentiation. If we conceive of being-with experiences as the result of an active integration of a distinct self with a distinct other, how can we conceive of the subjective social sense of being with an other? It is now no longer a given, as it was in Mahler's undifferentiated "dual-unity."

Clearly, the infant is deeply embedded in a social matrix, in which much experience is the consequence of others' actions. Why, then, is it not reasonable to think, from the infant's subjective viewpoint, in terms of a merged "self/other" or of a "we self" in addition to the solitary self and other? Is not the infant's initial experience thoroughly social, as the British object relations school has taught us? From the objective viewpoint there do appear to be amalgam-like events between self and other. How will these be experienced? Let us approach this problem of the social self by first considering the nature of the self with the social other as an objective event.

Self with Other as an Objective Event

The infant can be with an other such that the two join their activities to make something happen that could not happen without the commingling of behaviors from each. For example, during a "peek-a-boo" or "I'm going to getcha" game, the mutual interaction generates in the infant a self-experience of very high excitation, full of joy and suspense and perhaps tinged with a touch of fear. This feeling state, which cycles and crescendos several times over, could never be achieved by the infant alone at this age, neither in its cyclicity, in its intensity, nor in its unique qualities. Objectively, it is a mutual creation, a "we" or a self/other phenomenon.

The infant is with an other who regulates the infant's own self-experience. In this sense, the other is a *self-regulating other* for the infant.[1] In games like peek-a-boo, it is the regulation of the infant's arousal that is mainly involved. We can speak of a self-arousal-regulating other. Arousal, however, is only one of many possible self-experiences that others can regulate.

Affect intensity is another infant self-experience of arousal that is almost continually regulated by caregivers. For instance, in smiling interactions the dyad can increase by increments the level of intensity of the affect display. One partner increases a smile's intensity, eliciting an even bigger smile from the other partner, which ups the level yet again, and so on, producing a positive feedback spiral. (See Beebe [1973], Tronick et al. [1977], and Beebe and Kroner [1985] for fuller descriptions of these leadings and followings.)

Security or attachment is another such self-experience. All the events that regulate the feelings of attachment, physical proximity, and security are mutually created experiences. Cuddling or molding to a warm, contoured body and being cuddled; looking into another's eyes and being looked at; holding on to another and being held—these kinds of self-experiences with an other are among the most totally social of our experiences, in the straightforward sense that they can never occur unless elicited or maintained by the action or presence of an other. They cannot exist as a part of known self-experience without an other. This is true even if the self-regulating other is fantasied rather than actual. (The experience of hugging demands a partner even in fantasy, or else it can only be performed but not fully experienced. This applies to hugging pillows as well as people. The issue is not whether the pillow hugs back, only that the pillow be physically present or the sensation of it be imagined. In this sense there is no such thing as half a hug or half a kiss.)

1. "Self" is used here not reflexively but, as elsewhere in the book, to denote the infant's self. A self-regulatory other is thus one who regulates the infant, not the other.

Attachment theorists have stressed the indispensable role played by others in the regulation of security. While attachment is of enormous importance as an index of the quality of the parent/child relationship, it is not however, synonymous with the entire relationship. There are many other self-experiences regulated by others that fall outside the proper boundaries of attachment. Excitation has already been described, and others will be described later.

Parents can also regulate what affect category the infant will experience. Such regulation may involve interpreting the infant's behavior, asking questions like, "Is that face to be taken as funny or surprising?" "Is that cup-banging to be taken as amusing or hostile or bad?" In fact, from two to seven months an enormous sector of the entire affective spectrum an infant can feel is possible only in the presence of and through the interactive mediation of an other, that is, by being with another person.

Both infant and caregiver also regulate the infant's attention, curiosity, and cognitive engagement with the world. The caregiver's mediation greatly influences the infant's sense of wonder and avidity for exploration.

Historically most notable, others regulate the infant's experiences of somatic state. These experiences are the ones that have traditionally preoccupied psychoanalysis, namely, the gratification of hunger and the shift from wakeful fatigue to sleep. In all such regulations, a dramatic shift in neurophysiological state is involved. One of the reasons why these events have received such attention in psychoanalysis, which eclipsed for a long while the ability to discern the importance of the other ways of being with a self-regulating other, is undoubtedly that they were more readily explicable in terms of libido shifts and the energetic model, which the other forms of being-with are not. And this way of being-with is clearly of great importance. It is these experiences and their representation, more than any others, that have been thought to approximate most closely the feeling of total merging, of obliterating self/object boundaries and fusing into a "dual-unity." There is no reason, however, why satiation of hunger or falling into sleep should be construed as passing into a state of dual-unity unless one assumes that "symbiosis" is the lived experience of having excitation fall to zero, when subjective experience of any import effectively stops, as is described and implied in the pleasure principle. Most traditional theories do in fact assume just that, and we will examine this assumption in detail in chapter 9. It is just as likely, however, that experiences of hunger reduction and other somatic state regulations are mainly experienced as dramatic transformations in self-state that require the physical mediation of an other (Stern 1980). In that case, the predominant experience would be being with a somatic-state-regulating other rather than merging.

There have now been enough observations of well-fed institutionalized infants and kibbutz babies, as well as of primate behavior, to make it clear that strong feelings and important representations are forged not necessarily by the very acts of being fed or put to sleep (that is, by somatic-state-regulating others) but rather by the manner in which these acts are performed. And the manner is often best explained by the previously listed forms of self-regulation by others. The great advantage of the feeding experience is that it puts into play and brings together, at one time, so many different forms of self-regulation. Finally, Sander (1964, 1980, 1983a, 1983b) has continued to point out that the infant's states of consciousness and activity are ultimately socially negotiated states, taking their form, in part, through the mediation of self-regulating others.

It is clear that the social action of self-regulating others is a pervasive objective fact bearing on the infant's experience, but how may this be experienced subjectively?

Self with Other as a Subjective Experience

Somehow the infant registers the objective experience with self-regulating others as a subjective experience. These experiences are the same ones that have been called mergings, fusings, security gratifications, and so on.

Psychoanalysis has made a distinction between primary mergers and secondary mergers, and the experience we are considering presumably falls into one or the other type. Primary fusions are those experiences of boundary absence, and therefore sensing oneself to be part of an other, because of a maturational inability—that is, the failure to differentiate self from other. Secondary mergers are those experiences of losing one's perceptual and subjective boundaries after they have been formed and, so to speak, being engulfed by or dissolving into an other's semipermeable personhood. These secondary merger experiences are thought to be re-editions of primary mergers, brought about by regression secondary to some wish-related defensive operation.[2]

In the position taken here, these important social experiences are neither primary nor secondary mergers. They are simply the actual experience of being with someone (a self-regulatory other) such that self-feelings are importantly changed. During the actual event, the core sense of self is not breached: the other is still perceived as a separate core other. The change in self-experience belongs to the core self alone. The changed core self also becomes related (but not fused) with the core other. The self-experience is indeed dependent upon the presence and action of the other, but it still belongs entirely to the self. There is no distortion. The infant has accurately represented reality. Let us examine these assumptions in the form of several questions.

First, why does the experience with a self-regulating other not breach or confuse the sense of a core self and a core other? To address this question, let us return to the earlier example of the infant's experience of excitation as regulated by an other in a peek-a-boo game. Why does the infant continue to experience the cycles of anticipation and joy as belonging to the core self? Similarly, why do the wonderful disappearing-reappearing antics belong to mother, as a core other? Why are neither selfhood nor otherness breached or dissolved?

The core senses of self and other do not get disrupted for several reasons. Under normal conditions, the infant has experienced similar joyful cycles of suspense buildup and punch line in other, slightly

2. The idea of subjective states of fusion was born of two quite separate concepts. The first concept embraced pathological states seen in older children (*symbiotic psychosis*), in which the child experiences the dissolution of self/other boundaries and resultant feelings of fusion. It also embraces the wish for merger and the fear of engulfment, which are not uncommon clinical features in adult patients. The second concept is the now-familiar assumption that the infant experiences a protracted period of self/other undifferentiation. It was not a long retrospective leap backward in time to assume that if infants could not discriminate self from other, they too would experience states of self/other unity of merger like those reported by older patients. In this way, the notion of primary fusion experiences was historically inspired by the observation of secondary fusion experiences. Primary fusion was a pathomorphic, retrospective, secondary conceptualization.

different situations: "I'm gonna get you" games, "walking fingers," "tickle the tummy," and a host of other suspense games that are standard fare at this age. The infant is also likely to have experienced a dozen or more variations of the peek-a-boo game to begin with: diaper over baby's face, diaper over mother's face, mother's face gets covered by baby's feet as they are brought together, her face rises above and sets below the horizon of the bed, and so on. No matter how mother does it, the infant experiences her antics as belonging to her as a core other; this is only one of the many ways of experiencing her organization, cohesion, and agency.

Moreover, the same general feeling state is engendered in the infant, regardless of which way the mother plays the game. And it is likely that this family of games has been played with the infant by others—father, babysitter, and so on. The particular affect, then, remains, despite variations in the interaction and changes in the interactants. It is only the feeling state that belongs to the self, that is a self-invariant.

Variety is what permits the infant to triangulate and identify what invariants belong to whom. And normal parent/infant interactions are, of course, necessarily extremely variable. To highlight the crucial role of variety of experience in distinguishing self-invariants from other-invariants, imagine the following:

Suppose that an infant experienced joyful cycles of anticipation and resolution only with mother, and that mother always regulated these cycles in the *exact* same way (virtually impossible). That infant would be in a tricky spot. In this particular, unchanging activity, mother would be sensed as a core other because her behavior would obey most of the laws (agency, coherence, continuity) that specify others as against selves. However, the infant could not be sure to what extent his or her feeling state was an invariant property of self or of mother's behavior since both would invariably accompany this feeling. (This is close to the picture of self/other undifferentiation assumed by many, except that we have derived it from the mother's limitations rather than from the infant's.)

Under the normal conditions of inevitable variety, then, the infant should have no trouble in sensing who is who and what belongs to whom in these kinds of encounters. There are, however, many games and routines in which a great degree of similarity of behavior between parent and infant is the rule. May not these present a more difficult task for the infant in distinguishing self from other and from "us"? These include early forms of pat-a-cake, where mother makes her hands and the infant's hands do the same thing, various imitation routines, affect leading and following as in the mutual escalation of smiles, and many more. One could imagine that at such times the cues that specify self-invariants and other-invariants could partially break down, because in imitative interactions, the behavior of the other may be isomorphic (similarly contoured as far as intensity and vitality affects are concerned) and often simultaneous or even synchronous with the behavior of the infant. One might expect that these experiences are the ones that come closest to the notions of merging or of dissolution of self/other boundaries, at least on perceptual grounds (Stern 1980).

Even under these conditions, however, it is quite unlikely that enough of the differentiating cues can be obliterated. Infants' timing capacities are superb. They can detect split-second deviations from simultaneity. For instance, if a mother's face is shown to an infant of three months on a television screen but her voice is delayed by several hundred milliseconds, the infant picks up the discrepancy in synchrony and is disturbed by it, as by a badly dubbed movie (Trevarthan 1977; Dodd 1979). Similarly, it is the ability to estimate time in the split-second range that permits the infant to distinguish the sounds /ba/ and /pa/, which differ only in timing of voice onset (Eimas et al. 1971, 1978). Even if the parent could act like a perfect mirror, the memorial continuity of a core sense of self could not be obliterated.[3]

What happens to the sense of self in those mutual interactions

3. Moments of self/other similarity tend to occur at times of high arousal and retain throughout life their ability to establish a strong feeling of connectedness, similarity, or intimacy, for good or ill. Lovers assume similar postures and tend to move toward and away from one another roughly simultaneously, as in a courting dance. In a political discussion that divides a group into two camps, those of the same opinion will be found to share postural positions (Scheflin 1964). Mothers and infants, when feeling both happy and excited, will tend to vocalize together. This has been given several different names: coacting, chorusing, matching, and mimicking (Stern et al. 1975; Schaffer 1977).

On the negative side, staring, facial or postural mimicking, and "shadow-talking" are all used by children to infuriate peers or adults. There is something intolerably invasive in the sense of negative intimacy in these particular experiences of self/other similarity (not self/ other unity). However, this sense of negative intimacy could not arise in infants in the domain of core-relatedness. It requires the assumption of the existence of separate other minds with intentions, and that is not available until the domain of intersubjective relatedness opens up later.

involving the regulation of the infant's security or state transformations? While these interactions are no more devoted to affective alterations than the interactions already discussed, they are historically considered more conducive to experiences of mergers. During these experiences, the parent's behaviors are complementary to the infant's (holding the infant, who is being held). In this sense, each partner is generally doing something quite different from the other. The intactness of self and other is therefore readily maintained, since the perceptual cues reveal the other to be following a different temporal, spatial, intensity, and/or movement organization from the self. In other words, all the cues that specify self-invariants or other-invariants (discussed in chapter 4) are undisturbed, so that no confusion in the sense of self versus sense of other need occur at the level of core-relatedness. It is thus reasonable that the sense of a core self and a core other need not be breached by the presence of self-regulating others, even when the experience concerns the infant's affect state.

A second question now arises. What is the relationship between the altered self-experience and the regulating role of the other who helped alter the infant's self-experience? Or, more to the point, how is that relationship experienced by the infant? We can answer for an adult or older child. Sometimes it screams out and seems to fill the entire attentional field, as in the powerful feelings of being with someone when you are insecure or scared, being enfolded in that person's arms and engulfed in something like security, of almost falling into the other's personhood (what a normal "merger" experience is purportedly like).

At other times, the relationship between the altered self-experience and the regulatory role of the other is silent and goes unnoticed. This situation is analogous to the silent or invisible presence of the "self-other" as well expressed in the terminology of Self Psychology by Wolf (1980) and Stechler and Kaplan (1980).

> Setting aside, for the moment, any particular age-appropriate form of the selfobject need, one may compare the need for the continuous presence of a psychologically nourishing selfobject milieu with the continuing physiological need for an environment containing oxygen. It is a relatively silent need of which one becomes aware sharply only when it is not being met, when a harsh world compels one to draw the breath in pain. And so it goes also with the selfobject needs. As long as a person

> is securely embedded in a social matrix that provides him with a field in which he can find, but does not have to be actually utilizing the needed mirroring responses and the needed availability of idealizable values, he will feel comfortably affirmed in his total self and, paradoxically, relatively self-reliant, self-sufficient, and autonomous. But, if by some adversity of events this person would find himself transported into a strange environment, it will be experienced as alien and even hostile, no matter how friendly it might be disposed toward him. Even strong selves tend to fragment under such circumstances. One can feel loneliest in a crowd. Solitude, psychological solitude, is the mother of anxiety. (Wolf 1980, p. 128)

Whether the relationship between altered self-experience and the regulating role of the other is obvious or unobtrusive, the alteration in self-experience always belongs entirely to the self. Even in the obvious situation of a security need being met, the other may appear to provide—may actually even seem to possess—the "security" before enfolding you. But the feeling of becoming secure belongs only to the self. In those situations when the regulatory role of the other goes unnoticed, the experience of self-alteration belongs only to the self by default.

The previous discussion addressed the question of who subjectively owns, so to speak, the alteration in self-experience—the self, the other, or some "we" or fused amalgam. The answer seems to be that it falls completely within the domain of the sense of self. This issue of subjective ownership, however, leaves unanswered the question of how the relationship is sensed.

Some relationship must come to exist between the change in self-experience and the regulating role, obvious or unobtrusive, of the other, simply because they tend to occur together. They become related as do any attributes of a repeated lived experience. They are not elements that are fused or confused; they are simply related. They are two of the more salient elements (that is, attributes) of any particular lived experience with a self-regulating other. Merger experiences at this age are simply a way of being with someone, but someone who acts as a self-regulating other. Any such lived experience includes: (1) significant alterations in the infant's feeling state that seem to belong to the self even though they were mutually created by self with an other, (2) the other person, as seen, heard, and felt at the moment of the alteration, (3) an intact sense of a core self and core other against which all this occurs, and (4) a variety of contextual and situational events. How can all of these be yoked to form a subjective unit that is neither a fusion nor a we-self nor a cool cognitive association between distinct selves and others? This yoking occurs in the form of an actual episode of life as lived. The lived episode—just as in memory—is the unit that locks the different attributes of the experience into relationships one with the other. The relationships are those that prevailed at the actual happening.

Viewed this way, the altering self-experiences and the regulatory role of the other are not simply associated in a learned way. Rather, they are embraced by a larger common unit of subjective experience, the episode, that includes them both along with other attributes and preserves their natural relations. Similarly, the altering self-experience and the perceptions of the other do not have to collapse into one another and become fused or confused. Rather, they can remain as distinct and separate components of the larger subjective unit, the episode.

Lived episodes immediately become the specific episodes for memory, and with repetition they become generalized episodes as described in chapter 4. They are generalized episodes of interactive experience that are mentally represented—that is, representations of interactions that have been generalized, or RIGs. For example, after the first game of peek-a-boo the infant lays down the memory of the specific episode. After the second, third, or twelfth experience of slightly different episodes, the infant will have formed a RIG of peek-a-boo. It is important to remember that RIGs are flexible structures that average several actual instances and form a prototype to represent them all. A RIG is something that has never happened before exactly that way, yet it takes into account nothing that did not actually happen once.

The experience of being with a self-regulating other gradually forms RIGs. And these memories are retrievable whenever one of the attributes of the RIG is present. When an infant has a certain feeling, that feeling will call to mind the RIG of which the feeling is an attribute. Attributes are thus recall cues to reactivate the lived experience. And whenever a RIG is activated, it packs some of the wallop of the originally lived experience in the form of an active memory.

I am suggesting that each of the many different self-regulating other relationships with the same person will have its own distinctive RIG. And when different RIGs are activated, the infant re-experiences different forms or ways of being with a self-regulating other. The activation of different RIGs can influence different regulatory functions, ranging from the biological and physiological to the psychic.[4]

Another question concerns the issue of being with self-regulating others who are present as compared with those who are absent, which in turn brings up the issue of "internalized" relationships. If the lines of argument presented here are followed, the distinction between present and absent self-regulating other does not loom so large, because in both cases infants must deal with their history with others. And this involves the subjective experience of being with an historical self-regulating other that may best be captured by the notion of being with an *evoked companion.*

Evoked Companions

Whenever a RIG of being with someone (who has changed self-experience) is activated, the infant encounters an evoked companion. This can be conceptualized as shown schematically in figure 5.1.

Suppose that the infant has already experienced six roughly similar specific episodes of a type of interaction with a self-regulating other. These specific episodes will be generalized and encoded as a Repre-

4. In discussing the psychobiology of bereavement in light of animal experimentation, Hofer remarks,

> Could the elements of the inner life that we experience with people who are close to us come to serve as biological regulators, much the way the actual sensorimotor interactions with the mother act for the infant animal in our experiments? And could this link internal object relations to biological systems? I think this may be possible. Certainly associative or Pavlovian conditioning is a well-known mechanism by which symbolic cues, and even internal time sense, can come to control physiological responses. Thus, it seems possible that the regulating action of important human relationships upon biological systems may be transduced, not only by sensorimotor and temporal patterning of the actual interactions, but also by the internal experiences of the relationship as it is carried out in the minds of the people involved. A permanent loss is sustained at both levels of organization, so that both representational and actual interactions are affected by the reality of the event. (Hofer 1983, p. 15)

Field (in press), in her work on the response of infants to extended maternal separation, reaches toward a similar conclusion as Reite et al. (1981) in their work on infant monkeys.

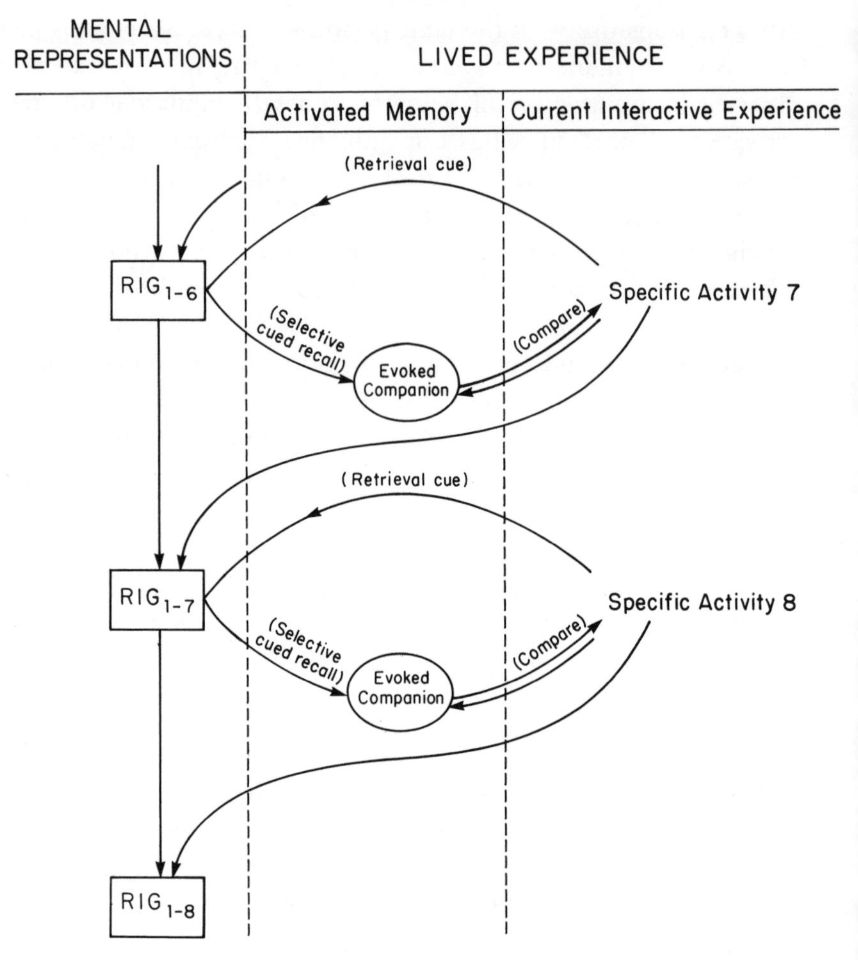

Figure 5.1

sentation of Interaction that has been Generalized ($RIG_{1\text{-}6}$). When a similar but not identical specific episode is next encountered (specific episode #7), some of its attributes act as a retrieval cue to the $RIG_{1\text{-}6}$. The $RIG_{1\text{-}6}$ is a representation and not an activated memory. The retrieval cue evokes from the RIG an activated memory which I will call an *evoked companion.* The evoked companion is an experience of being with, or in the presence of, a self-regulating other, which may occur in or out of awareness. The companion is evoked from the RIG not as the recall of an actual past happening, but as an active exemplar of such happenings. This conceptualization seems necessary to explain the form in which such events are encountered in clinical and everyday life—to put some experiential flesh on an abstract representation. Abstract representations such as RIGs are not experienced in the form of life as lived. They must be instantiated in the form of an activated memory that can be part of lived experience.[5] (The evoked companion is not a companion in the sense of a comrade but in the sense of a particular instance of one who accompanies another.)

The evoked companion functions to evaluate the specific ongoing interactive episode. The current interactive experience (specific episode #7) is compared with the simultaneously occurring experience with the evoked companion. This comparison serves to determine what new contributions the current specific episode (#7) can make in revising the $RIG_{1\text{-}6}$. To the extent that specific episode #7 is unique, it will result in some alteration in the RIG, from $RIG_{1\text{-}6}$ to $RIG_{1\text{-}7}$. The RIG will thus be slightly different when it is later encountered by the next specific episode (#8), and so on. In this fashion RIGs are slowly updated by current experience. However, the more past experience there is, the less relative impact for change any single specific episode will have. History builds up inertia. (This is essentially what Bowlby means in stating that working models of mother, a different unit of representation from RIGs, are conservative.)

Evoked companions can also be called into active memory during episodes when the infant is alone but when historically similar episodes involved the presence of a self-regulating other. For instance, if a six-month-old, when alone, encounters a rattle and manages to grasp it and shake it enough so that it makes a sound, the initial pleasure may quickly become extreme delight and exuberance, expressed in smiling, vocalizing, and general body wriggling. The extreme delight and exuberance is not only the result of successful mastery, which may account for the initial pleasure, but also the historical result of similar past moments in the presence of a delight- and exuberance-enhancing (regulating) other. It is partly a social response, but in this instance it occurs in a nonsocial situation. At such moments, the initial pleasure born of successful mastery acts as a retrieval cue to activate the RIG, resulting in an imagined interaction with an evoked companion that includes the shared and mutually induced delight about the successful mastery. It is in this way that

5. Psychoanalysis also struggles with the same problems in considering representations. Are they to be treated as images in memory, concepts, abstractions, or a report on overall mental functioning about a focus of interest (see Friedman 1980)?

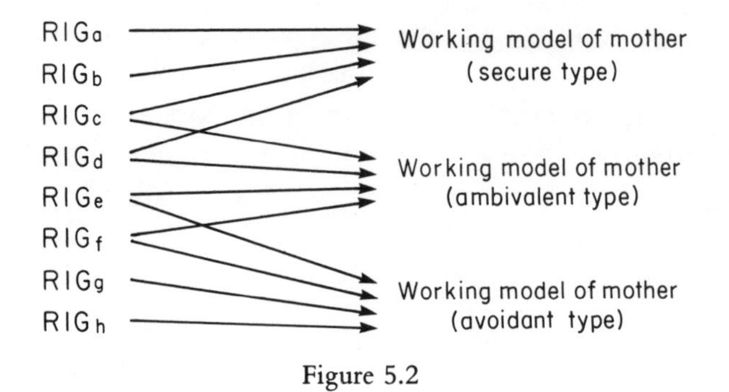

Figure 5.2

an evoked companion serves to add another dimension to the experience, in this case, extra delight and exuberance. So that even if actually alone, the infant is "being with" a self-regulating other in the form of an activated memory of prototypic lived events. The current experience now includes the presence (in or out of awareness) of an evoked companion.

The notion of RIGs and evoked companions bears important similarities to and differences from other postulated phenomena, such as the "working models of mother" in attachment theory, the selfobjects in Self Psychology, merger experiences in Mahlerian theory, early proto-forms of internalization in classical psychoanalytic theory, and "we" experiences (Stechler and Kaplan 1980). All these notions have arisen to fill a clinical need and a theoretical void.

The concept of the RIG and the evoked companion and the working model of attachment are different in several respects. First, they are of a different size and order. An individual RIG concerns the representation of a specific type of interaction. A working model concerns an assembly of many such interactions into a larger representation of a person's repertoire under certain conditions. The RIG can be conceptualized as the basic building block from which working models are constructed. This is shown schematically in figure 5.2.

Working models, as a larger construct, change as new RIGs are included and others are deleted and as the hierarchical structure of RIGs that constitute the working model are reorganized. Nonetheless, there has recently been a remarkable confluence of concern with the nature of the earliest representations or internal working models of mother. The current work of Sroufe (1985), Sroufe and Fleeson (1985), Bretherton (in press), and Main and Kaplan (in press) is all consistent with the general outlines of this approach. They have also found it necessary to turn to episodic memory as a fundamental process in the formation of these personal representations.

Second, RIGs are different from the working model of attachment theory in that working models, at least historically, concern expectations about the regulation primarily of security-attachment states. RIGs embody expectations about any and all interactions that can result in mutually created alterations in self-experience, such as arousal, affect, mastery, physiological state, state of consciousness, and curiosity, and not just those related to attachment.

Finally, the working model is conceived in highly cognitive terms and operates much like a schema that detects deviations from average expectation. The evoked companion as an activated RIG is conceived in terms of episodic memory and lends itself better to the affective nature of being with others, since the affective attributes of the lived and retrieved experience do not get transformed into cognitive terms that simply appraise and guide. In this sense, also, the evoked companion comes closer to the vividness of subjective experience, rather than taking the more experientially remote position of a guiding model. Nonetheless, evoked companions function like working models in two respects. First, they are prototypic memories that are not restricted to one past occurrence. Rather they represent the accumulated past history of a type of interaction with an other. Second, they serve a guiding function in the sense of the past creating expectations of the present and future.

The concept of the RIG and evoked companion differs importantly from selfobjects and mergers, in that the integrity of core sense of self and other is never breached in the presence of an evoked companion. It is also distinct from a "we" experience in that it is felt as an I-experience *with* an other. Finally, it differs from internalizations in that these in their final form are experienced as internal signals (symbolic cues), rather than as lived or reactivated experiences.

At some point in development there is no longer the necessity to retrieve the evoked companion and get a dose of the lived experience. The attribute alone serves as a cue that alters behavior, without a reliving of the generalized event. (This is no different from Pavlov's concepts of secondary signals in classical conditioning.) It remains an empirical question when this happens developmentally and whether, or under what circumstances, the secondary signal (the attribute) is really acting all alone or whether it usually activates the evoked companion to some extent. In either case, evoked companions never disappear. They lie dormant throughout life, and while they are always retrievable, their degree of activation is variable. In states of great disequilibrium such as loss, activation is very manifest.

Evoked companions operate during actual interactions with another person, as well as in the absence of others. They operate by becoming activated, so that a self-regulating other becomes "present" in the form of an active memory. Even during such interactions, in the presence of an other, evoked companions function to tell the infant what is now happening. They are a record of the past informing the present. For instance, if a mother plays a game of peek-a-boo in a very different manner from usual (let's say she is depressed and just going through the motions), the infant will use the companion evoked from the peek-a-boo RIG as a standard against which to check whether the current episode is something significantly changed, to be marked as a special variation, or an entirely new type of self-regulating-other experience. In this way evoked companions help to evaluate expectations and perform a stabilizing and regulating function for self-experience. This sounds like a working model in operation. But the detection of deviation may come about subjectively, in differences in the "presence" and "feel" of the evoked companion compared with the "actual" partner.

So far, we have discussed the use of RIGs mainly in the presence of the other, in fact, during an actual episode with the other. When that is the case, the infant needs only recognition memory to call to mind the evoked companion that is stored in memory, since the actual episode is happening now before the infant. But what about the retrieval of evoked companions in the absence of the other? This, after all, is when the concept of internalization is most generally needed for clinical purposes. The lived episode of being with an other must be recalled when the other is no longer present, requiring recall or evocative memory. It has traditionally been assumed that the infant's recall memory is not adequate to evoke the presence of someone absent until the age of nine to twelve months or so, as evidenced by separation reactions. Some theorists place the timing for evoking absent partners even later, in the second year, when symbolic functioning is available to be enlisted in the task of evocation. That would put these matters beyond the age period we are now considering. From what has already been said (see chapter 3), however, the evidence supports the view that the infant is capable of acts of cued recall memory beginning in the third month of life and perhaps before.[6]

In light of the infant's cued recall memory and memory for interpersonal happenings in terms of RIGs, it seems likely that the

6. It is generally assumed that the infant's elaboration of a "separation response" at nine months or so is the first major evidence of recall memory for interpersonal events. In addition to the other evidence of prior recall memory, there are several problems with this assumption. Schaffer et al. (1972), Kagan et al. (1978), and McCall (1979), among others, have criticized the more traditional view that separation distress comes about solely because the maturation of memory processes permits an internal representation of mother, so that at her departure the infant can evoke her memory and compare it against the condition of her absence, which reveals the infant's aloneness. Kagan et al. (1978), most notably, have raised such questions as, Why does the infant cry as the mother is moving away but still in sight? Why does the baby not cry when she leaves to go into the kitchen for the hundredth time that morning?

An alternate interpretation, basically similar to that proposed by Schaffer et al. (1972), suggests that two processes must come to maturation in order to produce separation distress. The first is the necessary, but not sufficient, condition that the infant has an enhanced ability to retrieve and hold a schema of past experience, that is, to evoke with recall memory an internal representation of the other. The traditional explanation stops here. The second necessary maturational ability to emerge at this age is the ability to generate anticipations of the future-representations of possible events. Kagan et al. (1978) describe this new capacity as the "disposition to attempt to predict future events and to generate response to deal with discrepant situations" (p. 110). If the child cannot generate a prediction or an instrumental response to deal with the prediction, uncertainty and distress result.

It may prove more helpful to break these two processes necessary for the separation reactions into three distinct processes: an improved recall (evocative) memory; the ability to generate future-representations of possible events; and the ability to generate communicative or instrumental responses to deal with the uncertainty and distress that are caused by incongruencies between present events and future representations of events. It is generally agreed that recall or evocative memory improves greatly toward the end of the first year of life. However, it is also clear that some recall memory is functioning long before the advent of separation distress at nine months. The notion, then, of "out of sight, out of mind" until nine months or so and "out of sight, but potentially in mind," thanks to recall memory (for people) after nine months, is not as clearcut as it seems.

In holding this view, we are closer both to Freud's original notion (1900) of the "hallucinated breast," in which he essentially invokes the newborn's use of cued recall memory (without calling it that), and to the recent findings on cued recall we have already alluded to. What Freud called the "hallucinated breast" could be called an attribute of a generalized episode of feeding. We would say that hunger acted as the cue to recall the other attribute, the breast. Freud would say that hunger created the tension that pushed for discharge, and in the face of a blocked motor discharge pathway, the impulse backed up and sought discharge through a sensory pathway, resulting in the hallucination. The sensory discharge was adaptive in that it would momentarily relieve the hunger, by the same amount as the sensory discharge reduced the tension.

Instead of emphasizing the discharge value of using a prototypic episode, we stress its organizing and regulating value. And instead of emphasizing the use of prototypic episodes under the presence of an acute need, we emphasize its continuous use in regulating and stabilizing all ongoing experience by providing continuity, that is, by contextualizing every experience in a history that is always being upgraded.

infant has almost constant rememberings (out of awareness) of previous interactions, both in the actual presence and in the absence of the other person involved in the interactions. I suggest that Freud's original model of the "hallucinated breast" was descriptively right, although it relied on the wrong mechanism. Whenever an infant encounters one part or attribute of a lived episode, the other attributes of that generalized episode (RIG) will be called to mind. Various evoked companions will be almost constant companions in everyday life. Is it not so for adults when they are not occupied with tasks? How much time each day do we spend in imagined interactions that are either memories, or the fantasied practice of upcoming events, or daydreams?

Another way to put all of this is that the infant's life is so thoroughly social that most of the things the infant does, feels, and perceives occur in different kinds of relationships. An evoked companion or internal representation or working model or fantasied union with mother is no more or less than the history of specific kinds of relationships (in Bowlby's terms, 1980) or the prototypic memory of many specific ways of being with mother, in our terms. Once cued recall memory has begun to function, subjective experiences are largely social, regardless of whether we are alone or not. In fact, because of memory we are rarely alone, even (perhaps especially) during the first half-year of life. The infant engages with real external partners some of the time and with evoked companions almost all the time. Development requires a constant, usually silent, dialogue between the two.

This view of being almost continuously with real and evoked companions encompasses what is generally meant when one says that the infant has learned to be trustful or secure in exploring the surrounding world. What could create trust or security in exploring, initially, if not the memory of past experiences with self and other in exploratory contexts? The infant is, in subjective fact, not alone but accompanied by evoked companions, drawn from several RIGs, who operate at various levels of activation and awareness. The infant is therefore trustful. This is a more subjective and more experience-near version of a working model.

The notion of self-with-other as a subjective reality is thus almost pervasive. This subjective sense of being-with (intrapsychically and extrapsychically) is always an active mental act of construction, however, not a passive failure of differentiation. It is not an error of maturation, nor a regression to earlier periods of undifferentiation. Seen in this way, the experiences of being-with are not something like the "delusion of dual-unity" or mergers that one needs to grow out of, dissolve, and leave behind. They are permanent, healthy parts of the mental landscape that undergo continual growth and elaboration. They are the active constitutions of a memory that encodes, integrates, and recalls experience, and thereby guides behavior.

BRIDGING THE INFANT'S SUBJECTIVE WORLD AND THE MOTHER'S SUBJECTIVE WORLD

We have discussed only the infant's subjective world and its relation to those interactive events that are observable to all. This was schematized in figure 5.1. But that is only half of the story. The mother also participates in the same observable interactive episodes, and she too brings her own history to influence her subjective experience of the ongoing observable interaction. In effect, the observable interaction in which both partners participate is the bridge between two potentially quite separate subjective worlds. In principle the dyadic system is symmetrical. The observable interaction acts at the interface. It is not symmetrical in practice, however, because the mother brings so much more personal history to each encounter. She has not only a working model of her infant, but a working model of her own mother (see Main 1985), a working model of her husband (who the baby may frequently remind her of), and various other working models, all of which will come into play.

Accordingly, we can expand figure 5.1 to include the mother's half as shown in figure 5.3. For the purpose of this expansion, what was called the "evoked companion" of the infant in figure 5.1 will be called more generically the "subjective experience of the observable event." To illustrate how this schematization might work, imagine a specific interactive episode: a baby boy, Joey, makes repeated attempts for attention, while mother ignores or refuses to acknowledge his appeals. This specific episode will evoke from the memories of both infant and mother a subjective experience in light of which the currently occurring interactive episode is apprehended. On the mother's side assume that the specific episode has evoked a particular RIG_k that is part of the mother's working model of her own mother as a mother (as indicated in figure 5.3). RIG_k, for example, is the

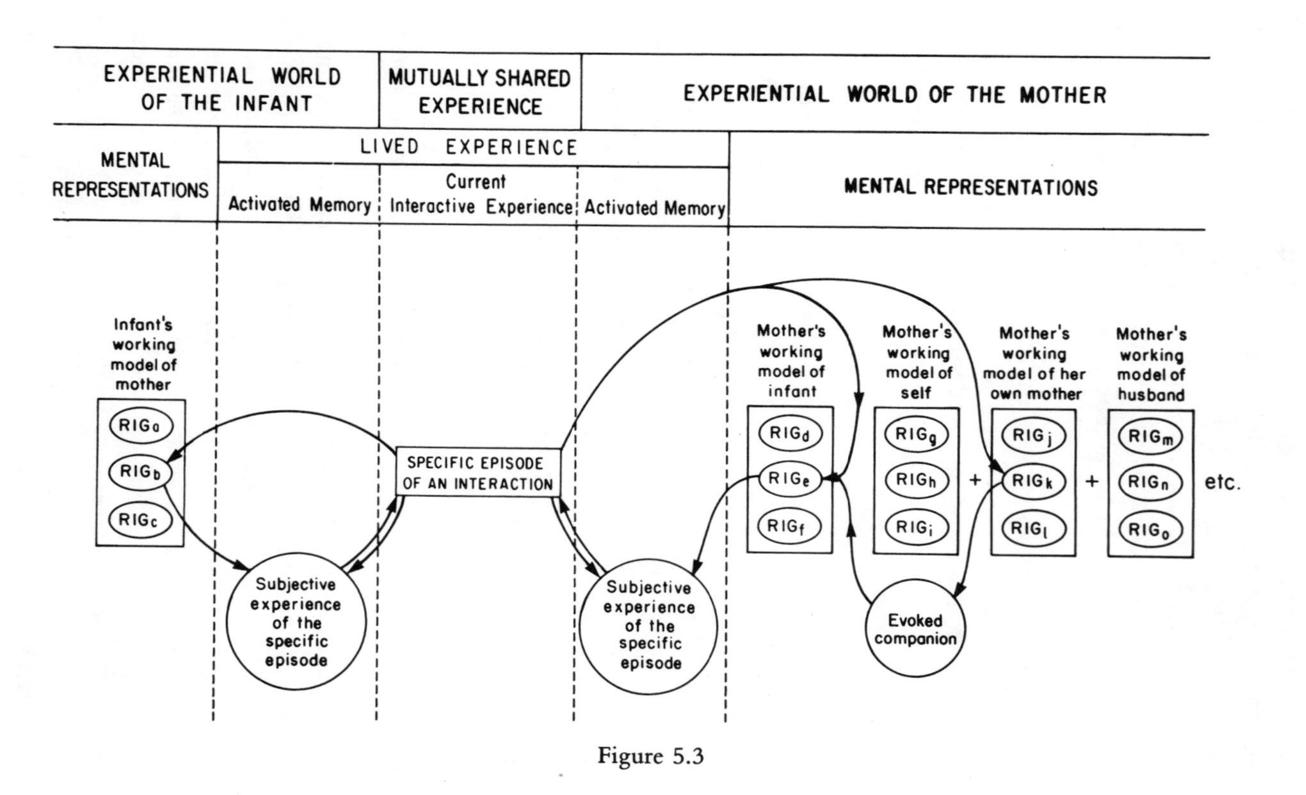
EXPERIENTIAL WORLD OF THE INFANT
MUTUALLY SHARED EXPERIENCE
EXPERIENTIAL WORLD OF THE MOTHER
MENTAL REPRESENTATIONS
LIVED EXPERIENCE
Activated Memory
Current Interactive Experience
Activated Memory
MENTAL REPRESENTATIONS
Infant's working model of mother
RIG_a
RIG_b
RIG_c
Subjective experience of the specific episode
SPECIFIC EPISODE OF AN INTERACTION
Subjective experience of the specific episode
Mother's working model of infant
RIG_d
RIG_e
RIG_f
Mother's working model of self
RIG_g
RIG_h
RIG_i
+
Mother's working model of her own mother
RIG_j
RIG_k
RIG_l
+
Mother's working model of husband
RIG_m
RIG_n
RIG_o
etc.
Evoked companion

Figure 5.3

specific representation of how the mother's mother tended to meet the appeals for attention (of Joey's mother when she was a child) with disdain and aversion. This particular aspect of the mother's mother becomes activated in the form of an evoked companion (a "ghost in the nursery," in Fraiberg's words, 1974). The evoked companion then plays a role in determining the choice of RIG_e to be evoked within the mother's working model of her own infant, Joey. The generalized interaction represented in RIG_e might be something like: Joey is always making unwanted, unreasonable demands for attention that are unpleasant. The evocation of the particular RIG_e will largely determine the mother's subjective experience of Joey's present appeal for attention.

In a similar fashion, the infant is forming a different subjective experience, from his past history, of the ongoing specific episode. It is in this way that the observable interactive event acts as a bridge between the two subjective worlds of infant and mother. In principal, this formulation is no different from that used in a global way by most psychodynamically-oriented clinicians. However, because it is conceptualized with more specificity and implies various discrete hierarchically arranged units and processes it may prove helpful in advancing our thinking about how maternal fantasies and attributions can influence not only the observable interaction but ultimately the shape of the infant's fantasies and attributions. It may also prove helpful in understanding how therapeutic interventions may operate to alter the parent's view of what her infant is doing and who that infant is. Further exploration of this enormous area is beyond the scope of this book, but active efforts in this direction are underway.[7]

We have attempted to retrieve what was missing in the last chapter, namely, the very social nature and presumably social subjective experience of the infant in the domain of core relatedness. There is one final issue to consider, which extends the social nature of the infant's experience even further.

7. Dr. Cramer and I are currently studying the interplay between the levels of observable interaction and maternal fantasies as well as the impact of intervention on both. (See B. Cramer and D. Stern, "A bridge between minds: How do the mother's and infant's subjective worlds meet?" [In preparation, to be presented at the World Association of Infant Psychiatry and Allied Professions, Stockholm, August 1986].) The above schematization was greatly contributed to by Dr. Cramer's group in Geneva.

Self-Regulating Experiences with Inanimate Things

Self-regulating experiences with things that have become personified can also occur at this age and level of relatedness. Such events fall at an early point on the developmental line that later includes transitional objects (like security blankets, which stand for and can be freely substituted for persons) and even later the larger realm of transitional phenomena embracing the worlds of art, as Winnicott (1971) has taught us.

During this period the mother very often enters into the infant's play by lending some things animate properties. She manipulates toys so that they swoop in and out and speak and tickle. They take on the organic rhythms and feelings of force, that is, the vitality affects of persons. And they elicit in the infant feeling states that are generally only elicited by persons. Both while and immediately after the mother imbues a toy with the actions, motions, vitality affects, and other invariant attributes of persons, the infant's interest in the toy is heightened. It is one of mother's main ways of maintaining the general flow of the infant's play with things. Once she has so imbued an object and withdraws, the infant is likely to continue to explore it alone, so long as it has the afterglow of personification. It has become, for the moment, a self-regulating person-thing, because like a self-regulating other it can dramatically alter experience of self.[8]

Well before the age of six months, infants appear to be able to discriminate animate from inanimate—that is, persons from things (Sherrod 1981). This means that they have identified the invariants that generally specify one or the other. Given this situation, a person-

8. We will encounter this again when the child starts to learn words, for a word can also become a personified thing. Fernald and Mazzie (1983) have shown that when a mother teaches a fourteen-month-old child the names of things, she uses a predictable strategy. When she wishes to mark a new or novel word in contrast to an old or familiar one, she does so by marking it with increased and exaggerated pitch contours, using both sharp pitch rises and rise-fall contours. Fernald points out that these marked pitch contours are intrinsically attention-getting, but she also implies that there is more to it than that. The most qualitatively special things to infants are the social behaviors of persons that are eliciting of and expressive of human vitality affects and regular emotions. When the mother intonationally marks a word, she is not simply raising the infant's attention nonspecifically; she is imbuing one particular word with human magic by making it a person-thing for the moment.

performed-thing will be viewed by the infant as some form of composite entity, a thing that has taken on some of the characteristics of a person. It has some of the invariant properties of both. The infant maintains an intact sense of things versus persons. The wonder of a personified thing lies in a successful constructionistic effort. It, too, is a success of integration, not a failure of differentiation.

At this point in the infant's development, a personified thing is a short-lived self-regulating person-thing. It is different, in several respects, from Winnicott's transitional objects: (1) the transitional object appears developmentally later; (2) the transitional object involves symbolic thinking, while the person-thing can be accounted for by episodic memory; (3) the existence of the transitional object, Winnicott assumed, implies some remaining lack of (or regression toward) self/other undifferentiation, while a personified thing does not.

The phenomena of self-regulating others and personified things indicate the degree to which the subjective world of infants is deeply social. They experience a sense of a core self and other, and along with these, they experience a pervasive sense of self being with other in multiple forms. All of these forms of being-with are active constructions. They will grow and become elaborated in the course of development, a process that results in the progressive socializing of experience.

Chapter 6

The Sense of a Subjective Self: I. Overview

THE NEXT QUANTUM LEAP in the sense of self occurs when the infant discovers that he or she has a mind and that other people have minds as well. Between the seventh and ninth month of life, infants gradually come upon the momentous realization that inner subjective experiences, the "subject matter" of the mind, are potentially shareable with someone else. The subject matter at this point in development can be as simple and important as an intention to act ("I want that cookie"), a feeling state ("This is exciting"), or a focus of attention ("Look at that toy"). This discovery amounts to the acquisition of a "theory" of separate minds. Only when infants can sense that others distinct from themselves can hold or entertain a mental state that is similar to one they sense themselves to be holding is the sharing of subjective experience or intersubjectivity possible (Trevarthan and Hubley 1978). The infant must arrive at a theory not only of separate minds but of "interfaceable separate minds" (Bretherton and Bates 1979; Bretherton et al. 1981). It is not, of course, a full-blown theory. It is rather a working notion that says something like, what is going on in my mind may be similar enough to what is going on in your mind that we can somehow communicate this (without words) and thereby experience intersubjectivity. For such an experience to occur, there must be some shared framework of meaning and means of communication such as gesture, posture, or facial expression.

When it does occur, the interpersonal action has moved, in part, from overt actions and responses to the internal subjective states that lie behind the overt behaviors. This shift gives the infant a different "presence" and social "feel." Parents generally begin to treat the infant differently and address themselves more to the subjective domain of experience. This sense of the self and other is quite different from what was possible in the domain of core-relatedness. Infants now have a new organizing subjective perspective about their social lives. The potential properties of a self and of an other have been greatly expanded. Selves and others now include inner or subjective states of experience in addition to the overt behaviors and direct sensations that marked the core self and other. With this expansion in the nature of the sensed self, the capacity for relatedness and the subject matter with which it is concerned catapult the infant into a new *domain of intersubjective relatedness.* A new organizing subjective perspective about the self emerges.

What relation does this new perspective bear to the already present sense of a core self? Intersubjective relatedness is built on the foundation of core-relatedness. Core-relatedness, with its establishment of the physical and sensory distinctions of self and other, is the necessary precondition, since the possibility of sharing subjective experiences has no meaning unless it is a transaction that occurs against the surety of a physically distinct and separate self and other. While intersubjective relatedness transforms the interpersonal world, however, core-relatedness continues. Intersubjective relatedness does not displace it; nothing ever will. It is the existential bedrock of interpersonal relations. When the domain of intersubjective relatedness is added, core-relatedness and intersubjective relatedness coexist and interact. Each domain affects the experience of the other.

When this leap in the sense of self occurs, how does the interpersonal world appear to be different? Empathy on the part of the caregiver now becomes a different experience. It is one thing for a younger infant to respond to the overt behavior that reflects a mother's empathy, such as a soothing behavior at the right moment. In the younger infant the empathic *process* itself goes unnoticed, and only the empathic *response* is registered. It is quite another thing for the infant to sense that an empathic process bridging the two minds has been created. The caregiver's empathy, that process crucial to the infant's development, now becomes a direct subject of the infant's experience.

At this stage, for the first time, one can attribute to the infant the capacity for psychic intimacy—the openness to disclosure, the permeability or interpenetrability that occurs between two people (Hinde 1979). Psychic intimacy as well as physical intimacy is now possible. The desire to know and be known in this sense of mutually revealing subjective experience is great. In fact, it can be a powerful motive and can be felt as a need-state. (The refusal to be known psychically can also be experienced with great power.)

Finally, with the advent of intersubjectivity, the parents' socialization of the infant's subjective experience comes to be at issue. Is subjective experience to be shared? How much of it is to be shared? What kinds of subjective experience are to be shared? What are the consequences of sharing and not sharing? Once the infant gets the first glimpse of the intersubjective domain and the parents realize this, they must begin to deal with these issues. What is ultimately at stake is nothing less than discovering what part of the private world of inner experience is shareable and what part falls outside the pale of commonly recognized human experiences. At one end is psychic human membership, at the other psychic isolation.

The Background of the Focus on Intersubjectivity

Given the far-reaching consequences of this quantum leap in the sense of self, how did it happen that we have been so slow to come upon the infant's discovery of intersubjective relatedness? Historically, several streams of inquiry flowed together to produce the recognition of this major developmental step. Philosophy has long dealt with the issue of separate minds. The necessity of assuming a developmental point when infants acquired a theory or working sense of separate minds is not alien to philosophical inquiry and, in fact, was often tacitly assumed (Habermas 1972; Hamlyn 1974; MacMurray 1961; Cavell 1984). Psychology, on the other hand, has been slower to deal with this issue in these terms, largely because the study of the development of subjective experience with persons, in comparison with the study of the development of knowledge of things, has been relatively neglected in recent academic psychology. Only now is the pendulum starting to swing back the other way, and pioneers such as Baldwin (1902), who firmly designated subjective experience of the self and other as the starting units for a developmental psychology, are being rediscovered in this country, as is Wallon (1949) in Europe.

Psychoanalysis has always been intensely concerned with the subjective experience of individuals. Except in the very special case of therapeutic empathy, however, it has not conceptualized intersubjective experience as a dyadic event, and this conceptualization is necessary to a generic view of intersubjectivity. It is also possible that the dominance of separation/individuation theory to explain the life period under discussion acted as an obstacle to a fuller appreciation of the role of intersubjectivity.

To be more specific on this point, ego psychoanalytic theory has viewed the period after seven to nine months as the time of emerging more fully ("hatching" is the metaphor) from the undifferentiated and fused state that preceded it. This phase was predominantly devoted to establishing a separate and individuated self, to dissolving merger experiences, and to forming a more autonomous self that could interact with a more separated other. Given this view of the major life task of this period, it is not surprising that the theory failed to notice that the appearance of intersubjective relatedness permitted, for the first time, the creation of mutually held mental states and allowed for the reality-based joining (even merging) of inner experience. Paradoxically, it is only with the advent of intersubjectivity that anything like the joining of subjective psychic experience can actually occur. And this is indeed what the leap to an intersubjective sense of self and other makes possible, just at the developmental moment when traditional theory had the tide beginning to flow the other way. In the present view, both separation/individuation and new forms of experiencing union (or being-with) emerge equally out of the same experience of intersubjectivity.[1]

1. The point is not to exchange symbiosis for intersubjectivity and reverse the order of developmental tasks. The point is that intersubjectivity is equally crucial for creating experiences of being with a mentally similar other and for furthering individuation and autonomy, just as core-relatedness is equally crucial for both physical autonomy and togetherness.

In spite of a general disregard of intersubjective experience as a dyadic phenomenon, theorists have regularly appeared, often just outside of the mainstream, who have held positions receptive to the concept of intersubjectivity or subjective relatedness. Vygotsky's notion of the "intermental" (1962), Fairbairn's of the infant's innate interpersonal relatedness (1949), and MacMurray's of the field of the personal (1961) as well as Sullivan's of the interpersonal field (1953), are influential examples. It was against this background that the recent findings of the developmentalists acted to bring the developmental leap of intersubjectivity into its present sharp focus. It is not surprising that these developmentalists were largely interested either in the role of intentionality in the mother-infant interaction or in how infants acquire language. Both routes would ultimately lead to the issue of intersubjectivity and its underlying assumptions, which the philosophers had long been dealing with.

The Evidence for Intersubjective Relatedness

What, then, is the evidence for the appearance of intersubjective relatedness at seven to nine months? Trevarthan and Hubley (1978) have provided a definition of intersubjectivity that can be operationalized: "a deliberately sought sharing of experiences about events and things." What subjective experiences does the infant give evidence of sharing or, at least, expecting the mother to share?

Recall that infants at this point in development are still preverbal. The subjective experiences that they can share must be of a kind that do not require translation into language. Three mental states that are of great relevance to the interpersonal world and yet do not require language come to mind. These are sharing joint attention, sharing intentions, and sharing affective states. What behaviors do infants show to suggest that they can conduct or appreciate these sharings?

SHARING THE FOCUS OF ATTENTION

The gesture of pointing and the act of following another's line of vision are among the first overt acts that permit inferences about the sharing of attention, or the establishing of joint attention. Mothers point and infants point. Let us start with the mother's pointing. For her pointing to work, the infant must know to stop looking at the pointing hand itself and look in the direction it indicates, to the target. For a long time it was believed that infants could not do this until well into their second year because they could not escape their egocentric position. But Murphy and Messer (1977) showed that nine-month-olds do indeed detach their gaze from the pointing hand and follow the imaginary line to the target. "What has been mastered at this stage is a procedure for homing in on the attentional focus of another. It is a disclosure and discovery routine . . . highly generative within the limited world inhabited by the infant in the sense that it is not limited to specific kinds of objects. It has, moreover, equipped the child with a technique for transcending egocentrism, for insofar as he can appreciate another's line of regard and decipher their marking intentions, he has plainly achieved a basis for what Piaget has called decentration, using a coordinate system for the world other than the one of which he is the center" (Bruner 1977, 276). Earlier than nine months, infants show a preliminary form of this discovery procedure: they follow the mother's line of vision when she turns her head (Scaife and Bruner 1975), just as the mother follows the infant's line of vision (Collis and Schaffer 1975).

So far, we have seen only a routine or procedure for discovering another's attentional focus. Infants of nine months, however, do more than that. They not only visually follow the direction of the point but, after reaching the target, look back at the mother and appear to use the feedback from her face to confirm that they have arrived at the intended target. This is now more than a discovery procedure. It is a deliberate attempt to validate whether the joint attention has been achieved, that is, whether the focus of attention is being shared, although the infant is not self-aware of these operations.

Similarly, infants begin to point at about nine months of age, though they do so less frequently than mothers do. When they do, their gaze alternates between the target and the mother's face, as when she is pointing to see if she has joined in to share the attentional focus.[2] It seems reasonable to assume that, even prior to pointing, the infant's beginning capacity to move about, to crawl or cruise, is crucial in discovering alternative perspectives as is necessary for joint attention. In moving about, the infant continually alters the perspective held on some known stationary sight. Perhaps this initial acceptance of serially different perspectives is a necessary precursor to the more generic "realization" that others can be using a different coordinate system from the infant's own.

These observations lead one to infer that by nine months infants have some sense that they can have a particular attentional focus, that mother can also have a particular attentional focus, that these two mental states can be similar or not, and that if they are not, they can be brought into alignment and shared. *Inter-attentionality* becomes a reality.

SHARING INTENTIONS

Researchers interested in infants' language acquisition have naturally been drawn to look at the most immediate origins of language use. These origins include the gestures, postures, actions, and nonverbal vocalizations that infants display just prior to and presumably as a precursor to language. Such protolinguistic forms have been examined closely by a number of researchers, all of whom agree in one way or another that beginning at about nine months the infant intends to communicate (Bloom 1973, 1983; Brown 1973; Bruner 1975, 1977, 1981; Dore 1975, 1979; Halliday 1975; Bates 1976, 1979; Ninio and Bruner 1977; Shields 1978; Bates et al. 1979; Bretherton and Bates 1979; Harding and Golinkoff 1979; Trevarthan 1980; Harding 1982). The intention to communicate is different from the intention simply to influence another person. Bates (1979) provides a working definition of intentional communication that we can use:

> Intentional communication is signaling behavior in which the sender is aware, a priori, of the effect that the signal will have on his listener, and he persists in that behavior until the effect is obtained or failure is clearly indicated. The behavioral evidence that permits us to infer the

2. Pointing is thought to originate in reaching, which gradually gets converted into a gesture (Bower 1974; Trevarthan 1974; Vygotsky 1966). In reaching, prior to age nine months, the child does not check back to mother's face; after nine months, in reaching that is more gesture than action, the infant does.

> presence of communicative intentions includes (a) alternations in eye gaze contact between the goal and the intended listeners, (b) augmentations, additions, and substitution of signals until the goal has been obtained, and (c) changes in the form of the signal towards abbreviated and/or exaggerated patterns that are appropriate only for achieving a communicative goal (p. 36).

The most straightforward and common examples of intentional communication are protolinguistic forms of requesting. For example, the mother is holding something the infant wants—say, a cookie. The infant reaches out a hand, palm up towards mother, and while making grasping movements and looking back and forth between hand and mother's face intones, "Eh! Eh!" with an imperative prosody (Dore 1975).[3] These acts, which are directed at a referent person, imply that the infant attributes an internal mental state to that person—namely, comprehension of the infant's intention and the capacity to intend to satisfy that intention. Intentions have become shareable experiences. *Interintentionality* becomes a reality. Once again, it need not be self-aware.

Soon after nine months of age, the beginning of jokes and teasing on the infant's part can be seen. Dunn has observed the interactions between older and younger siblings and has richly described many subtle events between them that imply that they have shared moments of intersubjectivity. For instance, a three-year-old and a one-year-old suddenly burst into laughter over a private joke for which no one else can find the eliciting cause. Similar eruptions of teasing episodes occur that also remain opaque to adult comprehension (Dunn 1982; Dunn and Kendrick 1979, 1982). Such events require the attribution of shareable mental states that involve intentions and expectations. You can't tease other people unless you can correctly guess what is "in their minds" and make them suffer or laugh because of your knowing.

SHARING AFFECTIVE STATES

Can infants also attribute shareable affective states to their social partners? A group of researchers (Emde et al. 1978; Klinert 1978;

3. This can rapidly become a "give and take" game, as commented on by Spitz (1965) and Piaget (1954). For a list of related examples see Trevarthan and Hubley (1978) and Bretherton et al. (1981).

Campos and Stenberg 1980; Emde and Sorce 1983; Klinert et al. 1983) have described a phenomenon they call social referencing.

The year-old infants are placed in a situation bound to create uncertainty, usually ambivalence between approach and withdrawal. The infant may be lured with an attractive toy to crawl across a "visual cliff" (an apparent drop-off, which is mildly frightening at one year of age or so) or may be approached by an unusual but highly stimulating object such as a bleeping, flashing robot like R2D2 from *Star Wars.* When the infants encounter these situations and give evidence of uncertainty, they look towards mother to read her face for its affective content, essentially to see what they should feel, to get a second appraisal to help resolve their uncertainty. If the mother has been instructed to show facial pleasure by smiling, the infant crosses the visual cliff. If the mother has been instructed to show facial fear, the infant turns back from the "cliff," retreats, and perhaps becomes upset. Similarly, if the mother smiles at the robot, the infant will too. If she shows fear, the infant will become more wary. The point for our purposes is that infants would not check with the mother in this fashion unless they attributed to her the capacity to have and to signal an affect that has relevance to their own actual or potential feeling states.

Recent preliminary findings in our laboratory (MacKain et al. 1985) suggest that infants at about nine months notice the congruence between their own affective state and the affect expression seen on someone's face. If infants are made sad and upset by several minutes' separation from mother (this is the age of acute separation reactions), as soon as they are reunited with her they stop being upset but remain solemn and are judged by mother and experimenters still to be sadder than usual. If then, right after the reunion when they are still sad, the infants are shown a happy face and a sad face, they prefer to look at the sad face. This does not happen if the infants are either made to laugh first or had not been separated in the first place. One conclusion is that the infant somehow makes a match between the feeling state as experienced within and as seen "on" or "in" another, a match that we can call *interaffectivity.*

Interaffectivity may be the first, most pervasive, and most immediately important form of sharing subjective experiences. Demos (1980, 1982a), Thoman and Acebo (1983), Tronick (1979), and others, as well as psychoanalysts, propose that early in life affects are both the primary *medium* and the primary *subject* of communication. This is in accord with our observations. And at nine to twelve months, when the infant has begun to share actions and intentions about objects and to exchange propositions in prelinguistic form, affective exchange is still the predominant mode and substance of communications with mother. It is for this reason that the sharing of affective states merits primary emphasis in our views of infants of these ages. Most protolinguistic exchanges involving intentions and objects are at the same time affective exchanges. (When the baby for the first time says "ba-a" and points to the ball, the people around respond with delight and excitement.) The two go on simultaneously, and findings that define a given event as primarily linguistic or primarily affective depend on perspective. However, the infant who is just learning the discursive mode appears to be far more expert in the domain of affect exchange. In a similar vein, Trevarthan and Hubley (1978) have commented that the sharing of affective moods and states appears before the sharing of mental states that reference objects, that is, things outside of the dyad. It seems clear that the sharing of affective states is of paramount importance during the first part of intersubjective relatedness, so much so that the next chapter will be devoted to a different view of the intersubjective sharing of feeling states.

The Nature of the Leap to Intersubjective Relatedness

Why does the infant suddenly adopt an organizing subjective perspective about self and others that opens the door to intersubjectivity? Is this quantum leap simply the result of a newly emergent, specific capacity or skill? Or does it result from the experience of social interactions? Or is it the maturational unfolding of a major human need and motive state? Piaget (1954), Bruner (1975, 1977), Bates (1976, 1979), and others whose primary approach is cognitive or linguistic view this achievement mainly in terms of an acquired social skill; the infant discovers generative rules and procedures for interactions that ultimately lead to the discovery of intersubjectivity. Trevarthan (1978) has called this a constructionist approach.

Shields (1978), Newson (1977), Vygotsky (1962), and others have understood this achievement more as the result of mother's entrance into "meaningful" exchanges, beginning at the infant's birth. She interprets all the infant's behaviors in terms of meanings; that is, she attributes meanings to them. She provides the semantic element, all by herself at first, and continues to bring the infant's behavior into her framework of created meanings. Gradually, as the infant is able, the framework of meaning becomes mutually created. This approach, based on social experience, might be called the approach of interpersonal meanings.

Many thinkers in France and Switzerland have independently approached the problem along similar lines and pushed the notion of maternal interpretation into richer clinical territory. They assert that mother's "meanings" reflect not only what she observes but also her fantasies about who the infant is and is to become. Intersubjectivity, for them, ultimately involves interfantasy. They have asked how the fantasies of the parent come to influence the infant's behavior and ultimately to shape the infant's own fantasies. This reciprocal fantasy interaction is a form of created interpersonal meaning at the covert level (Kreisler, Fair, and Soulé 1974; Kreisler and Cramer 1981; Cramer 1982, 1982b; Lebovici 1983; Pinol-Douriez 1983). The creation of such meanings has been called "interactions fantasmatique." Fraiberg et al. (1975) and Stern (1971) in the United States have also paid close attention to the relationship between maternal fantasy and overt behavior.

Trevarthan (1974, 1978) has stood relatively alone in maintaining that intersubjectivity is an innate, emergent human capacity. He points out that the other explanations for the appearance of intersubjectivity, especially the constructionist explanation, do not allow for any special awareness of humans or for the shared awareness that is so highly developed in humans. He sees this developmental leap as the "differentiation of a coherent field of intentionality" (Trevarthan and Hubley 1978, p. 213) and views intersubjectivity as a human capacity present in a primary form from the early months of life.[4]

4. In fact, what we are calling intersubjectivity Trevarthan calls "secondary intersubjectivity" (Trevarthan and Hubley 1978), the later differentiation of a uniquely human intersubjective function. Intersubjectivity does seem to be an emergent human capacity. However, it is not

All three viewpoints seem necessary for an adequate explanation of the emergence of intersubjectivity. Trevarthan is right that some special form of awareness must come into play at this point and that the capacity for it must unfold maturationally. And that special awareness is what we are calling an organizing subjective perspective. However, the capacity must have some tools to work with, and the constructivist approach has provided the tools in the form of rule structures, action formats, and discovery procedures. Finally, the capacity plus the tools would be operating in a vacuum without the addition of interpersonal meanings that are mutually created. All three taken together are required for a fuller account of intersubjective relatedness.

Once intersubjectivity has been tasted, so to speak, does it just remain as a capacity to be used or not, or as a perspective on self and other to be adopted or not? Or does it become a new psychological need, the need to share subjective experience?

We cannot cavalierly add to the list of basic psychological needs every time we come upon a new potentially autonomous capacity or need. The usual psychoanalytic solution to this problem, since the pioneering work of Hartmann, Kris, and Lowenstein (1946), is to call all such autonomously functioning capacities and need-like states "autonomous ego functions," rather than instincts or motivational systems. This label gives them their self-evident primary autonomous status but also puts them potentially at the service of the "basic" psychoanalytic needs, whose higher status is protected. (It is mainly in the area of infancy research that the presence and pervasiveness of newly recognized capacities and needs has become apparent and poses the problem.)

Up to a point, this solution of autonomous ego functions has proven extremely helpful and generative for the field. The question is, when does an autonomous ego function become of such magnitude that it is better conceived as a "basic need or motivational system?" Curiosity and stimulus seeking are good cases in point. These appear

---

meaningful to speak of primary intersubjectivity at three or four months of age, as Trevarthan does (1979). This can only refer to protoforms that lack the essential ingredients for being called intersubjectivity. Only Trevarthan's secondary stage is true intersubjectivity.

There is much reason to believe that other social animals, for example dogs, are also capable of intersubjectivity as the concept is used here.

to partake more of the quality of motivational systems than of mere autonomous ego functions.

What, then, about intersubjective relatedness? Are we to consider this another autonomous ego function? Or are we dealing with a primary psychobiological need? The answers to these questions are actually momentous for clinical theory. The more one conceives of intersubjective relatedness as a basic psychological need, the closer one refashions clinical theory toward the configurations suggested by Self psychologists and some existential psychologists.

From the perspective of infancy research, the question remains open. One consideration in this issue is to figure out what is so reinforcing about intersubjectivity. There is no question but that its reinforcing power can be related to achieving security needs or attachment goals. For instance, intersubjective successes can result in feelings of enhanced security. Similarly, minor failures in intersubjectivity can be interpreted, experienced, and acted upon as total ruptures in a relationship. This is often seen in therapy.

A parallel view is that an overriding human need develops for human-group-psychic-membership—that is, inclusion in the human group as a member with potentially shareable subjective experiences, in contrast to a nonmember whose subjective experiences are wholly unique, idiosyncratic, and nonshareable. The issue is basic. Opposite poles of this one dimension of psychic experience define different psychotic states. At one end is the sense of cosmic psychic isolation, alienation, and aloneness (the last person left on earth), and at the other end is the feeling of total psychic transparency, in which no single corner of potentially shareable experience can be kept private. The infant presumably begins to encounter this dimension of psychic experience somewhere in the middle, between the extreme poles, as most of us continue to do.[5]

Speaking teleologically, I assume that nature in the course of evolution created several ways to assure survival through group

5. The notion that the infant delegates omnipotence to the parent, imagining that the parent can always read the infant's mind, would predict that the infant could experience intersubjective experience like the psychotic at the total-transparency end of this dimension. This, however, would require a level of metacognition well beyond what is available at the age we are discussing. It is more likely that the infant starts in the middle, learning that some subjective states are shareable and others not.

membership in social species. Ethology and attachment theory have spelled out for us the behavior patterns that serve to assure those physical and psychological intermeshings of individuals that enhance survival. I suggest that nature has also provided the ways and means for any subjective intermeshings of individuals that would add survival value. And the survival value of intersubjectivity is potentially enormous.

There is no question that different societies could minimize or maximize this need for intersubjectivity. For instance, if a society were socially structured so that it was assumed that all members had essentially identical, inner subjective experiences, and if homogeneity of this aspect of felt life were stressed, there would be little need, and no societal pressure, to enhance the development of intersubjectivity. If on the other hand a society highly valued the existence and the sharing of individual differences at this level of experience (as ours does), then their development would be facilitated by that society.

Let us return to life as lived from moment to moment and examine more fully how affective experiences can enter the intersubjective domain, a phenomenon that I call *affect attunement.*

Chapter 7

The Sense of a Subjective Self: II. Affect Attunement

The Problem of Sharing Affective States

The sharing of affective states is the most pervasive and clinically germaine feature of intersubjective relatedness. This is especially true when the infant first enters this domain. Interaffectivity is mainly what is meant when clinicians speak of parental "mirroring" and "empathic responsiveness." Despite the importance of these events, it is not at all clear how they work. What are the acts and processes that let other people know that you are feeling something very like what they are feeling? How can you get "inside of" other people's subjective experience and then let them know that you have arrived there, without using words? After all, the infants we are talking about are only between nine and fifteen months old.

Imitation immediately comes to mind as a possible way one might show this. The mother might imitate the infant's facial expressions and gestures, and the baby would see her doing this. The problem with this solution is that the infant could only tell from the mother's imitation that mother got what the infant *did;* she would have reproduced the same overt behaviors, but she need not have had any similar inner experience. There is no reason why the infant should make the further assumption that mother also experienced the same feeling state that gave rise to the overt behavior.

For there to be an intersubjective exchange about affect, then, strict imitation alone won't do. In fact, several processes must take place. First, the parent must be able to read the infant's feeling state from the infant's overt behavior. Second, the parent must perform some behavior that is not a strict imitation but nonetheless corresponds in some way to the infant's overt behavior. Third, the infant must be able to read this corresponding parental response as having to do with the infant's own original feeling experience and not just imitating the infant's behavior. It is only in the presence of these three conditions that feeling states within one person can be knowable to another and that they can both sense, without using language, that the transaction has occurred.

To accomplish this transaction the mother must go beyond true imitations, which have been an enormous and important part of her social repertoire during the first six months or so of the infant's life (Moss 1973; Beebe 1973; Stern 1974b, 1977; Field 1977; Brazelton et al. 1979; Papoušek and Papoušek 1979; Trevarthan 1979; Francis et al. 1981; Uzgiris 1981, 1984; Kaye 1982; Malatesta and Izard 1982; Malatesta and Haviland 1983). Most of these investigators have described in detail how caregivers and infants mutually create the chains and sequences of reciprocal behaviors that make up social dialogues during the infant's first nine months. The Papoušeks describe this process in the vocal—in fact, musical—domain in great detail (1981). What is striking in these descriptions is that the mother is almost always working within the same modality as the infant. And in the leadings, followings, highlightings, and elaborations that make up her turn in the dialogue, she is generally performing close or loose imitations of the infant's immediate behavior. If the infant vocalizes, the mother vocalizes back. Similarly, if the infant makes a face, the mother makes a face. However, the dialogue does not remain a stereotypic boring sequence of repeats, back and forth, because the mother is constantly introducing modifying imitations (Kaye 1979; Uzgiris 1984) or providing a theme-and-variation format with slight changes in her contribution at each dialogic turn;

for example, her vocalization may be slightly different each time (Stern 1977).

When the infant is around nine months old, however, one begins to see the mother add a new dimension to her imitation-like behavior, a dimension that appears to be geared to the infant's new status as a potentially intersubjective partner. (It is not clear how mothers know this change has occurred in the infant; it seems to be part of their intuitive parental sense.) She begins to expand her behavior beyond true imitation into a new category of behavior we will call *affect attunement.*

The phenomenon of affect attunement is best shown by examples (Stern 1985). Affect attunement is often so embedded in other behaviors that relatively pure examples are hard to find, but the first five examples that follow are relatively unencumbered by other goings-on.

- A nine-month-old girl becomes very excited about a toy and reaches for it. As she grabs it, she lets out an exuberant "aaaah!" and looks at her mother. Her mother looks back, scrunches up her shoulders, and performs a terrific shimmy with her upper body, like a go-go dancer. The shimmy lasts only about as long as her daughter's "aaaah!" but is equally excited, joyful, and intense.
- A nine-month-old boy bangs his hand on a soft toy, at first in some anger but gradually with pleasure, exuberance, and humor. He sets up a steady rhythm. Mother falls into his rhythm and says, "kaaaaa-*bam,* kaaaaa-*bam,*" the "*bam*" falling on the stroke and the "kaaaaa" riding with the preparatory upswing and the suspenseful holding of his arm aloft before it falls.
- An eight-and-one-half-month-old boy reaches for a toy just beyond reach. Silently he stretches toward it, leaning and extending arms and fingers out fully. Still short of the toy, he tenses his body to squeeze out the extra inch he needs to reach it. At that moment, his mother says, "uuuuuh . . . uuuuuh!" with a crescendo of vocal effort, the expiration of air pushing against her tensed torso. The mother's accelerating vocal-respiratory effort matches the infant's accelerating physical effort.
- A ten-month-old girl accomplishes an amusing routine with mother and then looks at her. The girl opens up her face (her mouth opens, her eyes widen, her eyebrows rise) and then closes it back, in a series of changes whose contour can be represented by a smooth arch (⌒). Mother responds by intoning "Yeah," with a pitch line that rises and falls as the volume crescendos and decrescendos:

"Yeah." The mother's prosodic contour has matched the child's facial-kinetic contour.

A nine-month-old boy is sitting facing his mother. He has a rattle in his hand and is shaking it up and down with a display of interest and mild amusement. As mother watches, she begins to nod her head up and down, keeping a tight beat with her son's arm motions.

More often the attunement is so embedded in other actions and purposes that it is partially masked, as in the next example:

A ten-month-old girl finally gets a piece in a jig saw puzzle. She looks toward her mother, throws her head up in the air, and with a forceful arm flap raises herself partly off the ground in a flurry of exuberance. The mother says "YES, thatta girl." The "YES" is intoned with much stress. It has an explosive rise that echoes the girl's fling of gesture and posture.

One could easily argue that the "YES, thatta girl" functions as a routine response in the form of a positive reinforcer, and it certainly does do so. But why does the mother not just say "Yes, thatta girl"? Why does she need to add the intense intonation to "YES" that vocally matches the child's gestures? The "YES," I suggest, is an attunement embedded within a routine response.

The embedding of attunements is so common and most often so subtle that unless one is looking for it, or asking why any behavior is being performed exactly the way it is, the attunements will pass unnoticed (except, of course, that one will gather from them what we imagine to be "really" going on clinically). It is the embedded attunements that give much of the impression of the quality of the relationship.

Attunements have the following characteristics, which makes them ideal for accomplishing the intersubjective sharing of affect:

1. They give the impression that a kind of imitation has occurred. There is no faithful rendering of the infant's overt behavior, but some form of matching is going on.
2. The matching is largely cross-modal. That is, the channel or modality of expression used by the mother to match the infant's behavior is different from the channel or modality used by the infant. In the first example, the intensity level and duration of the girl's voice is matched by the mother's body movements. In the second example, features of the boy's arm movements are matched by features of the mother's voice.

3. What is being matched is not the other person's behavior *per se,* but rather some aspect of the behavior that reflects the person's feeling state. The ultimate reference for the match appears to be the feeling state (inferred or directly apprehended), not the external behavioral event. Thus the match appears to occur between the expressions of inner state. These expressions can differ in mode or form, but they are to some extent interchangeable as manifestations of a single, recognizable internal state. We appear to be dealing with behavior as expression rather than as sign or symbol, and the vehicles of transfer are metaphor and analogue.[1]

Affect attunement, then, is the performance of behaviors that express the quality of feeling of a shared affect state without imitating the exact behavioral expression of the inner state. If we could demonstrate subjective affect-sharing only with true imitations, we would be limited to flurries of rampant imitation. Our affectively responsive behavior would look ludicrous, maybe even robot-like.

The reason attunement behaviors are so important as separate phenomena is that true imitation does not permit the partners to refer to the internal state. It maintains the focus of attention upon the forms of the external behaviors. Attunement behaviors, on the other hand, recast the event and shift the focus of attention to what is behind the behavior, to the quality of feeling that is being shared. It is for the same reasons that imitation is the predominant way to teach external forms and attunement the predominant way to commune with or indicate sharing of internal states. Imitation renders form; attunement renders feeling. In actuality, however, there does not appear to be a true dichotomy between attunement and imitation; rather, they seem to occupy two ends of a spectrum.

Alternative Conceptualizations

One might well ask why I call this phenomenon affect attunement when there already exist several terms to encompass it. One reason is that these terms and their underlying concepts fail to capture the

1. Strictly speaking one could call this the imitation of selected features, in that one or two features of a behavior are chosen to be imitated while most other features are not so selected. The reason we have not chosen this term is that the imitated features are recast in a different form, creating the impression of referencing the inner state rather than the overt behavior.

phenomenon adequately. While the mother's attunings are often not even reasonably faithful imitations, the virtue of a loose definition of imitation can be argued. Kaye (1979) has pointed out that "modifying imitations" are intended to just miss the mark in order to maximize or minimize aspects of the original behavior. And Uzgiris refers to essentially the same issues with the terms "imitation" and "matching" (1984). Nonetheless, there is a limit beyond which fidelity cannot be stretched if "imitation" is still to keep its usual meaning.

A second problem is that of the representations necessary for imitation. "Deferred imitation," as meant by Piaget (1954), requires the capacity for acting on the basis of an internal representation of the original. The reproduction (or imitation) is guided by the blueprint provided by the internal representation. Piaget had in mind the *observed behaviors* as the referent which is represented. The nature of such representations is well conceptualized. But if the referent is the feeling state, how do we conceptualize its representation so that it can act as a blueprint? We are going to require a different notion of the nature of the representation that is operating, namely a representation of the feeling state, not its overt behavioral manifestation.

The terms "affect matching" or "affect contagion" have a similar appeal. These processes refer to the automatic induction of an affect in one person from seeing or hearing someone else's affect display. This process may well be a basic biological tendency among highly evolved social species, which becomes perfected in man (Malatesta and Izard 1982). The earliest affect contagion that has been demonstrated involves the human distress cry. Wolff (1969) found that two-month-old infants showed "infectious crying" when they heard tape recordings of their own distress cries. Simner (1971) and Sagi and Hoffman (1976) showed that contagious crying occurred in newborns. Newborns cried more to infant cries in general than to equally loud artificially produced sounds. Similarly, the contagious properties of the smile have been well documented in infancy, even though mechanisms for it may shift during development.

Affect matching with its probable basis in "motor mimicry" (Lipps 1906) cannot alone explain affect attunement, although it may well provide one of the underlying mechanisms on which that phenomenon is founded. By itself, affect matching, like imitation, explains only a reproduction of the original. It cannot account for the phenomenon of responding in different modes or with different forms of behavior, with the internal state as the referent.

"Intersubjectivity" as articulated by Trevarthan (1977, 1978, 1979, 1980) approaches the essence of the problem, although from a different direction. It concerns the mutual sharing of psychic states, but it refers mainly to intentions and motives rather than to qualities of feeling or affects. Its major concern is interintentionality, not interaffectivity. Intersubjectivity is an entirely adequate term and concept, but it is too inclusive for our purposes. Affect attunement is a particular form of intersubjectivity that requires some processes that are unique to it.

"Mirroring" and "echoing" represent the clinical terms and concepts that come closest to affect attunement. As terms, both run into the problem of fidelity to the original. "Mirroring" has the disadvantage of suggesting complete temporal synchrony. "Echoing," taken literally, at least avoids the temporal constraint. In spite of these semantic limitations, however, these concepts represent attempts to grapple with the issue of one person reflecting another's inner state. In this important respect, unlike imitation or contagion, they are appropriately concerned with the subjective state rather than the manifest behavior.

This meaning of reflecting inner state has been used mostly in clinical theories (Mahler et al. 1975; Kohut 1977; Lacan 1977), which have noted that reflecting back an infant's feeling state is important to the infant's developing knowledge of his or her own affectivity and sense of self. When used in this sense, however, "mirroring" implies that the mother is helping to create something within the infant that was only dimly or partially there until her reflection acted somehow to solidify its existence. This concept goes far beyond just participating in another's subjective experience. It involves changing the other by providing something the other did not have before or, if it was present, by consolidating it.

A second problem with mirroring as a term is the inconsistency and overinclusiveness of its usage. In clinical writings, it sometimes refers to the behavior itself—that is, to true imitation, a literal reflecting back, in the domain of core-relatedness—and sometimes to the sharing or alignment of internal states—in our terms, affect attunement in the domain of intersubjective relatedness. At still other times, it refers to verbal reinforcements or consensual validation at the level of verbal relatedness. "Mirroring" is thus commonly used to embrace three different processes. Moreover, it is not clear which subjective states are to be included in mirroring affects—intentions? motives? beliefs? ego functions? In short, while mirroring has focused upon the essence of the problem, the indeterminate usage has blurred what appear to be real differences in mechanism, form, and function.

Finally, there is "empathy." Is attunement sufficiently close to what is generally meant by empathy? No. The evidence indicates that attunements occur largely out of awareness and almost automatically. Empathy, on the other hand, involves the mediation of cognitive processes. What is generally called empathy consists of at least four distinct and probably sequential processes: (1) the resonance of feeling state; (2) the abstraction of empathic knowledge from the experience of emotional resonance; (3) the integration of abstracted empathic knowledge into an empathic response; and (4) a transient role identification. Cognitive processes such as these involved in the second and third events are crucial to empathy (Schaffer 1968; Hoffman 1978; Ornstein 1979; Basch 1983; Demos 1984). (Cognitive imaginings of what it must be like to be another person, however, are nothing more than elaborated acts of role taking and not empathy, unless they have been ignited by at least a spark of emotional resonance.) Affect attunement, then, shares with empathy the initial process of emotional resonance (Hoffman 1978); neither can occur without it. The work of many psychoanalytic thinkers concurs on this formulation (Basch 1983). But while affect attunement, like empathy, starts with an emotional resonance, it does something different with it. Attunement takes the experience of emotional resonance and automatically recasts that experience into another form of expression. Attunement thus need not proceed towards empathic knowledge or response. Attunement is a distinct form of affective transaction in its own right.

The Evidence for Attunement

What evidence exists for the phenomenon of attunement, and what kind of evidence could be developed to demonstrate it? The problem of demonstration boils down to this: the existence of an attunement is at first glance a clinical impression, perhaps an intuition. To operationalize this impression, it is necessary to identify those aspects of a person's behavior that could be matched without actually imitating them. Stern et al. (in press) reasoned that there were three general features of a behavior that could be matched (and thereby form the basis of an attunement) without rendering an imitation. These are intensity, timing, and shape. These three dimensions were then broken down into six more specific types of match:

1. *Absolute intensity.* The level of intensity of the mother's behavior is the same as that of the infant's, irrespective of the mode or form of the behavior. For instance, the loudness of a mother's vocalization might match the force of an abrupt arm movement performed by the infant.
2. *Intensity contour.* The changes of intensity over time are matched. The second example on page 140 provides a good instance of this type of match. The mother's vocal effort and the infant's physical effort both showed an acceleration in intensity, followed suddenly by an even quicker intensity deceleration phase.
3. *Temporal beat.* A regular pulsation in time is matched. The fifth example, on page 141, is a good example of a temporal beat match. The nodding of the mother's head and the infant's gesture conform to the same beat.
4. *Rhythm.* A pattern of pulsations of unequal stress is matched.
5. *Duration.* The time span of the behavior is matched. If the mother's and infant's behaviors last about the same time, a duration match has occurred. A duration match by itself is not considered to constitute a sufficient criterion for an attunement, however, because too many non-attunement, infant/mother response chains show duration matching.
6. *Shape.* Some spatial feature of a behavior that can be abstracted and rendered in a different act is matched. The fifth example, on page 141, provides an instance. The mother has borrowed the vertical shape of the infant's up-down arm motion and adapted it in her head motion. Shape does not mean the same form; that would be imitation.

The second step in examining the nature of affect attunements, once matching criteria were established, was to enlist the collaboration of mothers in answering a series of questions about their matchings. Why did she do what she did, the way she did it and when she did it? What did she think the baby felt at the moment that . . . ? Was she aware of her own behavior when she . . . ? What did she wish to accomplish . . . ?

Accordingly, mothers were first asked to play with their infants as they normally would at home. The play session took place in a pleasant observation room filled with some age-appropriate toys. The mother and infant were left alone for ten to fifteen minutes while their interaction was videotaped. Immediately afterwards, the mother and the experimenters watched a replay of the taped interaction. Many questions were then asked. The experimenters made every attempt to create a collaborative, easy, working atmosphere with the mothers, rather than an inquisitional or judgmental one. Most mothers felt that an alliance had been forged with the researchers. This "research-therapeutic alliance" is crucial to this kind of joint inquiry.

An important issue in the process was when to stop the taped flow of interaction and ask the questions. Entry criteria were set up to identify points at which to jump into the stream of interaction. The first such criterion was that the baby had made some affective expression—facial, vocal, gestural, or postural. The second was that the mother had responded in some observable way. And the third was that the baby had seen, heard, or felt her response. When an event meeting these criteria was viewed, the videotape was stopped and the questions were asked. The taped episode was replayed as often as necessary. The results of the experiments with ten mothers as participant-researchers and their infants aged eight to twelve months are reported elsewhere in detail (Stern et al., in press). The major findings that have relevance to the present discussion are summarized here.

1. In response to an infant expression of affect, maternal attunements were the most common maternal response (48 percent), followed by comments (33 percent), and imitations (19 percent). During play interactions attunements occurred at a rate of one every sixty-five seconds.

2. Most attunements occurred across sensory modes. If the infant's expression was vocal, the mother's attunement was likely to be gestural or facial, and vice versa. In 39 percent of the instances of attunement, the mothers used entirely different modalities from those used by the infant (cross-modal attunement). In 48 percent of the cases, the mothers used some modalities that were the same as those used by the infant (intramodal attunement) and some that were different. Thus 87 percent of the time, the mothers' attunements were partially, if not wholly, cross-modal.
3. Of the three aspects of behavior—intensity, timing, and shape—that a mother can use to accomplish an attunement, intensity matches were the most common, followed by timing matches and last by shape matches. In the majority of cases, more than one aspect of behavior was simultaneously matched. For instance, when the infant's up-and-down hand gesture was matched by the mother's head nodding up and down, both beat and shape were being matched. The percentages of all attunements that represented matchings of the various aspects are: intensity contour, 81 percent; duration, 69 percent; absolute intensity, 61 percent; shape, 47 percent; beat, 13 percent; and rhythm, 11 percent.
4. The largest single reason that mothers gave (or that we inferred) for performing an attunement was "to be with" the infant, "to share," "to participate in," "to join in." We have called these functions *interpersonal communion.* This group of reasons stands in contrast to the other kinds of reasons given: to respond, to jazz the baby up or to quiet, to restructure the interaction, to reinforce, to engage in a standard game. This later group can be lumped together as serving the function of communication rather than communion. Communication generally means to exchange or transmit information with the attempt to alter another's belief or action system. During many of these attunements the mother is doing none of these things. Communion means to share in another's experience with no attempt to change what that person is doing or believing. This idea captures far better the mother's behavior as seen by experimenters and by the mothers themselves.
5. Several variations on attunements occurred. In addition to *communing attunements,* true attunements in which the mother tried to match exactly the infant's internal state for the purpose of "being with" the baby, there were misattunements, which fell into two types. In *purposeful misattunement,* the mother "intentionally" over- or under-matched the infant's intensity, timing, or behavioral shape. The purpose of these misattunements was usually to increase or decrease the baby's level of activity or affect. The mother "slipped inside of" the infant's feeling state far enough to capture it, but she then misexpressed it enough to alter the infant's behavior but not enough

to break the sense of an attunement in process. Such purposeful misattunements were called *tuning.* There were also *nonpurposeful misattunements.* Either the mother incorrectly identified, to some extent, the quality and/or quantity of the infant's feeling state, or she was unable to find in herself the same internal state. These misattunements we called *true misattunements.*[2]

6. When mothers were shown the taped replay of their attunements, they judged themselves to have been entirely unaware of their behavior at the time of occurrence in 24 percent of cases; only partly aware of their behavior in 43 percent of cases; and fully aware of their behavior in 32 percent of cases.

Even in the 32 percent of cases where the mother said she was fully aware of her behavior, she was often referring to the desired consequences of her behavior more than to what she actually did. Thus the attunement *process* itself occurs largely unawares.

It is easy enough to determine experimentally that tunings and misattunements influence the infant: they usually result in some alteration or interruption of ongoing infant behavior. That is their purpose, and the result can be readily gauged. The situation with communing attunements is different. Most often after the mother has made such an attunement, the infant acts as if nothing special has happened. The infant's activity continues uninterrupted, and we are left with no evidence, only speculation, that the fact of attunement has "gotten in," taken hold, and had some psychic consequence. To get underneath this still surface, we chose the method of perturbing ongoing interactions and seeing what happens.

The approach of creating defined perturbations in naturalistic or seminaturalistic interaction is well established in infancy research. For example, the "still-face" procedure (Tronick et al. 1978) asks a mother or father to go "still-faced"—impassive and expressionless—in the middle of an interaction, creating a perturbation in the expected flow. Infants by three months of age react with mild upset and social withdrawal, alternating with attempts to re-engage the impassive partner. This kind of perturbation can be used with any and all parent/infant pairs. The perturbations of attunement, however, had to be tailored to a specific pair and aimed at a previously

2. The obvious clinical import of the characteristic and selective use of attunements, tuning, and misattunements in different affective contexts will be addressed in chapter 9.

identified and likely-to-recur attunement episode. No two pairs presented the same opportunity.

For each pair, the specific attunement episode chosen for perturbation was identified while the mother and researchers watched the replay of the videorecording. After discussing the structure of behaviors that made up the attunement episode, the researchers instructed the mothers in how to perturb the structure. The mothers then returned to the observation room, and when the appropriate context for the expectable attunement behavior arose, they performed the planned perturbation. Two examples will serve to illustrate the results.

In the videotape of the initial play period, a nine-month-old infant is seen crawling away from his mother and over to a new toy. While on his stomach, he grabs the toy and begins to bang and flail with it happily. His play is animated, as judged by his movements, breathing, and vocalizations. Mother then approaches him from behind, out of sight, and puts her hand on his bottom and gives it an animated jiggle side to side. The speed and intensity of her jiggle appear to match well the intensity and rate of the infant's arm movements and vocalizations, qualifying this as an attunement. The infant's response to her attunement is—nothing! He simply continues his play without missing a beat. Her jiggle has no overt effect, as though she had never acted. This attunement episode was fairly characteristic of this pair. The infant wandered from her and became involved in another toy, and she leaned over and jiggled his bottom, his leg, or his foot. This sequence was repeated several times.

For the first perturbation, the mother was instructed to do exactly the same as always, except that now she was purposely to "misjudge" her baby's level of joyful animation, to pretend that the baby was somewhat less excited than he appeared to be, and to jiggle accordingly. When the mother did jiggle somewhat more slowly and less intensely than she truly judged would make a good match, the baby quickly stopped playing and looked around at her, as if to say "What's going on?" This procedure was repeated, with the same result.

The second perturbation was in the opposite direction. The mother was to pretend that her baby was at a higher level of joyful animation and to jiggle accordingly. The results were the same: the infant noticed the discrepancy and stopped. The mother was then asked to go back to jiggling appropriately, and again the infant did *not* respond.[3]

One could argue that the jiggle, when performed within some band of speed/intensity, is simply a form of reinforcement, rather than a signal. There is no problem with this formulation except that it does not account for the fact that the acceptable band is determined by the relationship between the infant's and the mother's speed and level of intensity, not by the absolute level on the mother's part. And there is no problem with attunements also serving reinforcing functions. But simple reinforcement cannot explain away attunement. The two phenomena are undoubtedly embedded one within the other and serve different functions in the developing relationship. Interviews with the mother afterwards confirmed this dual function. She said that she did the regular attunement "to get into the playing with him," but she also said that she figured, in retrospect, that it probably "encouraged" him to continue.

In another example, the initial videotape shows an eleven-month-old going after an object with determination and excitement. He gets it and brings it to his mouth with much excitement and body tension. Mother says, "*Yeah,* ya *like* that." The infant does not respond to her utterance. When the mother was asked to over-shoot or under-shoot the pitch contouring, rate, and stress patterning of her standard utterance, compared with the perceived excitement and tension of her infant, the infant took notice and looked at her, as if for further clarification.

Many more such individualized perturbations have been performed, all indicating that the infant does indeed have some sense of the extent of matching. Closeness of match, in itself, is an expectation under some circumstances, and its violation is meaningful.

It is clear that interpersonal communion, as created by attunement, will play an important role in the infant's coming to recognize that internal feeling states are forms of human experience that are shareable with other humans. The converse is also true: feeling states that are never attuned to will be experienced only alone, isolated

3. Note that each time a perturbation was attempted the infant was at a somewhat different level of excitation and the mother had to adjust her "misjudgment" to his current level. It is also notable that some mothers found misjudgments hard to execute. One said that it is like trying to pat your head and rub your stomach at the same time.

from the interpersonal context of shareable experience. What is at stake here is nothing less than the shape of and extent of the shareable inner universe.

Underlying Mechanisms for Attunement

For attunement to work, different behavioral expressions occurring in different forms and in different sensory modalities must somehow be interchangeable. If a certain gesture by the mother is to be "correspondent" with a certain kind of vocal exclamation by the infant, the two expressions must share some common currency that permits them to be transferred from one modality or form to another. That common currency consists of amodal properties.

There are some qualities or properties that are held in common by most or all of the modalities of perception. These include intensity, shape, time, motion, and number. Such qualities of perception can be abstracted by any sensory mode from the invariant properties of the stimulus world and then translated into other modalities of perception. For instance, a rhythm, such as "long short" (—— -), can be delivered in or abstracted from sight, audition, smell, touch, or taste. For this to occur, the rhythm must at some point exist in the mind in a form that is not inextricably bound to one particular way of perceiving it but is rather sufficiently abstract to be transportable across modalities. It is the existence of these abstract representations of amodal properties that permits us to experience a perceptually unified world.

From what has gone before, it is clear that infants can perceive the world amodally from early on and that they get better at it during maturation. This position has been strongly put forth by developmentalists such as Bower (1974), who states that from the earliest days of life, the infant forms and acts upon abstract representations of qualities of perception.

The qualities of experience that lend themselves to intermodal fluency, which will be of paramount interest to us here, are the ones that were determined to be the best criteria for defining attunements—namely, intensity, time, and shape. This intermodal fluency is the phenomenon in want of an explanatory mechanism. What, then, is the evidence that infants can perceive or experience intensity, time, and shape amodally?

INTENSITY

Level of intensity, as we have seen, was one of the qualities most frequently matched in designating attunements. Most often the match was between the intensity of an infant's physical behavior and the intensity of the mother's vocal behavior. Can an infant match levels of intensity across the visual and auditory modalities? Yes, and quite well, as indicated in the experiment described in chapter 3 in which three-week-old infants matched levels of loudness of sounds to levels of brightness of lights (Lewcowicz and Turkewitz 1980). The ability to perform audio-visual cross-modal matches of the absolute level of intensity appears to be a very early capacity.[4]

TIME

The temporal qualities of behavior were the second most commonly matched in performing attunements. Here too, as mentioned in chapter 3, infants appear to be well endowed with the capacity to match temporal patterns across modes. In fact, intensity level and timing may be the perceptual qualities that the infant is best able to represent modally, and at the earliest points in development.

SHAPE

Intensity and time are quantitative properties of stimulation or perception, in contrast to shape, which is qualitative. What is known about the infant's competence in the intermodal coordination of shape or configuration? The Meltzoff and Borton (1979) experiment described on pages 47–48 is an example par excellence of the transfer of the shape of a static object from the tactile mode to the visual mode. After this demonstration, it was logical to ask whether correspondences in kinetic shapes could also be made, and whether correspondences would also occur across vision and audition as well as across vision and touch. After all, most human behavior consists

4. This intermodal capacity for matching relative level of intensity does not directly address the capacity for matching intensity contours, the profiles of change in intensity over time. This was the other intensity criterion for attunement—in fact, the most common type of match. An intensity contour also involves time and is in some ways closer to shape as a quality than to intensity as a quantity.

of kinetic shapes—that is, configurations that change in time—and vocalizations are one of the most pervasive kinetic shapes involved in attunements. As the experiments of MacKain et al. (1983) and Kuhl and Meltzoff (1982) have shown, infants should have no trouble at all in making these cross-modal transformations (see chapter 3).

The Unity of the Senses

It thus appears that shape, intensity, and time can all be perceived amodally. And, indeed, philosophy, psychology, and art have a long history of designating shape, time, and intensity to be amodal qualities of experience (in psychological terms) or primary qualities of experience (in philosophical terms) (see Marks 1978). These issues have a long history, because what is at stake is the unity of the senses, which ultimately boils down to the knowledge or experience that the world as seen is the same world that is heard or felt.

Aristotle first postulated a doctrine of sensory correspondence, or a doctrine of the unity of the senses. His sixth sense, the common sense, was the sense that could apperceive the qualities of sensation that are primary (that is, amodal) in that they do not belong exclusively to any one sense alone, as color belongs to vision, but are shared by all the senses. Aristotle's list of primary qualities that could be extracted from any modality, represented in abstract form, and translated among all sense modes included intensity, motion, rest, unity, form, and number. Philosophers since have argued about which attributes of perception meet the requirements of primary qualities, but intensity, form, and time are usually included.

Psychologists were probably first drawn to the issue of the unity of the senses by the phenomenon of synesthesia, in which stimulation in a single sense evokes sensations that belong to a different modality of stimulation. The most common synesthesia is "colored hearing." Particular sounds, such as a trumpet, produce the visual image of a particular color, perhaps red, along with the auditory percept (see Marks [1978] for a review). The existence of synesthesia was only part of the allure of unity of the senses, however. The issue of intramodal equivalences or correspondences has always been of interest to students of perception, and the developmental psychologists have recently picked up the age-old trail. The problem is subsumed under what Marks calls the Doctrine of Equivalent Information, which states that different senses can inform about the same features of the external world. Much of the theoretical work of the Gibsons (1959, 1969, 1979), Piaget (1954), T. Bower (1974), and others addresses this issue.

Therapists are so familiar with this phenomenon that it is taken for granted as a way to communicate feelings about important perceptions. When a patient says, "I was so anxious and uptight about how she would greet me, but as soon as she spoke it was like the sun came out—I melted," we understand directly. How could most metaphors work without an underlying capacity for the transposition of amodal information?

Artists, especially poets, have taken the unity of the senses for granted. Most poetry could not work without the tacit assumption that cross-sensory analogies and metaphors are immediately apparent to everyone. Certain poets, such as the French Symbolists during the nineteenth century, elevated the fact of the cross-modal equivalence of information to a guiding principle of the poetic process.

> There are odors fresh as the skin of an infant,
> Sweet as flutes, green as any grass,
> And others, corrupt, rich and triumphant.
>
> (Baudelaire, *Correspondences,* 1857)

In just three lines, Baudelaire asks us to relate smells to experiences in the domains of touch, sound, color, sensuality, finance, and power. A similar preoccupation has visited the other arts.[5]

5. Around the turn of the twentieth century, visual artists and musicians engaged in innumerable experiments at symphonic light shows, using novel instruments such as color organs to express in one medium or perceptual modality the qualities rendered in another. Such cross-sensory attempts were also conducted in traditional media; an example is Mussorgsky's *Pictures at an Exhibition.*

When sound film became possible, the opportunities for intermingling and integrating the qualities of sound and vision became obvious and irresistible for pioneers in the new medium. Sergei Eisenstein's attempts to integrate the two media are perhaps best known because of his extensive writing about film-making (1957) and the success of his genius in intramodal integration. In his classic film *Alexander Nevsky,* Eisenstein worked closely with Prokofiev, the composer of the score. Together they matched the visual structure of each film frame with the auditory structure of the music being played during that shot; the battle scene is perhaps still the most careful and painstaking artistic exploration of the integration of sight and sound

The point of this discussion about the unity of the senses is that the capacities for identifying cross-modal equivalences that make for a perceptually unified world are the same capacities that permit the mother and infant to engage in affect attunement to achieve affective intersubjectivity.

What Inner State is Being Attuned to?

It appears that both forms of affects—discrete categorical affects such as sadness and joy as well as vitality affects such as explosions and fading—are attuned to. In fact, most attunements seem to occur with the vitality affects.

In chapter 3, we identified vitality affects as those dynamic, kinetic qualities of feeling that distinguish animate from inanimate and that correspond to the momentary changes in feeling states involved in the organic processes of being alive. We experience vitality affects as dynamic shifts or patterned changes within ourselves or others. One of the reasons we went to such efforts there to establish vitality affects as entities in their own right, distinct from what is usually meant by activation as well as from categories of affect, is that now they become essential to an understanding of attunement.

During an average mother-infant interaction, discrete affect displays occur only occasionally—perhaps every thirty to ninety seconds. Since this is so, affective tracking or attuning with another could not occur as a continuous process if it were limited to categorical affects. One cannot wait around for a discrete categorical affect display, such as a surprise expression, to occur in order to re-establish attunement. Attunement feels more like an unbroken process. It cannot await

---

ever attempted. The works of Walt Disney achieve their various effects through the same impact of sound-sight coordination. And dance is the ultimate example—in fact, the prototype.

At a more mundane level, the pervasiveness of our familiarity with the unity of the senses is seen in many games. One variant of the parlor game of Twenty Questions depends upon this familiarity. The person who is "it," thinks of some person. Everyone else has to guess that person's identity by asking for intra- and cross-modal correspondences; for example, "If the person were a vegetable, what vegetable would he be?" "What kind of drink would she be?" "What kind of sound?" "What smell?" "What kind of geometric shape?" "What surface would he feel like?" and so on.

discrete affect eruptions; it must be able to work with virtually all behavior. And that is one of the great advantages of the vitality affects. They are manifest in all behavior and can thus be an almost omnipresent subject of attunement. They concern *how* a behavior, *any* behavior, *all* behavior is performed, not *what* behavior is performed.

Vitality affects therefore must be added to affect categories as one of the kinds of subjective inner states that can be referenced in acts of attunement. Vitality is ideally suited to be the subject of attunements, because it is composed of the amodal qualities of intensity and time and because it resides in virtually any behavior one can perform and thus provide a continuously present (though changing) subject for attunement. Attunements can be made with the inner quality of feeling of how an infant reaches for a toy, holds a block, kicks a foot, or listens to a sound. Tracking and attuning with vitality affects permit one human to "be with" another in the sense of sharing likely inner experiences on an almost continuous basis. This is exactly our experience of feeling-connectedness, of being in attunement with another. It feels like an unbroken line. It seeks out the activation contour that is momentarily going on in any and every behavior and uses that contour to keep the thread of communion unbroken.

Communicating Vitality Affects: Art and Behavior

Both categorical and vitality affects, then, are the subject matter for attunement. One can imagine how a categorical affect display such as sadness, once seen, is directly felt by the viewer. Evolution and experience have teamed up to make that transposition of feeling from one to another comprehensible. But how and why can we automatically make these transpositions with vitality affects? We have identified time-intensity contours as one of the salient perceptual qualities that undergo the transformation and the way in which this process relies on capacities for amodal perception. But we still have not fully answered how we get from perceptions of others to feelings in ourselves, when there are no specific prewired programs operating, as there appear to be for the discrete categorical affects.

The problem can be restated as follows. We tend automatically to transpose perceptual qualities into feeling qualities, particularly when the qualities belong to another person's behavior. For instance, we may gather from someone's arm gesture the perceptual qualities of rapid acceleration, speed, and fullness of display. But we will *not* experience the gesture in terms of the perceptual qualities of timing, intensity, and shape; we will experience it directly as "forceful"—that is, in terms of a vitality affect.

How, then, do we get from intensity, timing, and shape to "forcefulness"? This is the question that lies at the heart of understanding one aspect of how art works, and perhaps a look at how the question has been approached in the domain of art may be helpful in understanding it in the domain of behavior.

Suzanne Langer (1967) has proposed a route for getting from perception to feeling. She suggests that, in works of art, the organization of elements seems to present an aspect of felt life. The feeling that is presented is in fact an apparition, an illusion, a virtual feeling. For instance, a two-dimensional painting creates the virtual feeling of three-dimensional space. What is more, virtual space can have the virtual properties of vastness, distance, advancing, receding, and so on. In a similar fashion, sculpture, an unmoving volume, can present virtual feelings of kinetic volume: leanings, liftings, and soarings. Music as an actual physical temporal event is one dimensional and homogeneous in time, yet it presents virtual time—that is, time as lived or experienced, rushing, tripping, drawn out, or suspenseful. Dance as actual effortful movement and gesture presents virtual "realms of power, a play of powers made visible" (Ghosh 1979, p. 69): explosions and implosions, restraint, meanderings, and effortlessness.

Is it possible that the activation contours (intensity in time) perceived in another's overt behavior become a virtual vitality affect when experienced in the self?

Spontaneous behaviors include conventionalized elements such as the configurations (the smiles and weeping) of the discrete categorical affects. These are analogous to conventionalized representational forms or iconic elements in painting, such as the Madonna and Child, except that their shared import comes about because of biological ritualization (by force of evolution), not by cultural convention, as in the case of the Madonna and Child.

The translation from perception to feeling in conventionalized forms (icons in art or discrete affect displays in spontaneous behavior) is the least interesting part of the problem, however. In both art and behavior, there is also the *rendering* of the conventional forms. In the case of the Madonna and Child, that might mean the exact treatment of the Madonna's robe and the background, how the colors contrast and harmonize, how the linear and planar tensions are resolved—in short, how the forms will be handled. This is the domain of style.[6] In spontaneous behavior, the counterpart to artistic style is the domain of vitality affects. As we have seen, these concern the manner in which conventionalized affect displays such as smiling and other highly fixed motor programs such as walking are performed. This is where the exact performance of the behavior, in terms of timing, intensity, and shape, can render multiple "stylistic" versions or vitality affects of the same sign, signal, or action.[7]

The translation, then, from perception to feeling in the case of style in art involves the transmutation from "veridical" perceptions (color harmonies, linear resolutions, and the like) into such virtual forms of feeling as calmness. The analogous translation from perception of another person's behavior to feelings involves the transmutation from the perception of timing, intensity, and shape via cross-modal fluency into felt vitality affects in ourselves. I am in no way making a case that art and spontaneous behavior are equivalent; I am simply pointing out some similarities that may be helpful in understanding how affect attunement works when the attunement is to a vitality affect.

6. In the manner in which the representational elements are rendered, a high degree of the conventionalization is a product of a particular historical, geographic, or cultural setting or even of momentary fashions. The same is true for behavior. Still, style and conventionalized form are distinguishable.

7. This is the area in which many of the dance or movement analysis pioneers have labored, for example, and which Kestenberg (1979) and Sossin (1979) have fruitfully applied to mother/infant interactions. A recent photography show (*Form and Emotion in Photography.* The Metropolitan Museum of Art, New York, March 1982) brought home the difference that vitality affects can make. Mark Berghash took six photographs of the same woman's face. He simply asked her to think about a subject and "get into it"; he then took a photograph. The six subjects were her mother, her father, her brother, her past self, her present self, her future self. Together, the six pictures were titled "Aspects of the True Self." In no photograph (except possibly one) did the woman display a recognizable or nameable categorical display; her face was largely neutral by behavioral display rules. But the "stylistic" differences spoke volumes. Each photograph was a captured vitality affect.

There is one crucial difference between art and behavior that highlights an important limitation in attunement. The apprehension of art (although not its creation) involves a certain kind of contemplative mode, which has long been an issue in aesthetics. Mrs. Canbell Fischer expresses the essence of this issue for our purposes: "My grasp of the essence of sadness . . . comes not from moments in which I have been sad, but from moments when [through art] I have seen sadness before me released from entanglements with contingency" (quoted in Langer [1967], p. 88). But spontaneous behavior between persons is invariably and irreversibly entangled with contingencies at innumerable levels. There are two consequences of this reality. The first is that while art can deal with an idea or ideal, spontaneous behavior deals only with a particular instance of an idea; the particulars are defined by the "entanglements." The second issue is that certain "entanglements with contingency" may even make it impossible to attune. Can you attune with anger that is directed at you? Certainly you can experience the level of intensity and quality of feeling that is occurring in the other and that may be elicited in yourself. But it can then no longer be said that you are "sharing in" or "participating in" the other's anger; you are involved in your own. The entangling contingency of threat and harm places a barrier between the two separate experiences such that the notion of communion is no longer applicable. The range of attunement has some limitations in the contingent world of interpersonal reality.

It is inescapable that the infant and child first learn about vitality affects, or in Langer's term "forms of feeling," from their interactions with their own behavior and bodily processes and by watching, testing, and reacting to the social behaviors that impinge on and surround them. They must also learn or somehow arrive at the realization that there are transformational means for translating perceptions of external things into internal feelings, besides those for categorical affects. These transformations from perception to feeling are first learned with spontaneous social behaviors. It seems that only after many years of performing these transformations and building up a repertoire of vitality affects is a child ready to bring this experience to the domain of art as something that is externally perceived but transposed into felt experience.

Attunement is more fully explicable when social behavior is seen, at least in part, as a form of expressionism. The apprehension of some behavior as a form of expressionism makes attunement a precursor to the experience of art. But attunements have achieved something else of developmental significance.

Attunement as a Stepping Stone Toward Language

An attunement is a recasting, a restatement of a subjective state. It treats the subjective state as the referent and the overt behavior as one of several possible manifestations or expressions of the referent. For example, a level and quality of exuberance can be expressed as a unique vocalization, as a unique gesture, or as a unique facial display. Each manifestation has some degree of substitutability as a recognizable signifier of the same inner state. And thus attunement recasting behaviors by way of nonverbal metaphor and analogue. If one imagines a developmental progression from imitation through analogue and metaphor to symbols, this period of the formation of the sense of a subjective self provides the experience with analogue in the form of attunements, an essential step toward the use of symbols, to which we now turn.

Chapter 8

The Sense of a Verbal Self

DURING THE SECOND YEAR of the infant's life language emerges, and in the process the senses of self and other acquire new attributes. Now the self and the other have different and distinct personal world knowledge as well as a new medium of exchange with which to create shared meanings. A new organizing subjective perspective emerges and opens a new domain of relatedness. The possible ways of "being with" another increase enormously. At first glance, language appears to be a straightforward advantage for the augmentation of interpersonal experience. It makes parts of our known experience more shareable with others. In addition, it permits two people to create mutual experiences of meaning that had been unknown before and could never have existed until fashioned by words. It also finally permits the child to begin to construct a narrative of his own life. But in fact language is a double-edged sword. It also makes some parts of our experience less shareable with ourselves and with others. It drives a wedge between two simultaneous forms of interpersonal experience: as it is lived and as it is verbally represented. Experience in the domains of emergent, core- and intersubjective relatedness, which continue irrespective of language, can be embraced only very partially in the domain of verbal relatedness. And to the extent that events in the domain of verbal relatedness are held to be what has really happened, experiences in these other domains suffer an alienation. (They can become the nether domains of experience.) Language, then, causes a split in the experience of the self. It also moves relatedness onto the impersonal, abstract level intrinsic to language and away from the personal, immediate level intrinsic to the other domains of relatedness.

It will be necessary to follow both these lines of development—language as a new form of relatedness and language as a problem for the integration of self-experience and self-with-other experiences. We must somehow take into account these divergent directions that the emergence of a linguistic sense of self has created.

But first, let us see what capacities have developed in the infant that permit a new perspective on the self to emerge and revolutionize the possible ways that the self can be with another and with itself.

New Capacities Available in the Second Year

Toward the middle of the second year (at around fifteen to eighteen months), children begin to imagine or represent things in their minds in such a way that signs and symbols are now in use. Symbolic play and language now become possible. Children can conceive of and then refer to themselves as external or objective entities. They can communicate about things and persons who are no longer present. (All of these milestones bring Piaget's period of sensorimotor intelligence towards an end.)

These changes in world perspective are best illustrated by Piaget's concept of "deferred imitation" (1954). Deferred imitation captures the essence of the developmental changes needed to lead to the sharing of meanings. At about eighteen months, a child may observe someone perform a behavior that the child has never performed—say dial a telephone, or pretend to bottle-feed a doll, or pour milk into a cup—and later that day, or several days later, imitate the dialing, feeding, or pouring. For infants to be able to perform such simple delayed imitations, several capacities are necessary.

1. They must have developed a capacity to represent accurately things and events done by others that are not yet part of their own action schemas. They must be able to create a mental prototype or representation of what they have witnessed someone else do. Mental representations require some currency or form in which they "exist" or are "laid down" in the mind; visual images and language are the two that first come to mind. (To get around the developmental problem of specifying what form the representation is being processed in, Lichtenberg has called this capacity an "imagining" capacity (1983, p. 198). (See also Call [1980]; Golinkoff [1983].)
2. They must, of course, already have the physical capacity to perform the action in their repertoires of possible acts.
3. Since the imitation is delayed and being performed when the original model is no longer doing it, perhaps not even around, the representation must be encoded in long-term memory and must be retrieved with a minimum of external cues. The infants must have good recall or evocative memory for the entire representation.

Children have already acquired these three capacities prior to the age of eighteen months. It is the next two capacities that make the difference and truly mark the boundary.

4. To perform delayed imitations, infants must have two versions of the same reality available: the representation of the original act, as performed by the model, and their own actual execution of the act. Furthermore, they must be able to go back and forth between these two versions of reality and make adjustments of one or the other to accomplish a good imitation. This is what Piaget meant by "reversibility" in the coordination of a mental schema and a motor schema. (The infant's capacity for recognizing maternal attunements during intersubjective relatedness falls short of what is now being described. In attunements the infant senses whether two expressions of an internal state are equivalent or not but does not need to make any behavioral adjustments on the basis of these perceptions. Moreover, only short-term memory is required for the registration of attunement, since the match is almost immediate.)
5. Finally, infants must perceive a psychological relationship between themselves and the model who performs the original act, or they would not embark on the delayed imitation to begin with. They must have some way of representing themselves as similar to the model, such that they and the model could be in the same position relative to the act to be imitated (Kagan 1978). This requires some representation of self as an objective entity that can be seen from the outside as well as felt subjectively from the inside. The self has

become an objective category as well as a subjective experience (Lewis and Brooks-Gunn 1979; Kagan 1981).

What is most new in this revolution about sense of self is the child's ability to coordinate schemas existing in the mind with operations existing externally in actions or words. The three consequences of this ability that most alter the sense of self and consequently the possibilities for relatedness are the capacity to make the self the object of reflection, the capacity to engage in symbolic action such as play, and the acquisition of language. These consequences, which we will take up in turn, combine to make it possible for the infant to negotiate shared meaning with another about personal knowledge.

THE OBJECTIVE VIEW OF SELF

The evidence that children begin at this age to see themselves objectively is thoroughly argued by Lewis and Brooks-Gunn (1979), Kagan (1981), and Kaye (1982). The most telling points in this argument are infants' behavior in front of a mirror, their use of verbal labels (names and pronouns) to designate self, the establishment of core gender identity (an objective categorization of self), and acts of empathy.

Prior to the age of eighteen months, infants do not seem to know that what they are seeing in a mirror is their own reflection. After eighteen months, they do. This can be shown by surreptitiously marking infants' faces with rouge, so that they are unaware that the mark has been placed. When younger infants see their reflections, they point to the mirror and not to themselves. After the age of eighteen months or so, they touch the rouge on their own faces instead of just pointing to the mirror. They now know that they can be objectified, that is, represented in some form that exists outside of their subjectively felt selves (Amsterdam 1972; Lewis and Brooks-Gunn 1978). Lewis and Brooks-Gunn call this newly objectifiable self the "categorical self," in distinction to the "existential self." It might also be called the "objective self" as against the "subjective self," or the "conceptual self" as against the "experiential self" of the previous levels of relatedness.

In any event, at about the same time infants give many other evidences of being able to objectify self and act as though self were an external category that can be conceptualized. They now begin to use pronouns ("I," "me," "mine") to refer to self, and they sometimes even begin to use proper names.[1] It is also at about this time that gender identity begins to become fixed. Infants recognize that the self as an objective entity can be categorized with other objective entities, either boys or girls.

It is also beginning around this time that empathic acts are seen (Hoffman 1977, 1978; Zahn-Waxler and Radke-Yarrow 1979, 1982). To act empathically the infant must be able to imagine both self as an object who can be experienced by the other and the objectified other's subjective state. Hoffman provides a lovely example of a thirteen-month-old boy who could, at that age, only incompletely sort out whose person (self or other) was to be objectified and whose subjective experience was to be focused upon. The failures in this case are more instructive than the successes. This child characteristically sucked his thumb and pulled on his ear lobe when he was upset. Once he saw his father clearly upset. He went over to his father and pulled the father's ear lobe but sucked on his own thumb. The boy was truly caught halfway between subjective and objective relatedness, but the coming months would see him performing more fully formed acts of empathy.

THE CAPACITY FOR SYMBOLIC PLAY

Lichtenberg (1983) has pointed out how the new capacities for objectifying the self and for coordinating mental and action schemas permit infants to "think" about or "imagine" about their interpersonal life. The clinical work of Herzog that Lichtenberg relies on illustrates this. In a study of eighteen- to twenty-month-old boys whose fathers had recently separated from the family, Herzog (1980) describes the following vignette. An eighteen-month-old boy was miserable because his father had just moved out of the home. During a play session with dolls, the boy doll was sleeping in the same bed as the mother doll. (The mother did, in fact, have the boy sleep in her bed after

1. Pseudo-proper names may appear earlier than semantically controlled pronouns (Dore, personal communication, 1984). There is some question about how much the infant initially sees the name or pronoun as an unencumbered, objectified referent for the self and how much as a referent for a more complex set of situational conditions involving caregiver and self in some activity: "Lucy don't do that!" In any event, the objectification process is well begun.

the father left.) The child got very upset at the dolls' sleeping arrangement. Herzog tried to calm the boy by having the mother doll comfort the boy doll. This did not work. Herzog then brought a daddy doll into the scene. The child first put the daddy doll in bed next to the boy doll. But this solution did not satisfy the child. The child then made the daddy doll put the boy doll in a separate bed and then get into bed with the mother doll. The child then said, "All better now" (Herzog 1980, p. 224). The child had to be juggling three versions of family reality: what he knew to be true at home, what he wished and remembered was once true at home, and what he saw as being enacted in the doll family. Using these three representations, he manipulated the signifying representation (the dolls) to realize the wished-for representation of family life and to repair symbolically the actual situation.

With this new capacity for objectifying the self and coordinating different mental and actional schemas, infants have transcended immediate experience. They now have the psychic mechanisms and operations to share their interpersonal world knowledge and experience, as well as to work on it in imagination or reality. The advance is enormous.

From the point of view of psychodynamic theories, something momentous has happened here. For the first time, the infant can now entertain and maintain a formed wish of how reality ought to be, contrary to fact. Furthermore, this wish can rely on memories and can exist in mental representation buffered in large part from the momentary press of psychophysiological needs. It can carry on an existence like a structure. This is the stuff of dynamic conflict. It reaches far beyond the real or potential distortions in perception due to immaturity or to the influence of "need state" or affect seen at earlier levels of relatedness. Interpersonal interaction can now involve past memories, present realities, and expectations of the future based solely on the past. But when expectations are based on a selective portion of the past, we end up with wishes, as in the case of Herzog's patient.

All these interpersonal goings-on can now take place verbally, or at least they will be reportable to the self and others verbally. The already existing knowledge of interpersonal transactions (real, wished for, and remembered) that involves objectifiable selves and others can be translated into words. When that happens, mutually shared meaning becomes possible and the quantum leap in relatedness occurs.[2]

THE USE OF LANGUAGE

By the time babies start to talk they have already acquired a great deal of world knowledge, not only about how inanimate things work and how their own bodies work but also about how social interactions go. The boy in Herzog's example cannot yet tell us verbally exactly what he wants and doesn't want, but he can enact what he knows and wishes with considerable precision. Similarly, children can point to the rouge on their own noses when they see it in a mirror before they can say "me," "mine," or "nose." The point is simply that there is a stretch of time in which rich experiential knowledge "in there" is accumulated, which somehow will later get assembled (although not totally) with a verbal code, language. And at the same time, much new experience will emerge along with the verbalization of the experience.

Such statements seem self-evident, yet until the 1970s most of the work on children's language acquisition was either concerned more with language itself, not experience, or focused on the child's innate mental devices and operations for making sense of language as a formal system, as in the work of Chomsky. There have also been fascinating and invaluable discoveries about the infant's perception of speech sounds, but these are largely outside the scope of this book.

It was mainly the seminal works of Bloom (1973), Brown (1973), Dore (1975, 1979), Greenfield and Smith (1976), and Bruner (1977) that insisted that world knowledge of interpersonal events was the essential key to unlocking the mysteries of language acquisition. As Bruner (1983) put it, a "new functionalism began to temper the formalism of the previous decades" (p. 8). Nonetheless, the words and structures of language have more than a one-to-one relationship to things and events in real experience. Words have an existence, a

2. The present description implies that concepts come first and that words are then attached, or that experiences established earlier get translated into words. Much current thinking suggests that felt-experience and words as an expression of felt-experience coemerge. The present argument does not depend upon this issue, which is crucial to the conception of language development *per se*.

life of their own that permits language to transcend lived experience and to be generative.

How world knowledge and language are assembled from the beginning of language acquisition remains at the cutting edge of experimental studies of child language in the interpersonal context (Golinkoff 1983; Brunner 1983). This issue has resurfaced simultaneously with a growing interest in the kinds of world knowledge and language structures our theories really look at and the kinds of interactions between experience and language we are imagining take place (Glick 1983). These considerations are necessary to our discussion because the essence of the question is how language may change the sense of self and what the acquisition of language, and all that it implies, makes possible between self and others that was not possible before. Since our subject is interpersonal relatedness rather than the equally enormous subject of language acquisition, we will very selectively draw on notions that have particular clinical relevance because they take into account the interpersonal motivational or affective context of language learning.

Michael Holquist (1982) suggests that the problem of different views of understanding language and its acquisition can be approached by asking who "owns" meanings. He defines three major positions. In Personalism, *I* own meaning. This view is deeply rooted in the western humanist tradition of the individual as unique. In contrast, a second view, more likely to be found in departments of comparative literature, holds that *no one* owns meaning. It exists out there in the culture. Neither of these views is very hospitable to our concerns, since it is hard to see how interpersonal events can influence the sharing or joint ownership of meaning in either case. However, Holquist defines a third view, which he calls Dialogism. In this view, *we* own meaning, or "if we do not own it, we may, at least, *rent* meaning" (p. 3). It is this third view that opens the door wide for interpersonal happenings to play a role, and it is from this perspective that the works of several students of language are of such interest.

The Effects of Language on Self-Other Relatedness: New Ways of "Being-With"

Vygotsky (1962) maintained that the problem of understanding language acquisition was, stated oversimply, how do mutually negotiated meanings (*we* meanings) "get in" to the child's mind? As Glick (1983) puts it, "The underlying conceptual problem is the *relationship* that exists between socialized systems of mediation (provided mainly by parents) and the individual's (infant's) reconstruction of these in an interior, and perhaps not fully socialized, way" (p. 16). The problem of language acquisition has become an interpersonal problem. Meaning, in the sense of the linkage between world knowledge (or thought) and words, is no longer a given that is obvious from the beginning. It is something to be negotiated between the parent and child. The exact relationship between thought and word "is not a thing, but a process, a continual movement back and forth from thought to word and from word to thought" (Vygotsky 1962, p. 125). Meaning results from interpersonal negotiations involving what can be agreed upon as shared. And such mutually negotiated meanings (the relation of thought to word) grow, change, develop and are struggled over by two people and thus ultimately owned by *us*.

This view leaves a great deal of room for the emergence of meanings that are unique to the dyad or to the individual.[3] "Good girl," "bad girl," "naughty boy," "happy," "upset," "tired," and a host of other such value and internal-state words will continue (often throughout life) to have the meanings uniquely negotiated between one parent and one child during the early years of assembling world knowledge and language. Only when the child begins to engage in an interpersonal dialectic with other socializing mediators such as peers can these meanings undergo further change. At that stage, new mutually negotiated *we* meanings emerge.

This process of the mutual negotiations of meaning actually applies to all meanings—"dog," "red," "boy," and so on—but it becomes most interesting and less socially constrained with internal state words. (There may be a difference between children in their interest

3. An extreme example is the "private speech" of twins.

in verbalizing things versus internal states. See Bretherton et al. [1981]; Nelson [1973]; and Clarke-Stewart [1973] for differences between individual styles and sexes.) When daddy says "good girl," the words are assembled with a set of experiences and thoughts that is different from the set assembled with mother's words "good girl." Two meanings, two relations coexist. And, the difference in the two meanings can become a potent source of difficulty in solidifying an identity or self-concept. The two diverse sets of experiences and thoughts are supposed to be congruent because they are claimed by the same words, "good girl." In the learning of language, we act overtly as though meaning lies either inside the self or somewhere out there belonging to anyone and meaning the same to all. This obscures the covert, unique *we* meanings. They become very hard to isolate and rediscover; much of the task of psychotherapy lies in doing so.

Dore has carried the notion of *we* meanings and negotiated shared meanings further in a manner that has implications for interpersonal theories. In the matter of the child's motivation to talk to begin with, Dore believes that infants talk, in part, to re-establish "being-with" experiences (in my terms) or to re-establish the "personal order" (MacMurray 1961). Dore (1985) describes it as follows:

> At this critical period of the child's life (. . . when he begins to walk and talk), his mother . . . reorients him away from the personal order with her, and towards a social order. In other words, whereas their previous interactions were primarily spontaneous, playful, and relatively unorganized for the sake of being together, the mother now begins to require him to organize his action for practical, social purposes: to act on his own (getting his own ball), to fulfill role functions (feeding himself), to behave well by social standards (not throwing his glass), and so on. This induces in the child the fear of having to perform in terms of non-personal standards (towards a social order) which orients away from the personal order of infancy. (p. 15)

It is in this context of pressure to maintain the new social order that the infant is motivated by the need and desire to re-establish the personal order with mother (Dore 1985). Dore is quick to point out that motivation alone, of this sort or any other, is not sufficient to explain the appearance of language. From our point of view, however, it adds an interpersonal motive (tenable but unproven) to the interpersonal process already pointed out by Vygotsky.

One of the major imports of this dialogic view of language is that the very process of learning to speak is recast in terms of forming shared experiences, of re-establishing the "personal order," of creating a new type of "being-with" between adult and child. Just as the being-with experiences of intersubjective relatedness required the sense of two subjectivities in alignment—a sharing of inner experience of state—so too, at this new level of verbal relatedness, the infant and mother create a being-with experience using verbal symbols—a sharing of mutually created meanings about personal experience.

The acquisition of language has traditionally been seen as a major step in the achievement of separation and individuation, next only to acquiring locomotion. The present view asserts that the opposite is equally true, that the acquisition of language is potent in the service of union and togetherness. In fact, every word learned is the by-product of uniting two mentalities in a common symbol system, a forging of shared meaning. With each word, children solidify their mental commonality with the parent and later with the other members of the language culture, when they discover that their personal experiential knowledge is part of a larger experience of knowledge, that they are unified with others in a common culture base.

Dore has offered the interesting speculation that language acts in the beginning as a form of "transitional phenomenon." To speak in Winnicott's terms, the word is in a way "discovered" or "created" by the infant, in that the thought or knowledge is already in mind, ready to be linked up with the word. The word is given to the infant from the outside, by mother, but there exists a thought for it to be given to. In this sense the word, as a transitional phenomenon, does not truly belong to the self, nor does it truly belong to the other. It occupies a midway position between the infant's subjectivity and the mother's objectivity. It is "rented" by "us," as Holquist puts it. It is in this deeper sense that language is a union experience, permitting a new level of mental relatedness through shared meaning.

The notion of language as a "transitional object" seems at first glance somewhat fanciful. However, observed evidence makes it seem very real. Katherine Nelson has recorded "crib talk" of a girl before and after her second birthday. Routinely, the infant's father put her to bed. As part of the putting-to-bed ritual, they held a dialogue in which the father went over some of the things that had happened that day and discussed what was planned for the next day. The girl participated actively in this dialogue and at the same time went through many obvious and subtle maneuvers to keep daddy present and talking, to prolong the ritual. She would plead, fuss-cry, insist, cajole, and devise new questions for him, intoned ingenuously. But when he finally said "good night" and left, her voice changed dramatically into a more matter of fact, narrative tone and her monologue began, a soliloquy.

Nelson gathered a small group consisting of herself, Jerome Bruner, John Dore, Carol Feldman, Rita Watson, and me. We met monthly for a year to examine how this child conducted both the dialogue with her father and the monologue after he left. The important features of her monologues were her practice and discovery of word usage. She could be seen to struggle with finding the right linguistic forms to contain her thoughts and knowledge of events. At times, one could see her moving closer and closer, with successive trials, to a more satisfying verbal rendition of her thinking. But even more striking, for the point at hand, is that it was like watching "internalization" happen right before our eyes and ears. After father left, she appeared to be constantly under the threat of feeling alone and distressed. (A younger brother had been born about this time.) To keep herself controlled emotionally, she repeated in her soliloquy topics that had been part of the dialogue with father. Sometimes she seemed to intone in his voice or to recreate something like the previous dialogue with him, in order to reactivate his presence and carry it with her toward the abyss of sleep. This, of course, was not the only purpose that her monologue served (she was also practicing language!), but it certainly felt as though she were also engaged in a "transitional phenomenon," in Winnicott's sense.

Language, then, provides a new way of being related to others (who may be present or absent) by sharing personal world knowledge with them, coming together in the domain of verbal relatedness. These comings-together permit the old and persistent life issues of attachment, autonomy, separation, intimacy, and so on to be re-encountered on the previously unavailable plane of relatedness through shared meaning of personal knowledge. But language is not primarily another means for individuation, nor is it primarily another means for creating togetherness. It is rather the means for achieving the next developmental level of relatedness, in which all existential life issues will again be played out.

The advent of language ultimately brings about the ability to narrate one's own life story with all the potential that holds for changing how one views oneself. The making of a narrative is not the same as any other kind of thinking or talking. It appears to involve a different mode of thought from problem solving or pure description. It involves thinking in terms of persons who act as agents with intentions and goals that unfold in some causal sequence with a beginning, middle, and end. (Narrative-making may prove to be a universal human phenomenon reflecting the design of the human mind.) This is a new and exciting area of research in which it is not yet clear how, why or when children construct (or co-construct with a parent) narratives that begin to form the autobiographical history that ultimately evolves into the life story a patient may first present to a therapist. The domain of verbal relatedness might, in fact, be best subdivided into a sense of a categorical self that objectifies and labels, and of a narrated self that weaves into a story elements from other senses of the self (agency, intentions, causes, goals, and so on).

The Other Edge of the Sword: The Alienating Effect of Language on Self-Experience and Togetherness

This new level of relatedness does not eclipse the levels of core-relatedness and intersubjective relatedness, which continue as ongoing forms of interpersonal experience. It does, however, have the capacity to recast and transform some of the experiences of core- and intersubjective relatedness, so that they lead two lives—their original life as nonverbal experience and a life as the verbalized version of that experience. As Werner and Kaplan (1963) suggest, language grabs hold of a piece of the conglomerate of feeling, sensation, perception, and cognition that constitutes global nonverbal experience. The piece that language takes hold of is transformed by the process of language-making and becomes an experience separate from the original global experience.[4]

Several different relationships can exist between the nonverbal global experience and that part of it that has been transformed into words. At times, the piece that language separates out is quintessential and captures the whole experience beautifully. Language is generally thought to function in this "ideal" way, but in fact it rarely does, and we will have the least to say about this. At other times, the language version and the globally experienced version do not coexist well. The global experience may be fractured or simply poorly represented, in which case it wanders off to lead a misnamed and poorly understood existence. And finally, some global experiences at the level of core- and intersubjective relatedness (such as the very sense of a core self) do not permit language sufficient entry to separate out a piece for linguistic transformation. Such experiences then simply continue underground, nonverbalized, to lead an unnamed (and, to that extent only, unknown) but nonetheless very real existence. (Unusual efforts such as psychoanalysis of poetry or fiction can sometimes claim some of this territory for language, but not in the usual linguistic sense. And this is what gives such power to these processes.)

Specific examples of particular experiences will illustrate this general issue of divergence between world knowledge and words. The notion of divergence, or slippage, between world knowledge and word knowledge is well known as it concerns knowledge of the physical world. Bower (1978) provides an excellent example of it. When a child is shown a lump of clay first rolled long and thin and then made into a fat ball, the child will claim that the ball version of the same amount of clay is heavier. According to the verbal account, the child does not have conservation of volume and weight. One would therefore expect that if the child is handed the two balls, first the thin one and then the fat one, the child's arm would rise up when it received the fat ball, since it was expected to be heavier and the muscles of the arm should be tensed to compensate for the difference. But a high-speed film shows that the arm does not move up. Bower concludes that the child's body, at the sensorimotor level,

4. We are not concerned here with the experiences that are created *de novo* by language. Some might claim that all experience rendered linguistically is experience *de novo,* but this position is not being assumed here.

has already achieved conservation of weight and volume, even though verbally the child seems to have lost or never to have had this capacity. Similar phenomena occur in domains that concern interpersonal world knowledge more directly.

The infant's capacity for amodal perception has loomed large in this overall account. The abilities to sense a core self and other and to sense intersubjective relatedness through attunement have depended in part on amodal capacities. What might happen to the experience of amodal perception when language is applied to it?

Suppose we are considering a child's perception of a patch of yellow sunlight on the wall. The infant will experience the intensity, warmth, shape, brightness, pleasure, and other amodal aspects of the patch. The fact that it is yellow light is not of primary or, for that matter, of any importance. While looking at the patch and feeling-perceiving it (à la Werner), the child is engaged in a global experience resonant with a mix of all the amodal properties, the primary perceptual qualities, of the patch of light—its intensity, warmth, and so on. To maintain this highly flexible and omni-dimensional perspective on the patch, the infant must remain blind to those particular properties (secondary and tertiary perceptual qualities, such as color) that specify the sensory channel through which the patch is being experienced. The child must not notice or be made aware that it is a visual experience. Yet that is exactly what language will force the child to do. Someone will enter the room and say, "Oh, *look* at the *yellow* sun*light*!" Words in this case separate out precisely those properties that anchor the experience to a single modality of sensation. By binding it to words, they isolate the experience from the amodal flux in which it was originally experienced. Language can thus fracture amodal global experience. A discontinuity in experience is introduced.

What probably happens in development is that the language version "yellow sunlight" of such perceptual experiences becomes the official version, and the amodal version goes underground and can only resurface when conditions suppress or outweigh the dominance of the linguistic version. Such conditions might include certain contemplative states, certain emotional states, and the perception of certain works of art that are designed to evoke experiences defying verbal categorization. Again, works of the symbolist poets serve as an example of the latter. The paradox that language can evoke experience that transcends words is perhaps the highest tribute to the power of language. But those are words in poetic use. The words in our daily lives more often do the opposite and either fracture amodal global experience or send it underground.

In this area, then, the advent of language is a very mixed blessing to the child. What begins to be lost (or made latent) is enormous; what begins to be gained is also enormous. The infant gains entrance into a wider cultural membership, but at the risk of losing the force and wholeness of original experience.

The verbal rendering of specific instances of life-as-lived presents a similar problem. Recall that in earlier chapters we distinguished *specific episodes* of life-as-lived (for example, "that one time when Mommy put me to bed to go to sleep, but she was distraught and only going through the motions of the bedtime ritual and I was overtired, and she couldn't help me push through that familiar barrier into sleep") and *generalized episodes* ("what happens when Mommy puts me down to sleep"). It is only the generalized ritual that is nameable as "bedtime." No specific instance has a name. Words apply to classes of things ("dog," "tree," "run," and so on). That is where they are most powerful as tools. The generalized episode is some kind of average of similar events. It is a prototype of a class of events-as-lived (generalized interactions [RIGs]): going to bed, eating dinner, bathtime, dressing, walk with Mommy, play with Daddy, peek-a-boo. And words get assembled with experiences of life-as-lived at this generalized level of the prototypic episode. Specific episodes fall through the linguistic sieve and cannot be referenced verbally until the child is very advanced in language, and sometimes never. We see evidence of this all the time in children's frustration at their failures to communicate what seems obvious to them. The child may have to repeat a word several times ("eat!") before the parent figures out what specific instance (which food) of the general class (of edible things) the infant has in mind and expects the adult to produce.

In the clinical literature, such phenomena have often been ascribed to children's belief in or wish for adults' omniscience and omnipotence. In contrast to that view, I suggest that such misunderstandings are not based on the child's notion that the mother knows what is in her child's mind to begin with. They are true misunderstandings about meaning. To the infant who says "eat," that means a specific edible thing. It requires only understanding, not mind-reading. The mother's misunderstanding serves to teach the child that the child's specific meaning is only a subset of her possible meanings. It is in this way that mutual meanings get negotiated. In such cases, we are observing the infant and mother struggling together with the peculiar nature of language and meaning. We are not observing ruptures and repairs in the infant's sense of an omniscient parent. The passions, pleasures, and frustrations seem to come more from the success and failure of mental togetherness at the levels of shared meaning, which the infant is motivated toward, not from anxiety at the loss of delegated omnipotence and/or from the good feeling of security when omnipotence is re-established. The misunderstandings simply motivate the infant to learn language better. They do not seriously rupture the child's sense of competence.

There may be more opportunities for such frustrations at the outset of language learning, because at the levels of core- and intersubjective relatedness the mother and infant have had a good deal of time to work out a nonverbal interactive system for relating. Negotiating shared meanings necessarily invokes much failing. To an infant who at prior levels has become accustomed to smoother transactions with mother concerning the import and intent of their mutual behaviors, this may be particularly frustrating.

Our point in demonstrating the many ways that language is inadequate to the task of communicating about specific lived-experience is not to minimize the import of language at all. Rather, it is to identify the forms of slippage between personal world knowledge and official or socialized world knowledge as encoded in language, because the slippage between these two is one of the main ways in which reality and fantasy can begin to diverge. The very nature of language, as a specifier of the sensory modality in use (in contrast to amodal nonspecification) and as a specifier of the generalized episode instead of the specific instance, assures that there will be points of slippage.

There are other points of slippage that should be noted. One of these is in the verbal accounts of internal states. Affect as a form of personal knowledge is very hard to put into words and communicate. Words to label internal states are not among the first to be used by children, even though children have presumably had long familiarity with the internal states (Bretherton et al. 1981). It is easier to label the categories of affective states (happy, sad) than the dimensional features (how happy, how sad). One problem is that the dimensional features of affect are gradient features (a little happy, very happy), while categorical features are not (happy versus not happy). Language is the ideal medium to deal with categorical information—that is partly what naming is all about—but it is at a great disadvantage in dealing with an analogue system, such as fullness of display, in ethological terms, which is geared to express gradient information. And it is the gradient information that may carry the most decisive information in everyday interpersonal communications.

The well-worn joke about the two psychiatrists passing on the sidewalk provides an illustration. They say "hello" and smile as they pass, and then each thinks to himself, "I wonder what he meant by that?" We can untrivialize this story by discussing it in terms of its categorical and gradient information. To begin with, greeting behaviors are conventionalized emotional responses containing elements from the Darwinian categories of surprise and happiness. As soon as one becomes aware that a greeting response will be initiated or responded to, one must tune in to the subtle but inevitable social cues that will be carried in the gradient features of the greeting. A number of factors will influence the gradient features and how each greeter will assess the greeting received: the nature of the relationship between the two greeters, the state of the relationship since their last meeting, the amount of time since they last met, their sexes, their cultural norms, and so on. In accordance with each participant's assessments of these factors, they expect each other to say a "hello" of a roughly specific volume, gusto, and intonational richness and to raise their eyebrows, widen their eyes, and open their smiles to a roughly expected height, width, and duration of display. Any significant variance from these expectations will occasion the question, "I wonder what he meant by that?" Each responder or recipient of the greeting will also be in the active position of gauging exactly how to adjust the delivery of his or her own greeting (Stern et al. 1983).

In this example, the work of interpreting the other person's behavior did not reside in the category of the signal. In fact, it did not even lie, as I have been implying, in the gradient features of the signal as performed. It lay in the discrepancy between the way the gradient features were actually performed and the way they were expected to be performed, given the context. The work of interpretation thus consists of measuring the distance between an imaginary performance (perhaps never before even seen in reality) and an actual performance of gradient features.

There is no reason why the situation should be much different for the child. The infant who hears mother say "Hi, honey" in an unaccustomed way would sense, but would not think to say, "You did not say it right." But the child would be wrong. What mother said, in linguistic fact, is right, but she did not act it (mean it) right. What is said and what is meant have a complicated relationship in the interpersonal domain.

When two messages, usually verbal and nonverbal, clash in the extreme, it has been called a "double-bind message" (Bateson et al. 1956). It is usually the case that the nonverbal message is the one that is meant, and the verbal message is the one of "record." The "on-record" message is the one we are officially accountable for.

Several authors, such as Scherer (1979) and Labov and Fanshel (1977), have pointed out that some of our communications are deniable, while others we are held accountable for. Gradient information is more easily denied. These different signals are going on simultaneously in various communicative channels. Furthermore, for the greatest flexibility and maneuverability of communication it is necessary to have this kind of mix (Garfinkel 1967). Labov and Fanshel (1977) describe this necessity very well in discussing intonational signals; for our purposes, their point applies equally well to other nonverbal behaviors:

> The lack of clarity or discreteness in the intonational signal is not an unfortunate limitation of this channel, but an essential and important aspect of it. Speakers need a form of communication which is deniable. It is advantageous for them to express hostility, challenge the competence of others, or express friendliness and affection in a way that can be denied if they are explicitly held to account for it. If there were not such a deniable channel of communication and intonation contours became so well recognized and explicit that people were accountable for their intonations, then some other mode of deniable communication would indoubtedly develop. (p. 46)

The surest way to keep a channel deniable is to prevent it from becoming a part of the formal language system. In learning a new word, a baby isolates an experience for clear identification and at the same time becomes accountable to mother for that word.)

This line of argument suggests that in a multi-channel communicative system there will exist constant environmental or cultural pressure to keep some signals more resistant to explicit accountable encoding than others, so that they will remain deniable. Because language is so good at communicating what, rather than how, something happened, the verbal message invariably becomes the accountable one. A year-old-boy was angry at his mother and in a fit of temper, while not looking at her, yelled, "Aaaaah!" and brought his fist down hard on a puzzle. Mother said, "Don't you yell at your mother." She would have been very unlikely to say, "Don't you bring your fist down like that at your mother." Neither message, the verbal one nor the nonverbal one, was more closely directed at her than the other. One is accountable very early for what one says, and this child is being prepared for that by making his vocalizations rather than his gestures the accountable act.

One of the consequences of this inevitable division into the accountable and the deniable is that what is deniable to others becomes more and more deniable to oneself. The path into the unconscious (both topographic and potentially dynamic) is being well laid by language. Prior to language, all of one's behaviors have equal status as far as "ownership" is concerned. With the advent of language, some behaviors now have a privileged status with regard to one having to own them. The many messages in many channels are being fragmented by language into a hierarchy of accountability/deniability.

There is another type of slippage between experience and words that deserves mention. Some experiences of self, such as continuity of coherence, the "going on being" of a physically integrated, nonfragmented self, fall into a category something like your heartbeat or regular breathing. Such experiences rarely require the notice needed to be verbally encoded. Yet periodically some transient sense of this experience is revealed, for some inexplicable reason or via psychopathology, with the breathtaking effect of sudden realization that your existential and verbal selves can be light years apart, that the self is unavoidably divided by language.

Many experiences of self-with-other fall into this unverbalized category; mutually gazing into one another's eyes without speaking qualifies. So does the sense of another person's characteristic vitality affects—the individual subtleties of physical style, which are also experienced as the child experiences a patch of sunlight. All such experiences are ineluctable, with the consequence of further distancing personal knowledge as experienced as word or thought. (It is little wonder we need art so badly to bridge these gaps in ourselves.)

A final issue involves the relation between life as experienced and as retold. How much the act of making an autobiographical narrative reflects or necessarily alters the lived experiences that become the personal story is an open question.

Infants' initial interpersonal knowledge is mainly unshareable, amodal, instance-specific, and attuned to nonverbal behaviors in which no one channel of communication has priviledged status with regard to accountability or ownership. Language changes all of that. With its emergence, infants become estranged from direct contact with their own personal experience. Language forces a space between interpersonal experience as lived and as represented. And it is exactly across this space that the connections and associations that constitute neurotic behavior may form. But also with language, infants for the first time can share their personal experience of the world with others, including "being with" others in intimacy, isolation, loneliness, fear, awe, and love.

Finally, with the advent of language and symbolic thinking, children now have the tools to distort and transcend reality. They can create expectations contrary to past experience. They can elaborate a wish contrary to present fact. They can represent someone or something in terms of symbolically associated attributes (for example, bad experiences with mother) that in reality were never experienced all together at any one time but that can be pulled together from isolated episodes into a symbolic representation (the "bad mother" or "incompetent me"). These symbolic condensations finally make possible the distortion of reality and provide the soil for neurotic constructs. Prior to this linguistic ability, infants are confined to reflect the impress of reality. They can now transcend that, for good or ill.

PART III

SOME CLINICAL IMPLICATIONS

Chapter 9

The "Observed Infant" as Seen with a Clinical Eye

BY SHIFTING the focus from different clinical developmental tasks, such as trust and autonomy, to different senses of the self as explanations of the major changes in the social organization of the infant, we have made it possible to examine different kinds of sensitive periods in early development. Since the major developmental shifts now involve the emergence of new senses of the self, the formative period for each sense of self can be considered sensitive. How critical these formative periods for each sense of the self will ultimately prove to be remains an open empirical issue. The weight of evidence from the neurological and ethological viewpoints, however, argues that the initial period of formation will prove relatively more sensitive than subsequent periods for later functioning (Hofer 1980).

In this chapter we will identify some of the patterns that are seen during the emergence of each sense of self, and we will speculate on how the initial form in which they are established may be critical for later functioning. First, however, several caveats are required.

When the development of an infant is observed with a clinical eye one sees almost no pathology, unless a preselected high-risk group has been chosen. Instead, there are characteristic patterns and some variant patterns, but there is very little basis for believing that any deviations from the norm are going to result in later pathology. When there are deviations, it is the relationship with the caregivers and not the infant alone that appears deviant. Often it is not even clear which variations are the most likely precursors of later pathology. And at each successive age, everything seems different, yet everything feels exactly the same, clinically. This is the paradox of continuity/discontinuity that fascinates and plagues the prospective view of development.

We have videotaped many mother/infant pairs at two, four, six, nine, eighteen, twenty-four, and thirty-six months, either at home or in the laboratory. Whenever we show a complete longitudinal series of tapes of one pair (shown in order, either forward or backward) to a group of students, whether new or experienced, they are forcibly struck by the sense that the two individuals are conducting their interpersonal business in a similar and recognizable fashion throughout. The same issues seem to get handled in the same general ways, although with different behaviors at different ages. The "feel" and even the subject matter of the interaction around these clinical issues is continuous, while the infant as a social person seems to be differently organized at each point.[1]

These impressions are one of the main reasons that we have shifted the focus from developmental tasks to senses of the self. Our emphasis, then, will be on the establishment of patterns of self-experience within each domain of senses of self that appear to have some clinical relevance for later functioning.

The problems of finding continuity of pattern and relating it to potential pathology are very real. These problems are beautifully exemplified in the recent history of attachment research. Initially, attachment was viewed as a specific developmental task of a particular life phase (Bowlby 1958, 1960; Ainsworth 1969). It became apparent that "quality of relatedness"—that is, attachment—extends beyond

1. This sense of continuity is reinforced by the fact that the people look the same physically from one time point to another. However, we find that during the first year after the infant's birth a large number of mothers go through a great number of drastic changes in hair style as they seek out their new identity, and they in fact look quite different from visit to visit.

the initial mother/infant bond and develops throughout childhood, applying to peers as well as to mother. In fact, it is a life-span issue. The question was how to discover the continuity in patterns of attachment. When one measured attachment with molecular behaviors such as gazes, vocalizations, proxemics, and so on, there appeared to be little continuity in quality of attachment from one age to another. It was only when researchers fell back on (or moved toward) a more global and qualitative summary measure of attachment such as the type of infant attachment—secure (type B), anxious/avoidant (type A), and anxious/resistant (type C) (Ainsworth et al. 1978)—that progress in the study of continuity could be made. Note that the summary measure of types of attachment yielded styles or patterns of attachment, not strength or goodness of attachment. Once this summary measure of patterns of attachment was available, researchers went on to show that type of attachment at twelve months correlated well with later patterns of relating.[2]

Indeed, it appears that quality of relationship at one year is an excellent predictor of quality of relating in various other ways up through five years, with the advantage to the securely attached infant compared with the resistantly or avoidantly attached infant. It has been suggested that the anxious attachment patterns at twelve months are predictive of psychopathology at age six in boys (Lewis et al., in press).

It would appear that resistant or avoidant attachment, which occurs in about 12 percent and 20 percent of middle-class U.S. samples, might be an indicator of later clinical problems. However, a caveat can be found in cross-cultural research. While data from a South German sample reflected U.S. norms, a North German sample had a preponderance of avoidant attachment (Grossmann and Grossmann, in press), and many Japanese children (37 percent) showed resistant attachment (Miyake, Chen, and Campos, in press). In this light, can type of attachment be considered a precursor to pathology? If so, it is quite culture-bound. More likely it is simply a style of conducting a motivational-clinical issue which may be a good nonspecific

2. The type of attachment shown at twelve months predicts: (1) type of attachment at eighteen months (Waters 1978; Main and Weston 1981); (2) frustratability, persistence, cooperativeness, and task enthusiasm at twenty-four months (Main 1977; Matas, Arend, and Sroufe 1978); (3) social competence of preschoolers (Lieberman 1977; Easterbrook and Lamb 1979; Waters, Wipman, and Sroufe 1979); and (4) self-esteem, empathy, and classroom deportment (Sroufe 1983).

indicator of general success in adaptation to life, however life is found (Sroufe and Rutter 1984; Garmenzy and Rutter 1983; Cicchetti and Schneider-Rosen, in press). But indicators of general adaptation are not precursors. Their relationship to later behavior is too nonspecific and indirect.

In this chapter, we will confine the discussion to patterns of self-experience that are of potential clinical relevance and are best conceptualized in terms of the different domains of sense of self.

Constitutional Differences and Emergent Relatedness

The capacities that permit the infant to yoke his diverse experiences of the social world are to an enormous extent constitutionally—that is, genetically—determined. Either they are present right away or they unfold on an innate timetable, given an intact central nervous system and an intact environment. For the immediate future, the study of individual differences of these capacities may prove to be the most fruitful area of clinical research on the development of psychopathology in the very young. Whenever new capacities are identified, especially those needed in social perception and competence, they naturally become the focus of intense scrutiny, speculation, and hope. The hope is that the earliest deviation in social and intellectual functioning will be traceable to abnormalities in these capacities. If so, we would have an understanding of the underlying mechanisms that would help explain the emergence of pervasive developmental disorder, autism, later learning disabilities, attention deficit, characterological differences, and various problems in social conduct and competence. Discrete therapeutic strategies would also be more obvious.

Let us look briefly at some possible clinical ramifications of deficits in these capacities. The capacity to transfer information from one modality to another is so central to integrating perceptual experience that the potential problems resulting from a deficit are almost limitless. One of the first to leap to mind is learning disabilities, since so much learning calls for a transposition of information from one sensory mode to another, especially back and forth between vision and audition. And indeed, Rose et al. (1979) now have suggestive evidence that learning-disabled children may be abnormal in specific cross-modal transfer capacities. Infants could also be socially and emotionally disabled by such deficits; intermodal fluency greatly facilitates the apprehension of the social behavior of other persons as well as the integrated actions, sensations, affects, and so on of one's own self. These findings are still too new for one to have any idea, as yet, of the limits of their psychopathological relevance.

In a different vein, the perennial search for early predictors of later general intelligence seems to have been revived by promising results that show the extent to which the infant's capacities for long-term recognition memory and other information-processing feats predict later intellectual functioning (Caron and Caron 1981; Fagan and Singer 1983). The study of episodic memory in infancy has only just begun.

Ever since the work of Thomas et al. (1970) on temperamental differences and the emphasis of Escalona (1968) on the importance of the "fit" between maternal and infant temperaments, it has been clear that all considerations of interaction from the clinical point of view must take temperament into full account. Clinically, most practitioners find it absolutely essential to keep issues of temperament and fit in mind. In spite of this, researchers have to date been fairly unsuccessful in documenting the continuity of temperamental differences in infancy when they are viewed prospectively. (See Sroufe [in press] for a discussion of the problems of considering temperamental determinants outside of a relational perspective.) Nonetheless, it is worth speculating about how a temperamental difference in something such as tolerance for stimulation might be viewed clinically.

Individual differences in infants' tolerance for stimulation or the capacity to regulate arousal may have relevance to issues such as later anxiety disorders, which have a significant constitutional component. One can think of the relationship between absolute stimulation and arousal or excitation in several different ways, only one of which is shown in figure 9.1,[3] as an example. The asterisks mark individually

3. For any one child, there is no one, single curve; rather, there is a family of curves. For example, if the mother stays at home all day and the father has a quick bout of interaction with the baby in the evening after work, he usually does so at a higher level of stimulus intensity than what has been going on all day with mother. His games will be more explosive,

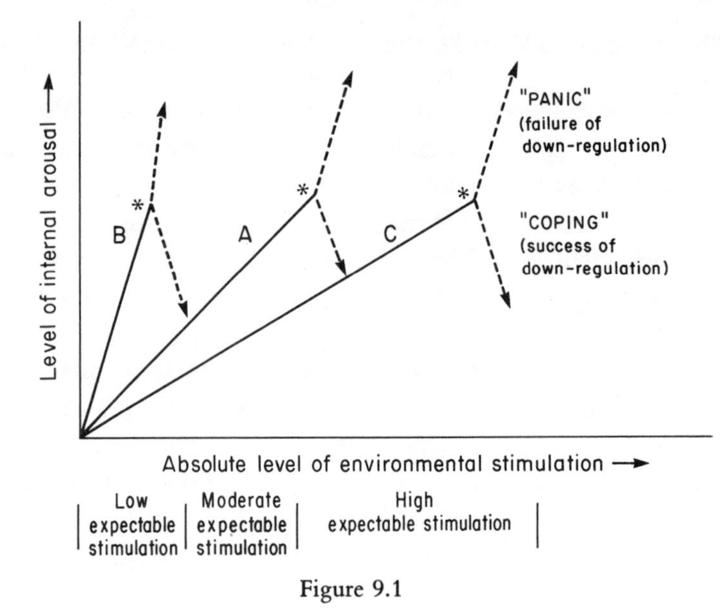

Figure 9.1

characteristic points at which the infant's capacity to cope with the stimulation level is about to be exceeded. At this point the child must down-regulate the level by dampening or terminating stimulus input through some coping maneuver, or the threshold for coping will be exceeded and the infant will experience something like panic. Assume that line A represents a normal curve. Suppose a baby had a characteristic curve like that shown in line B. The stimulation of normal daily events would exceed the infant's coping capacity and trigger anxiety episodes. Because the thresholds for external stimulation are set so low, it would look as though the anxiety attacks were spontaneous—that is, internally caused, as Klein (1982) suggests—when in fact they were simply promiscuously triggered by expectable, everyday stimulation arising from almost anywhere. In this regard, Brazelton's (1982) descriptions of the low stimulation tolerance of small-for-gestational-age infants may prove relevant.

There may also prove to be different thresholds of tolerance for different *kinds* of stimulation. It has long been suggested that autistic

with more throwing in the air and vigorous touching and kinesthetic stimulations. What is interesting is that the infant seems to expect and even want this higher level of excitement; the baby tolerates and even seeks higher levels of arousal and intensities of stimulation in the coming-home situation (Yogman 1982). If the father is a house-husband and mother goes to work, the parents reverse patterns and the two curves tend to switch. Still, each may have a characteristic limit.

children may have an extremely low tolerance for human stimulation (especially gaze), but not for nonhuman stimulation (Hutt and Ounsted 1966). Similarly, some people are predominantly aural or visual or tactile, and many investigators have proposed different sensitivities to stimulation in different modalities as a cause for mismatch in the regulation of arousal between mothers and infants (Greenspan 1981). Or again, the nature of the coping operation characteristically used may show wide individual differences, resulting in various pictures, such as shyness, avoidance, or vigilance.

While the potential of amodal and other constitutional capacities for the understanding of later psychopathology is great, it remains largely unresearched and fraught with many problems. First, there is the problem of specificity. We do not yet know if it is possible to have a severe disfunction in any one or two of these capacities without having disfunctions in almost all of them. Second, the relationship between severity of defect in these capacities and functional social behavior is unknown. Suppose something went drastically wrong with many of these capacities. What might result? In the most extreme case, one would predict pervasive developmental disorders (mental retardation with autistic features). Neither a core self nor a core other could be fully constituted, and social relatedness would be massively compromised. Unity of the senses would gel slowly, if at all, through experience. Causal relations would go largely undetected. The perceptual world would be disorganized and partially unconstructable. Memory would be limited, so that continuity of experience would be minimal. All transactions with the inanimate world as well as with the human world would be grossly compromised. The disorder would indeed be pervasive—so pervasive that it would be difficult or impossible to sort out which specific defects contributed to which specific disorders in function. And if a sense of a core self could not form, there would be no basis from which to form a sense of a subjective self, and so on.

Less drastic defects in these capacities could be the precursors of a spectrum of outcomes, from serious illness through subtle personal oddities, including differences in interpersonal, cognitive, or perceptual style. There is much new information that is very promising for later clinical issues. Now is the time to begin to evaluate its true clinical import. In particular, studies in individual differences with longitudinal follow-up are needed. Whatever the results, this early period of life will never again look the same clinically.

So far, this discussion has not directly concerned the infant's emergent sense of self. Since these capacities are the very ones involved in creating emergent experiences, however, the sense of the emergent self would be profoundly affected by deficits in any of these capacities. In the following sections we will focus more centrally on the clinical implications for the different senses of self. These will clearly have more relevance for the more characterological or neurotic features of pathology in contrast to the Axis I diagnostic categories of the *Diagnostic and Statistical Manual of Mental Disorders* (*DSM-III*).

Core-Relatedness

When watching an infant, can one get a clinical impression of future dangers to the core sense of self? Clinical vignettes will serve best to answer this question. The regulation of excitation, arousal, activation, stimulation, and tension are the aspects of self that clinicians focus on most in evaluating the health-promoting nature of the parent-infant relationship during the first half-year of life. Our major concern here, therefore, will be on the contouring of excitation as it is mutually performed by infant and parent.

Two statements first. There is no such thing as a perfect mutual contouring of excitation, either all the time or even for a short time. Interaction does not work that way. Constant failures of stimulation, overshooting, and under-shooting are built into the dynamic nature of an interaction. The goal or set point is always changing. These over- and under-shootings make up the ordinary repeating interactive patterns. Secondly, we are operating on assumptions, stated before, that the representational world is constituted mainly from the ordinary events of life, not from the exceptional ones. Exceptional moments are probably no more than superb yet slightly atypical examples of the ordinary. One can only address characteristic "mis-fittings" and their likely consequences.

EXPECTABLE AND TOLERABLE OVERSTIMULATION IN THE DOMAIN OF CORE-RELATEDNESS

Eric is a somewhat bland infant compared with his more affectively intense mother, but both are perfectly normal. His mother constantly likes to see him more excited, more expressive and demonstrative about feelings, and more avidly curious about the world. When Eric does show some excitement about something, his mother adroitly joins in and encourages, even intensifies, the experience a little—usually successfully, so that Eric experiences a higher level of excitement than he would alone. The cajoling, exaggerating, slightly overresponsive, eliciting behavior that she characteristically performs are in fact usually very enjoyable to Eric. Her behavior does not create a gross mismatch, but rather a small one. His tolerance for stimulation can encompass it, but at a level of excitement that he would not reach by his own efforts. It would not be accurate to call her controlling or intrusive. She does not try to disrupt or redirect his experience on the basis of her own needs or insensitivities. Rather, she is trying to augment the range of his experiences (granted, for her own reasons and in accord with her own temperamental type). It is a very common experience for any mother to try to expand her infant's tolerance for excitement or arousal and generally stretch her infant's world ("Did you realize that this old rattle could be that fascinating?"). It is no more than working in the infant's zone of proximal (affective) development, the place just beyond where he is and that he is developing toward.

What made the "constructive" mismatches more obvious in this case was the discrepancy in "temperamental" types between mother and son. But that only highlighted the situation. A mother of a temperament identical to her child's would have to act similarly at times to work in her infant's zone of proximal affective development.

In any event, Eric's self-experience of higher-than-usual excitement is, in fact, largely achieved and regulated by his mother's behavior. His experience of his own higher levels of excitement occurs only in the lived episodes in which her augmenting antics are a crucial attribute. She thus becomes for him a self-excitement-regulating other. Eric's self-experience of high positive excitement never occurs unless mother is there participating in it. Specific episodes coalesce to form a RIG. And the activated RIG takes the form of an evoked companion, the experience of whom can be captured by questions like: "What is it like to be with mother when I feel this way in myself? or, "How do I feel in myself when I am with mother?"

Now suppose Eric is alone or with another person. And by himself, he begins to exceed the level of positive excitement that is usual for him when he is not with his mother. (Maturation and development are proceeding rapidly day by day, making this experience frequent and inevitable.) He begins to "feel this way," that is, to reach a certain higher level of excitement. "Feeling this way" is one of the attributes of the RIG, the other indivisible attribute of which is mother's encouraging, experience-augmenting performance. Beginning to "feel this way" will serve as the attribute that unconsciously recalls to mind the evoked companion. (A representation has been reactivated.) Eric then experiences a fantasied being with mother. In some sense, she is functionally "there," and that helps him to stretch the level of excitement he has created for himself. The evoked companion as a self-regulating other is promoting development. There is no distortion of reality. Everything is reality-based. Let us now look at other RIGs, evoked companions, and their influence on development.

FORMS OF INTOLERABLE OVERSTIMULATION IN THE DOMAIN OF CORE-RELATEDNESS

The experience of overstimulation for the infant can only be understood in terms of what happens next, since that becomes part of the lived episode. It must be understood that by the age of three months or so, the infant's immediate response to overstimulation (short of excessive overstimulation) is *not* to cry and fall apart but rather to try to deal with it. After all, "it" is elicited by mother's or father's behavior, in an interaction for which the infant has a repertoire of regulating maneuvers. Coping and defensive operations form in the small space between the upper threshold of the infant's stimulation tolerance and final crying. This space is the growing and testing ground of adaptive maneuvers. And their performance becomes part of the lived experience of overstimulation.

In the case of Stevie, an overstimulating, controlling mother regularly forced the face-to-face interaction into a "game of chase and dodge," well described by Beebe and Stern (1977). In essence, when the mother overstimulated him, Stevie would avert his head to the side. Mother would respond to this dodge by chasing him with her face and escalating the stimulus level of her behavior to capture his attention. He would then execute another dodge, swinging his face away to the opposite side. Mother would follow his head with hers, still trying to maintain the vis-à-vis engagement at the level she wanted. Finally, if he was unable to avoid her gaze, Stevie would become more upset and end up crying. More often than not, however, his aversions were successful and mother would get the message long before he cried. This example is extreme, but the general pattern in milder form has been described over and over (Stern 1971, 1977; Beebe and Sloate 1982).

This kind of intrusive overstimulating behavior on the part of the mother can arise from many causes: hostility, need for control, insensitivity, or an unusual sensitivity to rejection such that mother interprets each infant head aversion as a "microrejection" and attempts to repair and undo it (Stern 1977). Whatever the reason for his mother's behavior, Stevie experiences the following RIG: a high level of arousal, maternal behavior that tends to push him beyond his tolerable limits, the need to self-regulate downward, and the (usually) successful self-regulation by persistent aversions. In Stevie's case, when he is experiencing the higher levels of excitement, his mother has become a different kind of evoked companion, a self-disregulating other.

Now let us suppose that Stevie is alone or with another person, and he begins to approach his upper level of tolerable stimulation, to "feel a certain way." Feeling that certain way will activate the RIG. Like Eric, he will experience an evoked being-with-mother, but in his case it is a disregulating union with mother that will result in his execution of potentially maladaptive behavior. He will unnecessarily avoid stimulation that threatens to exceed or has just exceeded his tolerance. If he is with someone else, he misses or does not stay open to the adjustments on the other's part that would permit him either to stay engaged or to re-engage. From observation of many infants such as Stevie, it is clear that they generalize their experience, so that they are relatively overavoidant with new persons. When they are alone, one of two things seems to happen. They cut short their potential positive excitement, most likely by activating a disregulating mother as the evoked companion, or they show freer access to their own pleasurable excitement and can even wallow in it, as if they inhibited or somehow prevented the activation of the RIG.[4]

We do not know why some infants seem able to regulate their excitement so much more successfully when alone than when interacting with a disregulating parent. Whether we are talking about inhibited evoked companions or selective generalization, it would appear that those children who are more successful at escaping the evoked presence of a problematic parent when alone gain the advantage of being able to utilize more of themselves. At the same time, they are dealt the disadvantage of living more alone in the world.

Molly and her mother illustrate a different form of intolerable overstimulation. Molly's mother was very controlling. She had to design, initiate, direct, and terminate all agendas. She determined which toy Molly should play with, how Molly was to play with it ("Shake it up and down—don't roll it on the floor"), when Molly was done playing with it, and what to do next ("Oh, here is Dressy Bessy. Look!"). The mother overcontrolled the interaction to such an extent that it was often hard to trace the natural crescendo and decrescendo of Molly's own interest and excitement. It was so frequently derailed or interrupted that it could hardly be said to trace its own course. This is an extreme form of disregulation of excitation. (Most experienced viewers who watch these televised interactions between Molly and her mother find themselves getting a tense feeling most often described as a knot in the stomach and slowly realize how enraged they are becoming. There is a co-opting of the child's self-regulating abilities that makes those who identify with Molly feel impotent and infuriated.)

Molly found an adaptation. She gradually became more compliant. Instead of actively avoiding or opposing these intrusions, she became one of those enigmatic gazers into space. She could stare through you, her eyes focused somewhere at infinity and her facial expressions opaque enough to be just uninterpretable, and at the same time remain in good contingent contact and by and large do what she was invited or told to do. Watching her over the months was like

4. All of these vignettes can also be explained in terms of traditional learning theory, generalization, and selective generalizations. However, these permit no account of the infant's subjective experience of performing these overt behaviors.

watching her self-regulation of excitement slip away. She appeared to let herself ride the stop-and-start course of arousal flow dictated by her mother. In fact, she seemed to have given up on the whole idea of self-regulation of this part of herself. When playing alone she did not recover it, remaining somewhat aloof from exciting engagements with things. This general dampening of her affectivity continued beyond this phase of development and was still apparent at age three years. She seems to have learned that excitement is not something that is equally regulated by two people—the self and the self-regulating other—but that it is mainly the self-regulating other who does all the regulating. (At some point in her development, anger, oppositionalism, hostility, and the like will be sorely needed to rescue her.)

FORMS OF INTOLERABLE UNDERSTIMULATION IN THE DOMAIN OF CORE-RELATEDNESS

Susie's mother was depressed, preoccupied with a recent divorce. She in fact had not wanted Susie to begin with except to hold the marriage together. She already had an older daughter, who was her favorite. Susie was a normally spunky infant, well endowed with all the capacities to appeal to and elicit social behavior from any willing adult, plus a lot of persistence to keep trying at the faintest hint of success. In spite of this, she was generally unsuccessful in getting her mother to join in for long. More important, she could not get her mother to spark enough so that the mother ever took over the up-regulation of excitation. The mother did not actually take control over the down-regulation of excitation, but her lack of responsitivity acted as a drag on Susie's attempts to up-regulate.

What is happening in this situation? Suppose that the mother were completely unresponsive and unmoveable, essentially not there, and Susie were left to her own devices to experience and regulate her own excitement (a variant of the situation that once prevailed for institutionalized babies). During the period of forming a sense of a core self, she could only experience a narrow band of pleasurable arousal, because it is only stimuli provided by the unique social behavior of adults towards infants that can, so to speak, blast the infant into the next orbit of positive excitation. The infant would be left without a certain range of experience. The actual and fantasied experiences with a self-regulating other are essential for encountering the normally expected range of self-experiences, and without the other's presence and responsive behavior, the full range simply does not develop. There is a maturational failure, a "self-regulating-other-deficiency disease." This is just another way of stating that only a selected portion of the whole spectrum of self-experiences of excitation may get exercized during this period resulting in a permanent influence during this sensitive period upon what experiences become part of the sense of a core self.

This is not exactly Susie's situation, but it is close to the situation that obtains when her experiences with her mother are particularly barren. Susie is persistent, however, and she is drawn on to be persistent because she is sometimes moderately successful and occasionally very successful. When she is, she experiences a much higher than ordinary sense of pleasurable excitement. What happens, then, is that she has to work hard to get mother to ignite and thereby sends herself the rest of the way. Susie's experience with self-excitement-regulating other forms a very different RIG from that of the other children. She does not expect and accept experiences of being with the self-excitement-regulating other, as Eric does. Nor does she need to dread them, as Stevie does, or tune them out, as Molly does.

She must actively strive and perform to set her mother into motion to create the being-with experiences she needs. This interactive pattern based on a specific RIG has remained characteristic of Susie for the first three years, and one can readily imagine its continuing and gathering in more and more aspects of the interpersonal world. She is already a "Miss Sparkle Plenty" and precociously charming. Her behavior lends support to the idea that we may be dealing with sensitive periods that put a stamp on the future.

Susie's is only one adaptive solution to a prevailing but not complete understimulation. Some infants, endowed with less persistence and spark, follow a depressive rather than a performance-oriented route.[5]

So far, we have discussed only the regulation of pleasurable excitement and the role of the other in that regulation. The issues

5. We have not pursued the developmental fate of each of the described RIGS. There are two reasons for this. We have not had the opportunity to conduct the needed longitudinal observations, and until recently we have not known in what forms to look for continuity at the next level of relatedness.

involved would be the same if we were discussing the regulation of security, curiosity/exploration, attention, and so on. Readers can trace from their own clinical experiences the line of development of those diverse self-regulating others and the RIGs they lend to.

Can potential problems in the formation of a sense of a core self be seen in these disregulations of contours of excitation? Does one see what look like possible precursors to "self pathology"? Is the period from two to six months a sensitive one for the formation of a sense of a core self?

These questions can only be answered in terms of how one conceptualizes a sense of a core self. The sense of core self, as a composite of the four self-invariants (agency, coherence, affectivity, and continuity), is always in flux. It is being built up, maintained, eroded, rebuilt, and dissolved, and all these things go on simultaneously. The sense of self at any moment, then, is the network of the many forming and dissolving dynamic processes. It is the experience of an equilibrium.

On one side, there are two general kinds of experiences that act continually to form or reconstitute these senses of self. There are the many events (such as deciding to sit up and doing so) that come and go and provide phasic perceptions that act to form and reform the sense of self. And there are the almost constant unattended events (remaining sitting up, with all the constant but out-of-awareness readjustments of antigravity and postural muscle tone) that provide tonic perception acting to maintain the sense of self. On the other side are all the influences that disrupt the organized perception of self: overstimulation, situations that disrupt the flow of tonic perceptions that maintain the sense of self (being thrown too high in the air with too long a fall); experiences of self/other similarity that confound the self/other boundary cues; maternal understimulation that reduces certain tonic and phasic self-experiences. The question of later clinical consequences boils down to whether the prevailing dynamic equilibrium of the sense of a core self, when the sense of a core self is first forming, influences the later sense of self.

The sense of a core self, since it is a dynamic equilibrium, is always in potential jeopardy. And indeed, it is a common life event to experience and/or fear major perturbations in the sense of a core self. Winnicott has made a list of what he calls the "primitive agonies" or "unthinkable anxieties" to which children are heir.

These are "going to pieces," "having no relation to the body," "having no orientation," "falling forever," "not going on being," and "complete isolation because of there being no means of communication" (Winnicott 1958, 1960, 1965, 1971). Such anxieties seem to be fairly ubiquitous in older children. They are common material for the fears, nightmares, favorite stories, and fairy tales of children. As adults, are any of us totally free of such fears, either waking or dreaming? In more severe form, they make up psychotic pathological experiences of fragmentation (ruptures of coherence), paralysis of action and/or will (ruptures of agency), annihilation (ruptures of continuity), and dissociation (ruptures in ownership of affectivity).

The infant, then, like everyone else, experiences the sense of a core self as having a fluctuating dynamic status. This is the normal state of existence. As one gets older, however, the forces of maintenance are so predominant that severe disequilibriums are infrequently felt under normal conditions, and then usually only as a hint or cue or "signal."

This picture leaves much room for individual differences in the prevailing dynamic equilibrium experienced by any one individual. And it is the prevailing dynamic equilibrium that may get established as a characteristic pattern during this early period. The question is not, then, does a sense of agency, coherence, affectivity, or continuity get established once and for all during this period? Nor is the question whether the sense of a core self gets established well or poorly. What seems to get established are some of the properties of the dynamic equilibrium that determines the sense of a core self.

In clinical terms, some patients have a relatively well-formed sense of a core self, which is stable but requires an enormous amount of maintaining input, in the form of both tonic and phasic contributions from others. When that input fails, the sense of self falls apart. Others have a less well-formed sense of self which, while equally stable, requires much less maintenance. And still others are most characterized by the great lability of this sense of self that cannot be fully explained by changes in maintaining input.

It is likely that these aspects of a sense of a core self receive a characteristic impress during the initial period of formation of the sense of a core self; the earlier in formation, the more lasting the likely influence. However, the sense of a core self does not stop forming, so there is much time after the initial phase of formation to provide compensatory influences. In any event the early formation of these three parameters of the core sense of self (degree of formation, maintenance needs, and lability) says more about the nature of the sense of self and less about the ultimate severity of any potential pathology.

In keeping with the focus on the infant's likely subjective experience, nothing has yet been said about how the infant might experience disequilibrations in the dynamic sense of a core self. Do infants experience anxiety as the (momentary and partial) dissolution of the sense of a core self, as adults generally do?

It is likely that in the domain of core-relatedness infants do not experience "unthinkable anxieties" about *potential* disruptions in the sense of a core self, but they may experience "primitive agonies" about *actual* disruptions. It is reasonable to assume that infants do not experience anxieties about these matters until later, because anxieties are ultimately fears, and fear is generally thought not to emerge as a full emotion until the second half of the first year of life (Lewis and Rosenblum 1978). Fear is not even seen as a facial display until after six months (Cicchetti and Sroufe 1978). Also, fear in the form of anxiety results from the cognitive appraisal of an immediate future, and the ability to anticipate an immediate future does not appear to be sufficiently present until after the age of six months or so.

The infant, then, should be left free of anxieties about the core self, at least during the short period during which this sense is first being formed. But how about "primitive agonies"? Assume that "primitive agonies" are some form of nonlocalizable distress that relies on *affect appraisals* of a situation, rather than *cognitive appraisals.* Affect appraisals ("Is it pleasurable or unpleasurable?" "Is it to be approached or avoided?") are presumed to be more primitive than cognitive appraisals. In other words, they are potentially independent of and developmentally prior to the cognitive appraising processes. Affect appraisals are therefore presumably operating prior to the emergence of fears and anxieties. They appraise the present.

Affect appraisal usually refers to the perception of external stimuli (a sweet or a bitter taste, a sudden loud voice, and so on), and the consequences of these appraisals are pleasures, unpleasures, approaches, or withdrawals (see Scheirla 1965). Other affect appraisals refer to the perception of internal stimuli specific to physiologic need states (hunger, thirst, physical comfort, oxygen). There is also a third source of affect appraisals, made up of the many interpersonal goal states that the young human is designed to achieve or maintain, which are ultimately necessary for species survival but do not involve physiological needs. These are the needs for specific social and self organizations (Bowlby 1969). We can add to these the need to organize perceptions such that a core sense of self agency, cohesion, affectivity, and continuity results. These, too, are essential for survival in a social world.

When there is a negative affect appraisal about the self required to meet those social and self-organizational goal states, what is felt? And what name can be given to this feeling? "Primitive agonies" is a good choice. It is meant to imply a nonlocalizable distress that does not attach to physiological state. (Physiological distress is better captured by Mahler's term "organismic distress . . . that forerunner of anxiety proper" [1968, p. 13].) "Primitive agonies" is specifically meant to capture failures in the ongoing functions needed to maintain essential social or interpersonal states. Borrowing from Winnicott, then, we can use it to describe this category of infant life experience.

The infant should experience "primitive agonies" whenever temporary and partial dissolutions of the sense of a core self occur. Furthermore, these agonies should occur during the period of core-relatedness well before cognitive appraisals of the exact same events add anxiety to the experience of agony, after about six months.

These considerations add a fourth property to the prevailing dynamic equilibrium that gets established: the presence or absence—or better, the dosage—of agony that characteristically accompanies the maintenance of a sense of a core self. This, too, can be carried forward in time as a characteristic feature of experience.

THE ISSUE OF PSYCHOPATHOLOGY DURING CORE-RELATEDNESS

During the formative phase of the domain of core-relatedness, an infant can readily present clinical problems. These are usually presented as sleep or eating problems. They are not signs or symptoms of any intrapsychic conflict within the infant, however. They are the accurate reflection of an ongoing interactive reality, manifestations of a problematic interpersonal exchange, not psychopathology of a psychodynamic nature.

In fact, at these early ages there are no mental disorders in infants, only in the relationships in which infants participate. (Mental retardation, Down's syndrome, and autism represent partial exceptions.)

One of the most common examples is sleeping problems. Usually the infant will not go to sleep, keeps crying until the mother returns to the bedside, sputters along until she has reenacted her put-down-to-sleep ritual, may or may not get some milk or water, and then cries again after she leaves for the third or fifth time. The infant's behavior in this situation is not a sign or symptom in the usual sense. Given the uncertain and unclear limit-setting by the mother, the natural fears of being alone or in the dark, the reinforcement of the behavior, and so on, the infant is acting in a manner concordant with current reality. In the vast majority of such common cases, there is nothing wrong with the infant per se. The behavior is simply a characteristic, predictable pattern that has become a family problem.

Intersubjective Relatedness

The clinical issues at stake during the formation of intersubjective relatedness are the same as those encountered during the formation of core-relatedness. But now the focus shifts from the regulation of behaviorally overt self-experience by the other to the sharing of subjective experience between self and other and the influencing of one another's subjective experience. To begin with sharing, can you share your inner experience with an other at all? And can others share their inner experience with you? If you both can share some subjective experiences, which ones are shareable and which are not? What is the fate of experiences that are not shareable? What is the fate of experiences that are shareable? And finally, what are some of the possible interpersonal consequences of sharing?

We stated that the focus shifts from regulating experiences to sharing them. This is true only to the extent that intersubjective sharing can now begin—not that the mutual regulation of experience stops—to give way to this new form. Now they can proceed together.

The following patterns with clinical relevance are describable in this domain.

NON-ATTUNEMENT: UNSHAREABILITY OF SUBJECTIVE EXPERIENCE

It is hard to imagine a situation in which there is no interaffective sharing. In its extreme form it is probably only encountered in severe psychosis or among normal persons in science-fiction plots in which the hero is the only human among robots or an alien species whose inner experiences are impenetrable. This fictional situation is particularly apt, because the human and the aliens can have physical relatedness (if the aliens are attractive enough) and can even communicate about external matters. But if affective subjectivity is impossible, a cosmic loneliness ensues in the hero. Milder versions of this state of affairs occur in character disorders and neuroses. But in these conditions there is the wish for, or illusion of, or bungled attempts at, possible intersubjective sharing. In the psychotic or science-fiction situation, no possibility of affective intersubjectivity exists a priori.

The extreme condition of lack of interaffective sharing might apply to the institutionalized infants described decades ago or to a mother sufficiently depressed or psychotic that she is judged as no longer able to care adequately for her baby. What follows is a description of the last-mentioned situation and is intended to illustrate how nonshareability of inner experience can occur and at the same time not scream out as a clinical fact.

A twenty-nine-year-old divorced mother was admitted to the psychiatric ward of a community hospital because of decompensation of her chronic paranoid schizophrenic condition. She had had two previous hospitalizations and had been maintained on antipsychotic medication. She had a ten-month-old daughter, who was rooming on the pediatric ward. The child was kept there because no extended family was available to take her and because some of the psychiatric ward staff did not think she was safe with her mother. Others felt that the baby was safe and urged that she be returned to the mother and live on the ward around the clock with her, instead of having just two supervised visits daily. Those who wanted separation thought that the mother's overconcern for the child's safety and her fear that someone or something might hurt the girl were ominous projections indicating hostile destructive wishes of her own. Those who wanted the girl to live on the ward felt that the projections were less of a threat than the real distress experienced by mother and child because of the separation.

The mother was usually quite compensated and could pull herself together. She was not overtly psychotic. Rather, she was secretive and unrevealing of her thoughts. She cared for the baby adequately and had been doing so for the ten months prior to admission. The baby was healthy. The entire ward staff felt that the mother was extremely overidentified with her daughter and that there was a symbiotic loss of boundaries, with the mother melting into the child. We—Lynn Hofer, Wendy Haft, John Dore, and I—were called in to help resolve the stalemate on the ward.

When we first observed the baby arriving for one of her visits, the child was asleep. The mother gently took her sleeping baby and began to lay her on the bed so she would stay asleep. The mother did this with enormous concentration that left us closed out. After she had ever-so-slowly eased the baby's head onto the bed, she took one of the baby's arms, which was awkwardly positioned, and with her two hands carefully guided it to a feather-like landing on the bed, as though the arm were made of eggshells and the bed made of marble. She poured herself into this activity with complete and total participation of her body and preoccupation of her mind. Once that was done, she turned to us and picked up the interrupted topic of conversation in a normal manner. It was incidents like this that made the staff feel that she was overidentified, had a loss of boundaries, was reacting against harmful impulses within herself, and at the same time was a competent caregiver—so far.

The mother also felt that she had some unspecified insecurities about her caregiving and about being overidentified with the child. With the promise of trying to help her in that area, we asked her to collaborate with us in our data collection and scoring technique for evaluating attunement as described in chapter 7.[6]

6. It is a common procedure in our laboratory to have a mother with some complaint, problem, or question about her caregiving first try to recreate for us "naturally" the events or situation in question while being videotaped and then to conduct the interview with the videotape to refer to as the focus. Routine consultation procedure and the data collection procedure for the attunement observation were therefore basically the same. We find that in

What emerged from this procedure was that of all the mothers we had ever observed, this mother was the *least* attuned. In the course of two observations on different days, she performed no behaviors that met our criteria for affect attunement. (They usually occur once a minute, using strict criteria.) Yet at the same time she was attentive to the baby, overly so; she hovered to make sure that no harm befell her, tried to anticipate all her needs, and was totally absorbed by these tasks.

When this became apparent, we commented to her that she seemed so attentive to potential sources of danger for her daughter that she seemed unable to share in her daughter's experiences. We did this by asking her about several instances when she had been protective without apparent external reason and also about several instances when she had missed responding to a particular expression or other behavior by the girl, opportunities for real engagement. Gradually, over four visits (she had two such sessions alone with Lynn Hofer), she revealed to us that she was almost exclusively attentive to the external environment and not to her daughter. She concerned herself with the hard edges of the desk, the sharp things on the floor, and the sounds from outside. If the horn that she had just heard beeping, beeped a second time, she would alter what she was doing with the baby at the moment. If it did not beep again, she would continue doing what she was doing and await some other external signs, all of which were nonspecific to her and open to her interpretation. Because of her preoccupation with trying to both read and control the external world impinging on her baby, she remained unavailable to enter into the baby's experiences and share them. The mother was aware of this. The baby had presumably become accustomed to the shifting of the mother's interactional tack. She seemed to have adapted passively, falling in with the mother's new direction of activity when it shifted. This compliance on the baby's part, along with the mother's rapt attention, made the interactions look far more harmonious and in accord than they in fact were.

This mother was partially in touch with her baby at the level of core-relatedness, but entirely out of touch at the level of intersubjective

dealing with nonverbal events, such as occur between parent and infant, it is often hard for the parent to verbalize a problem without a concrete instance to refer to. Lebovici (1983) has also commented on the power of video to evoke emotion and memory in a therapeutic situation.

relatedness. She provided the girl with no experiences of intersubjectivity. The initial impression of excessive intimacy was a partial illusion. The mother was in communion with her own delusions and unable to break away to "be with" her child.

This vignette is remarkable on several scores. It illustrates the almost complete lack of attunement that is possible even while physical and physiological needs are being met. It implies that most observers of human behavior (including the ward staff and us, initially) so expect attuning behaviors to be embedded in other communicative or caregiving behaviors that we tend to assume their presence and may read them in even when they are not there. (Recall the initial impression of this mother's behavior.) Finally, it illustrates one way that an infant can temporarily adapt to the absence of intersubjective relatedness—namely, to become very compliant at the level of core-relatedness. The future of such an adaptation would ultimately be disastrous for the child, if the mother could not change and if no others were available to open up the intersubjective world. We would anticipate a pervasive feeling of aloneness—not loneliness, because the child would never have experienced the presence and then loss of subjective sharing. It would probably be hard for such a child at an older age not to get some hint that things were going on between other people about which she had only a glimpse but no real experience. Then she would truly experience an ego-alien aloneness and would probably fear the possibility of such a form of intimacy. If, however, she never got to know that she didn't know, she would experience an ego-syntonic, acceptable, chronic isolation at the level of intersubjective relatedness.[7]

SELECTIVE ATTUNEMENTS

Selective attunement is one of the most potent ways that a parent can shape the development of a child's subjective and interpersonal life. It helps us account for "the infant becoming the child of his particular mother" (Lichtenstein 1961). Attunements are also one of the main vehicles for the influence of parents' fantasies about their

7. For the sake of readers who want more closure on such case material, the mother did gain some insight from working in this way with us for two weeks and began to show the ability either not to attend to or, at least, not to get fully captured by her delusions and illusions and to enter more, but still not fully, into the child's subjective world. She was discharged and lost to follow-up before we could evaluate these beginnings any further.

infants. In essence, attunement permits the parents to convey to the infant what is shareable, that is, which subjective experiences are within and which are beyond the pale of mutual consideration and acceptance. Through the selective use of attunement, the parents' intersubjective responsivity acts as a template to shape and create corresponding intrapsychic experiences in the child. It is in this way that the parents' desires, fears, prohibitions, and fantasies contour the psychic experiences of the child.

The communicative power of selective attunement reaches to almost all forms of experience. It determines which overt behaviors fall inside or outside the pale (Is it "all right"—within the intersubjective pale—to bang toys hard and noisy? to masturbate? to get real dirty?). It includes preferences for people (Is it all right to find delight in Aunt Ronnie but not in Aunt Lucy, who then says, "My nephew just doesn't take to me"?). And it includes degrees or types of internal states (joy, sadness, delight) that can occur with another person. It is these internal states rather than overt activities *per se* that we will focus on most, since they have generally been less emphasized in this context.

In a sense, parents have to make a choice, mostly out of awareness, about what to attune to, given that the infant provides almost every kind of feeling state, covering a wide range of affects, a full spectrum of the gradations of activation, and many vitality affects. This process of creating an intergenerational template is part of ordinary everyday transactions. It has an almost infinite number of opportunities to develop, some taken, some missed. The process does not divide the world sharply into black and white but rather into many shades of gray. An example from the experience of "enthusiasm" and its opposite will illustrate.

Molly's mother very much valued and sometimes appeared to overvalue "enthusiasm" in Molly. This was lucky in that Molly seemed to be well endowed with it. Together, they most characteristically made attunements when Molly was in the throes of a bout of enthusiasm. This is easy enough to do, since such moments are of enormous appeal and the explosive behavioral manifestations of infant enthusiasm are most contagious. The mother also made attunements with Molly's lower states of interest, arousal, and engagement with the world, but less consistently so. These lower states were not selected out and left totally unattuned; they simply received relatively and absolutely less attunement.[8]

One could argue that parental attunement with states of enthusiasm could only be a good thing. When it is relatively selective, however, the infant accurately perceives not only that these states have special status for the parent but that they may be one of the few ways of achieving intersubjective union. With Molly, one could begin to see a certain phoniness creep into her use of enthusiasm. The center of gravity was shifting from inside to outside, and the beginning of a particular aspect of "false self" formation could be detected. Her natural assets had joined forces with parental selective attunement, probably to his later disadvantage.

The situation with Annie was quite different. She was equally well endowed with enthusiasm, but her mother more characteristically attuned when her bubble of enthusiasm had just broken, when the gods had left. This mother made relatively more of an intersubjective alliance with the depleted Annie than with the filled-up Annie ("Oh, that's all right, honey." "That is hard, isn't it?"). The mother did this partly to soothe and comfort but also to buoy her up in a different form of intersubjective union, which we might call "*ex*thusiasm." Annie's mother was in fact more comfortable with a subjective partnership in exthusiasm than in enthusiasm. The latter seemed more dangerous to her.

For an infant to be a subjective partner only in enthusiasm will place the more depressive-like states of exthusiasm outside the pale of shareable personal experience. And, on the other hand, to be a partner only in exthusiasm will place the positively exciting states of enthusiasm outside of shareable personal experience.

In being themselves, parents inevitably exert some degree of selective bias in their attunement behaviors, and in doing so they create a template for the infant's shareable interpersonal world. This applies to all internal states; enthusiasm and exthusiasm are only examples.

8. Attunement with states of enthusiasm would certainly promote what are considered to be desirable and healthy feelings of omnipotence and grandiosity. In this light, the linguistic roots of the word "enthusiasm" are of interest. It literally means to have a god enter into one, to be imbued with his or her spirit or presence. This idea raises the question of whether enthusiasm is in fact possible without the infusion of someone else's real or fantasied spirit—an other's subjective experience—into one's feeling state. How different is this from the earlier formulation of an evoked companion?

And this is clearly how the "false self" can begin—by utilizing that portion of inner experience that can achieve intersubjective acceptance with the inner experience of an other, at the expense of the remaining, equally legitimate, portions of inner experience. The notions of the "false self" (Winnicott 1960), or of alienating interpersonal events that create the "not me" experiences of Sullivan (1953), or of the disavowal or repression of one's own experience (see Basch 1983) are all future elaborations of what we are discussing. We are describing the first step in that process, the exclusion from intersubjective sharing of certain experiences. Whatever happens next, whether the experience excluded from the interpersonal sphere becomes a part of the "false self" or a "not me" phenomenon, whether it is simply relegated out of consciousness, one way or another, or whether it remains a private but accessible part of self, the beginning lies here.

Similarly, the use of selective attunements continues to be seen throughout childhood, acting in the fashion described but for developmentally changing purposes. For instance, in considering the earliest masturbation practices of children (see Galenson and Roiphe 1974), how may prohibition or the ultimate need for disavowal or repression get transmitted? In discussing the potential clinical impact of selective attunement, Michael Basch put the case clearly:

> How, to use Freudian terminology, could the superego of the parents be conveyed so exquisitely accurately to the infant and young child? Take, for example, masturbatory practices . . . How, if the parents are psychologically enlightened and determined not to either shame the child or make it feel guilty for those activities, does it get the idea that these activities are beyond the pale of acceptance? Although the parents may say nothing to the child in the way of criticism or censure, they do not share the activity through cross-modal attunement, and that sends the message loud and clear. (Basch, personal communication, 28 September 1983)

The clinical processes I have just described have usually been discussed in terms of mirroring. I maintain that mirroring is really three different interpersonal processes, each having an age-specific use: appropriate responsivity and regulation (during core-relatedness); attunement (during intersubjective relatedness); and reinforcement shaping and consensual validation (during verbal relatedness). Taken together, these are what is usually meant by mirroring.

Before leaving the subject of selective attunement, we should note that as we move from core-relatedness to intersubjective relatedness, we can now begin to see separate continuous lines of development for separate internal states. The same phenomena (enthusiasm, for example) are seen to be under similar developmental pressures from the self-regulating other and from the subjective state-sharing other that is, from the mother, in different domains of relatedness. The self-regulating other acts with her physical presence, the state-sharing other acts with her mental presence—but both act in concert over time to create characteristic patterns that may last a lifetime.

Misattunement and Tuning

Misattunements and tunings are yet another way in which the parent's behavior (and the desires, fantasies, and wishes behind that behavior) act as a template to shape and create corresponding intrapsychic experiences in the child. Misattunement and tuning are difficult to isolate and define for research purposes, but they are clinically quite recognizable. The reason why misattunements are troublesome is that they fall somewhere between a communing (well-matching) attunement and a maternal comment (that is, an affectively nonmatching response). They fall closer towards attunements; in fact, their main feature is that they come close enough to true attunements to gain entry into that class of event. But they then just miss achieving a good match, and it is the amount that they miss by that packs the wallop.

Sam's mother was observed characteristically to just undermatch the affective behaviors of her ten-month-old son. For instance, when he evidenced some affect and looked to her with a bright face and some excited arm-flapping, she responded with a good, solid, "Yes, honey" that, in its absolute level of activation, fell just short of his arm-flapping and face-brightness. Such behavior on her part was all the more striking because she was a highly animated, vivacious person.

In our usual fashion, we asked her our routine questions—why she did what she did when she did it the way she did it—for each such interchange. Her answers to the first questions—why, what, and when—were quite expected and unremarkable. When we asked her why she did it the way she did it, more was revealed. In particular, when asked if she had intended to match the infant's level of enthusiasm in her response to him, she said "no." She was vaguely aware of the fact that she frequently undermatched him. When asked why, she struggled toward verbalizing that if she were to match him—not even overmatch, but just match him—he would tend to focus more on her behavior than on his own; it might shift the initiative over from him to her. She felt that he tended to lose his initiative if she joined in fully and equally and shared with him. When asked what was wrong if the initiative passed over to her some of the time, she paused and finally said that she felt he was a little on the passive side and tended to let the initiative slip to her, which she prevented by undermatching.

When the mother was asked what was wrong with the child's being relatively more passive or less initiatory than she at this life phase, she revealed that she thought he was too much like his father, who was too passive and low-keyed. She was the initiator, the spark plug in the family. She was the one who infused enthusiasm into the marriage, decided what to eat, whether to go to the movies, when to make love. And she did not want her son to grow up to be like his father in these ways.

Both mother and we were surprised to find that this one piece of behavior, purposeful slight misattunements, carried such weight and had become a cornerstone of her upbringing strategy and fantasy. Actually, it should not have been surprising. After all, there has to be some way in which attitudes, plans, and fantasies get transposed into palpable interactive behavior to achieve their ultimate aim. We happened to uncover one such point of transposition. Attunement and misattunement exist at the interface between attitude or fantasy and behavior, and their importance lies in their capacity to translate between the two.

One of the fascinating paradoxes about her strategy is that left alone, it would do exactly the opposite of what she intended. Her underattunements would tend to create a lower-keyed child who was less inclined to share his spunk. The mother would inadvertently have contributed to making the son more like the father, rather than different from him. The lines of "generational influences" are often not straight.

Clearly, misattunements are not attempts at communion, straightforward participation in experience. They are covert attempts to change the infant's behavior and experience. What, then, might the experience of maternal misattunement be like from the infant's viewpoint? We speculate as follows. Sometimes the infant seems to treat such events as if they were not even in the class of attunement and are like any other nonattuning response. In such cases, the misattunement simply fails. It is not close enough to a communing attunement to gain entrance. "Successful" misattunements must feel as though the mother has somehow slipped inside of the infant subjectively and set up the illusion of sharing, but not the actual sense of sharing. She has appeared to get into the infant's experience but has ended up somewhere else, a little way off. The infant sometimes moves to where she "is," to close the gap and establish (or re-establish) a good match. The misattunement then has been successful in altering the infant's behavior and experience in the direction the mother wanted.

This is a very common and necessary technique, but if it is used excessively or selectively for certain types of experiences it may throw open to question the infant's sense of and evaluation of his or her own internal states or those of the other. It also reveals some of the potential dangers of the whole realm of selective attunements and misattunements. Intersubjectivity and attunement, like most potent things, can be a mixed blessing.

Misattunements can be used not only to alter an infant's experience but to steal it, resulting in "emotional theft." There are dangers to letting someone inside your subjective experience, even at these young ages. The mother may attune to the infant's state, establishing a shared experience, and then change that experience so that it is lost to the child. For instance, the baby takes a doll and starts to chew on its shoes with gusto. The mother makes a number of attunements to his expressions of pleasure, enough so that she is seen as a mutually ratified member of the ongoing experience. This membership gives her the entrée to take the doll from the baby. Once she has the doll she hugs it, in a way that breaks the previously established chewing experience. The baby is left hanging. Her act is actually a prohibitive or preventive act to stop the infant from mouthing, and also a teaching act: dolls are to be hugged, not chewed. The prohibition or didactic act is not accomplished straightforwardly, however. She does not simply prohibit or teach. She slips inside the infant's experience by way of attunement and then steals the affective experience away from the child.

This type of exchange can happen in many ways, and it is not always an actual object-experience that is lost. For instance, a parent can make an attunement with the infant's ongoing state and then gradually tune up or vary her behavior to a point where the infant can no longer follow. The infant is left with the initial experience ebbing away, watching the parent go on with yet another variation of the infant's own original experience.

These simple examples, which are not uncommon, are intriguing, because one of their main features for the infant is the danger in permitting the intersubjective sharing of experience, namely that intersubjective sharing can result in loss. This is likely to be the point of origin of the long developmental line that later results in older children's need for lying, secrets, and evasions, to keep their own subjective experiences intact.

When viewing the ways attunement can be used, for good or ill, one might get the impression that dangers lurk everywhere, but that is no more true here than in any other form of human activity. After all, parents, at best, are only "good enough." That leaves room, on both sides of the optimal, for the infant to learn the necessary realities about attunement—that it is a key that unlocks the intersubjective doors between people; and that it can be used both to enrich one's mental life, by a partial union with an other, and to impoverish one's mental life, by bending or appropriating some part of one's inner experience.

AUTHENTICITY OR SINCERITY

At the level of intersubjective relatedness, the authenticity of the parent's behavior looms as an issue of great magnitude. This is obviously true for the formation of psychopathology, but it is also true for normal development.

The issue is not authentic versus unauthentic. There is a spectrum, not a dichotomy. The issue is, how authentic? Because of the natural asymmetries in the mother/infant relationship, in their knowledge, skills, plans, and so on, much of the time the mother is conducting several agendas of her own simultaneously, while the infant can only entertain and participate in one of these. Some of these multiple agendas have already been alluded to; the aim of Sam's mother of playing with her infant but not letting him become "passive" is one example. Then there are a host of more mundane multiple agendas: encouraging play with an object while directing the infant how to and how not to play with it; directing an infant's attention away from something relatively dangerous to something safe, as though the whole event were really only a game; wanting to show off the baby's responsivity or precocity, without appearing to; letting an exciting game proceed, but with one foot on the brakes as the baby starts to show the first signs of fatigue or overload. All these situations may necessarily involve some blend of sincere and insincere behaviors.

The pervasiveness of this issue became apparent when we tried to observe how a mother prohibits her infant. During this research project, we learned most from its problems and our failures. Three of us formed a team that we thought was well suited to the task of determining how a mother goes about prohibiting an infant at various ages. John Dore was expert at analyzing speech acts and covered the domain of the pragmatics and semantics of what mother said. Helen Marwick was expert in voice quality analysis and covered the domain of the paralinguistic messages of the mother. I had the responsibility of analyzing the facial, postural, and gestural maternal behaviors.

Our first problem came in defining an act of prohibition. Dore laid out what seemed appropriate linguistic and speech act criteria for prohibitives, but they did not work. Sometimes the mother would say, "Don't do that," an excellent prohibitive from the linguistic viewpoint, but she would say it in the sweetest, most playful voice and with a smile. Was that a prohibitive? At other times she would say just the baby's name or ask, "Do you want to do that?" and we would all agree, from her tone of voice and facial expression, that it served as a prohibitive, although it was not one linguistically. We ended up not being able to define in linguistic terms the very act we wished to study.

We therefore decided to switch tactics. We picked a mother who we knew hated to see her infant mouthing or sucking on anything and invariably tried to prohibit this behavior. We would study all interchanges that took place when the mother saw the infant mouthing or bringing something to his mouth. We were now no longer studying "prohibitives" but rather maternal responses to infant behaviors that were a priori designated "prohibitable." The subject of study became "prohibitables," not "prohibitives."

We categorized her behavior according to the different channels in which it occurred, realizing that mixed messages across channels would be the rule. The maternal communicative channels analyzed were: linguistic (pragmatic and semantic), paralinguistic (larangeal tension, pitch contour, absolute pitch, loudness, stress, nasality, creek, and whisper), facial (category of affect and fullness of display), gestural, positional, and proxemic. We also gave each behavior a subjective rating of our impression of her seriousness or authenticity and aim.

Our overall impression was that the mother sent out the "authentic" prohibition in one or more channels and then used the other channels to modify, contradict, or support the prohibitive message or to send out a competing "authentic" message. The situation was very similar to that so beautifully described by Labov and Fanshel (1977) in their analysis of the multiple messages sent via the different channels during a psychotherapy hour. We had expected adults to be able to deal with this level of complexity, but we did not foresee that infants too, almost from the beginning, have to learn to decipher mixed messages. To put the situation more strongly, the infant's very acquisition of communicative skill emerges in a complex medium, and this fact must have some impact on how the signal system is learned.

It was clear that when the mother was maximally serious and authentic—for instance, when the infant was about to play with an electric wall plug—all of her behaviors in all of the communicative channels lined up exactly as one would predict for a prohibition, and there were no competing, contradicting, or modifying signals. She yelled, "No!" with great vocal tension, flat pitch, great stress, full facial display, and a rush forward. Such behaviors stopped the infant short. It was thus clear that the infant was given occasional opportunities to see a pure array of prohibitives assembled. Most of the time, however, this was far from the case.

The question of how the infant reads the seriousness of the mother's diverse simultaneous behaviors may miss a major point. It assumes that there is *a* way to read them. It treats them as signals to be decoded, signals that have an absolute meaning. What is missed in this approach is that these behaviors are put out as part of a progressive negotiating process. Any one set of behaviors does not *in itself* have a knowable signal value, but only an approximate one, with built-in ambiguity. The more precise signal value is determined by what went before, in what direction the negotiation is tending, and other factors. Separate moves have limited meaning alone; they derive specific meanings in the context of the whole sequence.

This is a different way of viewing the problem of interpersonal signal interpretation and, more specifically, the problem of determining the degree of authenticity of someone's behavior. The situation is analogous to what is called the sincerity or felicity conditions in speech act theory, the essence of which is how much a speaker intends and expects an utterance to be taken as fully meant (Austin 1962; Searle 1969). What the infant is learning in these situations is to recognize the sincerity conditions of nonverbal behaviors. Since the term *sincerity condition* applies to speech acts, we will refer to *authenticity conditions.* It is crucial for the infant to learn what constitute the authenticity conditions for any interpersonal transaction.

UNAUTHENTIC ATTUNEMENTS

Attuning behavior can be quite good even when your heart isn't in it. And as every parent knows, your heart can't always be in it, for all of the obvious reasons from fatigue through competing agendas to external preoccupations that fluctuate from day to day. Going through the motions is an expectable part of everyday parental experience. Attunements, then, vary along the dimension of authenticity, as well as of goodness of match. And the infant would do well to start learning this, too. One of the great advantages of interpersonal conventions or standards is that by being varied along the authenticity dimension they can achieve infinitely more signal potential. (Recall the "hello" of the two psychiatrists meeting on the street in chapter 8.)

As observers, we do not have much trouble determining how authentic any given attunement is. The more obviously unauthentic attempts at attunement end up as misattunements. Unlike most misattunements, however, they do not have a characteristic covert intent. They are more like unsystematic failures at communion than like potential successes at systematically altering the infant's behavior in a known way. There is no consistent pattern, and mother is experienced as less consistent.

The difference between purposeful (covert or unconscious) misattunements and unauthenticity is like the difference between "magnetic north" which is not really at the top of the world and systematically distorts the compass reading of true north, and local magnetic interferences that cause a compass to behave erratically and jump all over the place. To the extent that communing attunements are the ultimate reference point (true north) for measuring affective intersubjectivity, misattunements are a systematic distortion (magnetic north) but gross unauthenticity leaves one without a working interpersonal compass for intersubjective relatedness.

So far in our research, the more subtle unauthenticities in attunements have escaped our ability to analyze them. It is not simply a matter of attuning well in one modality and poorly in another, although that is true of most people. It has more to do with slight violations in expectation of the profile of attunement. We do not know the extent of infants' abilities to pick up these subtle unauthenticities, but to the extent that they can discriminate them it would be like having an only slightly fluky interpersonal compass. Intersubjectivity would still rest on a shaky set of coordinates; it would not have the certainty of dead reckoning. This entire area of the negotiation, rather than the signaling, of the status of intersubjectivity and the emergence of the infant's ability to gauge authenticity conditions needs much more actual observation and theoretical attention.

OVERATTUNEMENT

Occasionally, we have seen a mother who appears to overattune. This is a form of "psychic hovering" that is usually accompanied by physical hovering. The mother is so overidentified with her child that she seems to want to crawl inside of the infant's every experience. If any such mother were a perfect and invariable attuner, if she never missed any opportunity to attune and hit each one exactly right (which is of course impossible), the infant might have the feeling of sharing a single dual mentality with the mother, similar to that proposed by "normal symbiosis," while still having a separate and distinct core boundary not proposed in normal symbiosis. Or, because of the continued presence of a sense of a core self and other, the child in this imaginary situation might have the sense of a transparent subjectivity and an omniscient mother. Mothers, even overattuners, do not attune with the vast majority of infant experiences, however, and even when they do they achieve only relative success. The infant learns that subjectivity is potentially permeable but not transparent and that mother can reach toward it but not automatically divine it. Overattunement is the psychic counterpart of physical intrusiveness, but it can never steal the infant's individual subjective experience; luckily, the process is too inefficient. This assures constant differentiation of self from other at the subjective level. Maternal psychic hovering, when complied with on the infant's part, may slow down the infant's moves toward independence, but it does not interfere with "individuation."

THE CLINICAL POSITION OF INTERSUBJECTIVITY AND EMPATHY

Intersubjectivity has currently become a cardinal issue in psychotherapy as viewed from the perspective of Self Psychology. The patient-therapist "system" is seen either implicitly (Kohut 1971, 1977, 1983) or explicitly as an "intersection of two subjectivities—that of the patient and that of the analyst . . . [in which] . . . psychoanalysis is pictured . . . as a science of the intersubjective" (Stolerow, Brandhoft, and Atwood 1983, p. 117–18). Seen in this light, the parent-infant "system" and the therapist-patient "system" appear to have parallels. For instance, "negative therapeutic reactions" refer to those paradoxical clinical situations in which an interpretation that is given to a patient makes the patient worse rather than better, in spite of the fact that all current and subsequent evidence supports the correctness of the interpretation. Stolerow, Brandhoft, and Atwood (1983) explain these reactions in terms of "intersubjective disjunctions" (p. 121), rather than as masochism, resistance, unconscious envy, or other defensive maneuvers, or simply poor timing, which are the traditional explanations. An "intersubjective disjunction" appears to be analogous to a misattunement. More broadly, "empathic failures" (of which the "negative therapeutic reactions" resulting from "intersubjective disjunction" are only an instance) and "empathic successes" are the cardinal therapeutic processes of Self Psychology (Kohut 1977, in press; Ornstein 1979; Schwaber 1980a, 1980b, 1981). These appear to be analogous to the spectrum of nonattunements, misattunements, selective attunements, and communing attunements.

I wish to inject some caution in drawing these analogies too closely, however. What is meant by the therapeutic use of empathy is enormously complex from our point of view. It involves an integration of features that include what we are calling core-, intersubjective, and verbal relatedness as well as what Schafer (1968) has called "generative empathy" and Basch (1983) has called "mature empathy." Attunement, functioning at the level of intersubjective relatedness prior to the advent of verbal relatedness, is thus a necessary precursor to one of the components of therapeutic empathy, but that is not the same as an analogous relationship. The two do have some important similarities in function, especially the mutual influence of one person's subjective state upon that of another, but attunement between mother and infant and empathy between therapist and patient are operating at different levels of complexity, in different realms, and for ultimately different purposes.

There is a related issue. Self Psychology has suggested that it is the failures in maternal empathy in the beginning of life that later are responsible for the deficits and weaknesses in self-cohesion that are manifest as borderline disorders. Once again, on the basis of these similarities, it is tempting to point the finger at the level of intersubjective relatedness as the "critical" or "sensitive" period for the origin of empathy-related failures in self development. And such may prove to be the case. But while the normal or abnormal developmental line for the cohesive self—or self-concept, as designated in Self Psychology—receives invaluable structuring at the level of intersubjective relatedness, so did it at the level of core-relatedness, and so will it at the level of verbal relatedness. The similarities and close relationship between attunement and empathy should not bias us toward attributing undue importance to the level of intersubjective relatedness, compared with other levels, in the clinical issue of sense of self development. Its appropriate importance is sufficiently obvious.

SOCIAL REFERENCING AND INFLUENCING THE INFANT'S AFFECTIVE EXPERIENCE

A group of researchers in Denver has identified a phenomenon occurring around the same time as affect attunement which they call *social referencing* (Emde et al. 1978; Klinert 1978; Campos and

Stenberg 1980; Emde and Sorce 1983; Klinert et al. 1983). The prototype situation has already been described, in chapter 6. A year-old infant is lured across an apparent visual cliff by an attractive toy and a smiling mother. On reaching the apparent drop-off, the child stops and appraises the dangers versus the desirability of crossing over. Placed in this position of uncertainty, the infant invariably looks up at the mother to read her face and get a secondary appraisal. If she smiles, the infant crosses over, but if she looks frightened, the infant retreats and gets upset ("It is not O.K."). The mother's affective state determines or modifies the infant's affective state.

One could argue that the infant is not only looking at mother for an appraisal, a fairly cognitive view, but is also looking to see which of the infant's own conflicted feeling states is being matched or attuned to. After all, in this situation the infant's position is not simply one of cognitive uncertainty but of affective ambivalence between fear at the visual drop—an innate fear—and pleasure in exploration. The infant seeks mother to resolve the ambivalence by attuning with one emotion and not the other, thereby tipping the scales. These two interpretations are complementary, not contradictory. The processes they describe are simultaneously in operation much of the time.

This same group of researchers points out that it is possible for the mother to influence the infant's affective state to the extent of instilling a new affect that was not part of the infant's original experience. To demonstrate this they have utilized a variety of situations that, unlike the visual cliff, do not elicit and rely on an affective conflict: collapsing castles, and staged accidents, for example. In these situations, mothers can successfully signal what an infant is to feel, but the infant's looking for an affective match cannot be called upon as an explanation.

A very common example of mother's influencing or even determining what a child will feel occurs when the child falls down and starts to cry. If the mother quickly moves into a fun-surprise mode, "Oh, what an interesting and funny thing just happened to you," the infant is likely to switch gears into a gleeful state. One might conclude that the mother brought the infant from one feeling state to an entirely different one. However, the mother's maneuver would never have worked if the level of arousal she showed in her fun-filled surprise had not matched the infant's initial level of negatively toned arousal. Some degree of attunement may have been necessary to permit a successful social referencing.

In any event the signalling of affect states adds another dimension to the one described for attunement and has equally important clinical implications. For instance, how might a mother make an infant feel some kind of badness about a neutral event without resorting to punishment or explanations? If we return to the study on prohibitions in light of the work on social referencing, the answer seems simpler. Let us assume that mouthing—teething on objects during the nine- to twelve-month period—is an experience made up of some pleasure and some pain for the infant and is morally neutral for most mothers these days. We have observed mothers who find the mouthing of objects disgusting, for intrapsychic reasons unrelated to cleanliness and health. Such mothers can instill a feeling of disgust by signaling disgust whenever the infant references her during a mouthing. One mother consistently flashed a disgusted facial display and said, "Yuuuck! That's icky—yuuuck!" while wrinkling up her nose. This began to serve as an effective prohibition, and the infant occasionally stopped mouthing an object and put it down while intoning a "yuuuck"-like noise and wrinkling up his nose in disgust. The mother had successfully introduced a "badness"-tinged feeling quality into the infant's total affective experience of mouthing.

In a similar fashion, another mother used "depressive-signals" just as the previous mother used "disgust-signals." Whenever her son did something maladroit, as is expectable in a one-year-old, so that something got knocked over or a toy was disarranged, the mother would let out a multi-modal depressive signal. This consisted of long expirations, falling intonations, slightly collapsing postures, furrowing the brows, tilting and drooping the head, and "Oh, Johnnys" that could be interpreted as "Look what you've done to your mother again," if not "What a tragedy that your clumsiness with that toy train has caused the death of another dozen people."

Gradually, Johnny's exuberant exploratory freedom became more circumspect. His mother too had brought an alien affective experience into an otherwise neutral or positive activity. She may also have succeeded in making it part of the infant's own affective experience during that activity, which then became a quite different kind of lived experience, to be recorded as a quite different kind of prototypic episodic memory, available to influence the future.

Social referencing and affect attunement are deeply complementary processes. Social referencing permits the mother to determine and alter to some extent what the infant actually experiences. It has real limitations, however, in that the mother can only tune the infant's subjective experience; she cannot create it wholly. And affect attunement permits the infant to know if what he or she experiences is shared by the mother and thus falls into the realm of the shareable. Selective attunement helps tune the infant's subjective experience by accentuating parts of that experience at the expense of others.

PSYCHOPATHOLOGY DURING THE FORMATIVE PERIOD OF INTERSUBJECTIVE RELATEDNESS

Three different forms of potential psychopathology are visible during the period beginning at seven to nine months and ending at about eighteen months: neurotic-like signs and symptoms; characterological malformations; and self pathology.

Potential characterological and self pathological malformations have already been alluded to. These are readily explicable on the basis of an infant's accurately perceiving the interpersonal reality created by the primary caregiver and making some adaptive coping response to that reality, which then becomes habitual. Examples are the girl mentioned on pages 197–98, who really did have to "sparkle plenty" to get mother to respond to her, and the two other little girls, Annie and Molly, who were being forced by the different attuning responses of their mothers to make exthusiasm rather than enthusiasm the socially sanctioned predominant experience of self. These kinds of adaptations can become maladaptive, and in that sense pathological, when they are used in new contexts and with new people, so that the infant's own patterns are no longer responsive to the new realities. The problem is one of overgeneralization and/or of experiencing one's self not simply as using one form of adaptation but being defined by and limited to it. This is the most common situation of "disorder" seen at this point in development, and it appears to be relevant for the developmental psychopathology of relatively stable individual differences of the kind that are usually meant by character traits or personality types, or adaptive styles—that is, the Axis II disorders from the *DSM-III* phenomenology. They may also have the fixity of patterns first established during a sensitive period.

There are some circumstances, however, in which it looks as though the infant, by a year of age, has elaborated a neurotic-like sign and symptom. These signs and symptoms are particularly interesting, because they may require different explanatory models from those of overgeneralization and delimited senses of the self. The most common example is "one-year phobias," those inexplicably strong fears that otherwise unfearful infants develop toward one particular thing, such as vacuum cleaners. Such phobias can be explained on the basis of having been frightened by the thing on one or more occasions (and vacuum cleaners are universally frightening when they start up unexpectedly, because of the rapid acceleration in loudness). An association has been made between the sight and the fearful experience, or an episodic memory is retrieved by the visual sight alone. Why the fear persists despite many opportunities for extinction and/or many opportunities to form other, unfearful lived episodes with the vacuum cleaner is not obvious. These phobias are not quite neurotic, because the infant's signs and symptoms are unelaborated compared with the original fear response that the vacuum cleaner probably elicited the first time it scared the infant. No condensation, displacement, or other elaborations are involved in the "symptom."

In contrast, it is possible to see an infant prior to age twelve months elaborate a symptom or sign that has many of the characteristics of a neurotic symptom, especially the condensation and displacement of diverse experiences into one particular object. For instance, Bertrand Cramer and his colleagues at Service de Guidance Infantile in Geneva presented the following case (a fairly common one in a clinic that deals with infant and family problems during the first years of life). A young Italian couple living in Geneva were referred because their nine-month-old daughter had general feeding problems, with a moderate but subclinical failure-to-thrive (weight was in the 25th percentile). The most remarkable feature of the child's behavior was that she would manifest violent negative reactions to the bottle, but to nothing else. It was not necessary to try to feed her with it to trigger the reactions; they could be triggered by handing the bottle to her or simply having it in sight. Her response was a mix of different behaviors. She would have a tantrum and at the same time show fear (shrinking back) and anger (throwing the bottle away). What was most convincing was that she acted as though the bottle itself contained the qualities that made her fearful, anxious, and angry. The strong impression was not that the bottle simply evoked or recalled unpleasant experiences, but that the bottle had come to represent them.

These were the major known facts bearing on this symptom:

1. The couple had been living together for years but chose not to marry, nor had they plans to do so. It was felt by all of us who witnessed the intake interview (via videotape) that the future of the marital relationship was at issue. The child represented the most binding reality that made the parents a couple. The major clinical questions one wished to ask the father and mother were: How can your relationship continue to grow? How can it best be nourished? What kind of nourishment will be best for it? And which of you will provide what portion? The parents did covertly struggle as to which one of them was to feed the baby what, and when. From the clinical perspective it seemed reasonable to infer that the infant's feeding problems had become the focus for, and somehow reflected, this overall family problem.
2. The mother had been brought up by a cold, nongiving mother. She had written her own mother off when she left Italy. She seemed to have insecurities about her own caregiving abilities and was unsure about her ability to feed the baby appropriately and well.
3. The father's mother had been the most powerful figure in his family. He admired her power and even held it in awe, but he did not experience it as always benign. So the father, too, had dynamic reasons to be ambivalent about women, about his "wife" in her feeding role, and about his own identification with his strong mother when feeding the baby.

All together, there is a current dynamic issue concerning the marriage that fuels the feeding problem. And each parent brings a past history of conflicts that contributes to the present situation. The problem is multiply determined such that it was never fully resolved who was to feed the baby, what, and when, with what degrees of confidence, with what consequences for the "marital" relationship, and with what fantasied meanings to the parents as to their identities.

Somehow—and this is the crucial part—for this infant these intrapsychic phenomena and their overt manifestations in behavior appeared to take as their final common path the form of the bottle. She could have simply become a poor eater or a compliant good one, but instead she elaborated a symptom.

The bottle in this symptom does not symbolize the various conflicts surrounding feeding. It is not at all an arbitrary signifier. It does seem to act as an object representing the many conflicts. How this could happen might best be understood in terms of the dynamic episodic memory model. Some of the prototypic episodes (RIGs), of which the bottle is always an attribute, invoke anger or tentativeness in the mother alone; others involve anger or tentativeness in the father alone; others include tension between the parents felt by the girl; others include intrusive overfeedings and felt anger on the child's part; still others contain signals of depression from either parent, with corresponding feelings in the child; and some involve disruptions in the smooth flow of the caregiving routine. If the girl is capable of reindexing, so to speak, these various troublesome prototypic interaction episodes (RIGs) in terms of their invariant attributes, she comes upon the bottle as that which best represents her various sources and forms of agony. The bottle no longer represents one single form of lived experience. It serves to bring together and condense diverse forms of lived experience. And in that sense it serves as a "neurotic signal" that transcends any single experienced reality. It is in this fashion that neurotic symptoms can form in advance of a true capacity for symbolization.

Verbal Relatedness

Paradoxically, while language vastly extends our grasp on reality, it can also provide the mechanism for the distortion of reality as experienced. As we have seen, language can force apart interpersonal self-experience as lived and as verbally represented. The "false self," "not-me experiences," the extent of disavowal and splitting of direct experience, and those experiences that are simply always kept private will all be further determined by the way the divisions between experience as lived and experience as represented in language are created and repaired. It is for this reason that so much of what is clinically important when language emerges is invisible and silent. It includes everything that is not expressed verbally and involves the choices about what is being left unspoken as well as what is being said. How can one best think about the situation in which there is a lived-experience version (in episodic memory) and a verbally represented version (in semantic memory)? Basch (1983) has provided a helpful clarification. He points out that in *repression,* the path from lived experience to its representation in language is blocked. (The felt experience of a parent's death cannot be translated into the verbal form necessary for conscious attention.) On the other hand, in *disavowal* the path from language representation to the lived, felt experience of those represented events is blocked. (One recognizes the reality of the semantic version that the parent is factually dead, but this recognition does not lead to the felt, affective experiences attached to that fact. These are disavowed.) In *denial,* there is a distortion of the perception itself ("My parents are not dead"). In disavowal only the emotional-personal significance of the perception is repudiated. There is a splitting of experience in which two different versions of reality are kept apart.

Using this terminology, one can approach the various relationships between the two versions of reality. In the creation of a "false self" and a "true self," personal experience of the self becomes split into two types. Some self-experiences are selected and enhanced because they meet the needs and wishes of someone else (the false self), regardless of the fact that they may diverge from the self-experiences that are more closely determined by "internal design" (the true self). We have seen how this process of splitting begins during core-relatedness and is greatly furthered during intersubjective relatedness through the use of selective attunement, misattunement, and nonattunement on the part of the parent. What happens at the level of verbal relatedness is that language becomes available to ratify the split and confer the privileged status of verbal representation upon the false self. ("Aren't you being gentle with the teddy bear! Sally's always so gentle." Or "Isn't this exciting! We're having such a wonderful time." Or "That thing is not so interesting, is it? But look at this one.")

Gradually, with the cooperation between the parent and the child, the false self becomes established as a semantic construction made of linguistic propositions about who one is and what one does and experiences. The true self becomes a conglomerate of disavowed experiences of self which cannot be linguistically encoded. Disavowal can only occur when the infant is able to treat the previously present core distinctions between self and other on a symbolic level. It requires a *concept* of self which can be held outside of immediate experience for reflection and in which experiences or attributes can be assigned personal meaning and affective significance. That is, disavowal separates the true personal, emotional meaning from the linguistic statement of what is reality. Since language provides the major vehicle for relating knowledge of the self to the self, the disavowal experiences are less able than other experiences to inform self-knowledge, and they remain less integrated because they are cut off from the organizing power existing in language.

For the first time we can speak of self-deception and distortion of reality on the part of the infant. The discrepancies with reality, however, are more acts of omission than acts of commission. There is not yet the active distortion of perception or meaning under the influence of a wish. ("There is too a penis on that little girl, it's just very small still—or there used to be one.") Instead there is a splitting into two equally "real" experiences, but only one of them is given full weight.

What is the pressure or motive that activates disavowal to keep the true and false selves separated? Primarily, it is the need for experiences of being with the other. It is only in the domain of false self that the infant is able to experience the communion of subjective sharing and the consensual validation of personal knowledge. In the domain of the true self, the mother holds herself unavailable, acting, in fact, as if it did not exist.

The development of the "domain of the private" (that which one will not share, and which may not even occur to one to share, with another) is related to the development of a false self. The domain of the private stands somewhere between the true disavowed self and the false or social self, but the private self has never been disavowed. It consists of self-experiences that have not been attuned with, shared, or reinforced but that when manifested would *not* have caused parental withdrawal. These private self-experiences do not cause interpersonal disengagement, nor do they provide a route to experiences of being-with. The infant learns simply that they are not part of what one shares, and they do not need to be disavowed. These private experiences have access to language and can become well known to the self and undergo more integration than the disavowed self-experiences.

The notion of a private self as distinct from a true but disavowed self is essential, because there is enormous individual and cultural variability in what constitutes self-experience that is to be shared and that which is not to be shared. Some of these differences are the result of different social pressures for disavowal, but some are not. They are conventions observed without imperative.

Because the domain of the private lacks the mechanism of disavowal for maintaining its position, this domain is the most changeable through experience. Much of growing up, learning to love, and learning to protect one's self realistically involves shifting the boundary lines of the domain of the private.

Implications of present or impending character pathology have become attached to the terms "true self" and "false self." Winnicott did not originally intend this. I believe he intended to imply that some splitting into true and false self was inevitable, given the imperfect nature of our interpersonal partners. Perhaps, then, we should adopt a different terminology and divide developing self-experiences into three categories: the "social self," the "private self," and the "disavowed self." The issue of how "true" or "false" the selves are or how much any of them hurts or suffers is a clinical issue of great complexity, but it is a clinical issue and not one of development *per se.* And the degree to which any of these selves has developed closest to the rhumb line of "internal design" is an issue to be debated after the direction of a whole life can be viewed (Kohut 1977). Perhaps it can never be known.

The fact that language is powerful in defining self to the self and that parents play a large role in this definition does not mean that an infant can readily be "bent out of shape" by those forces and become totally the creation of others' wishes and plans. The socialization process, for good or ill, has limits imposed by the biology of the infant. There are directions and degrees to which the child cannot be bent without the emergence of the disavowed self, which then makes claims on linguistic ratification.

We have so far delineated three domains of self-experience, the social, the private, and the disavowed. There is a fourth, the "not me" experience. Sullivan speculated that some self-experiences, such as masturbation, can become so tinged with resonant anxiety, set up in the infant but originating in the parent, that the experience could not be assimilated or integrated into the rest of self-experience.

Alternatively, if the experience is already partially integrated, the force of anxiety would dis-integrate it—dislodge it, so to speak—from its place within the organized experience of self. Clinical phenomena fitting this description are certainly known in older persons. Could it happen or begin in infancy, as Sullivan suggests? It all depends on the disintegrating or integration-inhibiting effect of anxiety or other extremely disruptive feeling states.

What is likely to happen is that the original disintegration or nonintegration occurs at the level of core-relatedness, so that the "not me" experience is not included in or gets dislodged from the sense of a core self. When this situation is enacted at the level of verbal relatedness, we have a part of self that is truly repressed, not disavowed. It has no access to language and thus cannot get in touch with the private or social self, or even the disavowed self.

We have only just begun to touch upon the clinical implications of language acquisition. Still to come in the child's development are the active ability to distort perceptions and meaning through defense and all the other variations on reality made possible by a truly symbolic vehicle such as language. However, these are rarely observed until after the age of two years and therefore are beyond the scope of this book. We stop our account at the earlier stages of language development, where the infant remains a relatively faithful recorder of reality and all deviations from the normal are close to the accurate reflections of the impress of interpersonal reality.

Chapter 10

Some Implications for the Theories Behind Therapeutic Reconstructions

THE CONCERN in this chapter is with the theories about development that operate in the therapist's mind and that therefore influence the creation of the reconstructed "clinical infant." These theories will be examined in the light of new knowledge about the "observed infant" and the development of the different domains of sense of self.

It is important to recall that an assessment of clinical theory from the perspective of direct infant observation says nothing about the validity of clinical theories as therapeutic constructs. Nor can it say much about the same theories as they apply to children past infancy, when symbolic functions are more in place. (We have suggested before that psychoanalytic developmental theory may make a better fit with direct observations during childhood than with observations during infancy.) What such an assessment can do is to measure and describe the distance between the two views, so that the tension between the two, when clarified can operate as a corrective to both.

Knowledge of the observed infant seems to have the greatest

potential impact on a number of theoretical issues at the level of metapsychology. They will be addressed by issue, in loose chronological order rather than by school of thought.

The Stimulus Barrier, the Early Handling of Stimulation and Excitation, and the Notion of a Normal Autistic Phase

It is a traditional psychoanalytic notion that during the first months of life, the infant is protected from external stimuli by a stimulus barrier, a "protective shield against stimuli" (Freud 1920). As described by Freud, this barrier was of intrinsic biological origin, in the form of heightened sensory thresholds except to internal stimuli. It was postulated that the infant was unable to handle stimulation that broke through the shield. There has been an active dialogue as to whether the stimulus barrier at some point came under some control of the infant, as an antecedent of ego defensive operations, or whether it remained as an essentially passive mechanism (Benjamin 1965; Gediman 1971; Esman 1983). Giving the infant more active control of the barrier altered the view of the concept somewhat.

An irrevocable change in our view of the stimulus barrier concept came with Wolff's (1966) description of the recurring states of consciousness that infants go through, beginning with neonates. The most important state, for this issue, is alert inactivity, the "window" during which questions can be posed to infants and answers given, as we saw in chapter 3. In this state the infant is quiet and not moving but has eyes and ears trained on the external world. It is not simply a passively receptive state; the infant is actively—in fact, avidly—taking it all in. If a stimulus barrier exists, either its threshold sinks to zero at times or the infant periodically reaches through it.

At the first International Conference of Infant Psychiatry in 1981, Eric Erikson was invited to give a special address. He told the audience that in preparation for his talk, he thought he had better go look closely at a newborn, for it had been a while since he had done so. So he went to a nursery for newborns, and the strongest impression he carried away was of the infants' eyes. He described the infants' gaze as "fierce" in their avidness to take the world in.

For parents who are at the other end of this fierce gaze, it is a compelling experience.[1]

It is true that the young infant's tolerance for stimulation, even during alert inactivity, is far less at one week or one month of age than it will be months or years later. But the very young infant, like anyone else, has optimal levels of stimulation, below which stimulation will be sought and above which stimulation will be avoided. As we saw in chapter 4, this is a general rule of infant interaction with stimuli (Kessen et al. 1970), and it has been amply described in the social interactive setting (Stechler and Carpenter 1967; Brazelton et al. 1974; Stern 1974b, 1977). What is different about the "stimulus barrier" period, then, is only the levels of stimulation and the durations of engagement with external stimulation that are acceptable or tolerable. There is no basic difference in the active regulatory engagement that the infant makes with the external environment. And this is the most telling point.

The infant engages in the same kind of active regulatory traffic with the external world as does anyone at any age. Different people or different psychiatric illnesses can be described as having different thresholds, set at characteristically higher or lower levels for tolerable amounts of stimulation and for tolerable durations of exposure. The relationship of the infant to external stimulation is *qualitatively* the same throughout the life span.

The stimulus barrier is a pivotal concept, because it is an instance, in the case of infancy, of Freud's pleasure principle and constancy principle (1920). In this view, the buildup of internal excitation is experienced as unpleasure, and one of the major roles of the entire mental apparatus is to discharge energy or excitation, so that the level of excitation within the psychic system is always minimized. Since in the eyes of classical psychoanalysis the infant does not have sufficient (if any) mental apparatuses for discharging the excitation that the outside world might impose in large quantities, the stimulus barrier is required to save the day. Actually, what is really at fault in the classical view of the stimulus barrier is not so much the idea itself. After all, infants' tolerance levels are limited, and they change,

1. Klaus and Kennel (1976) have remarked on the long periods of visual alertness that follow a nonmedicated birth and have allotted to the infant's gaze a role in bonding the parent to the infant. Bowlby (1969) has viewed the same event as playing a role in the other direction, bonding the infant to the parent.

perhaps even in quantum leaps. The problem is with the basic assumption that required the presence of the barrier to begin with. As we have seen in chapters 3 and 4, the infant does have the capacities to deal with the world of external stimulation, granted with some help from mother. Clearly, the complex of reasoning that resulted in the notion of a stimulus barrier, and that notion itself, should simply be discarded. Esman (1983), Lichtenberg (1981, 1983), and others all arrive at a similar conclusion and argue for major revision.

The basic reasoning that compelled the construction of the stimulus barrier is also at the foundation of the notion of an initial phase of "normal autism" to describe the infant's social interactions from birth through the second month of life (Mahler 1969; Mahler, Bergman, and Pine 1975). The idea of normal autism as an expectable phase of life has more immediate clinical implications, however, since it has been conceived as a developmental point at which fixation can occur and to which regression can lead back. The status of such a phase in light of new information is therefore no small matter for clinical theory.

If by autism we mean a primary lack of interest in and registration of external stimuli, in particular of human stimuli, then the recent data indicate that the infant is never "autistic." Infants are deeply engaged in and related to social stimuli. Even if they could not tell human from nonhuman stimuli, as some suggest, they are still avidly involved with both kinds, albeit indiscriminately. In autism there is a generally selective lack of interest in or avoidance of human stimuli. That is never the case with normal infants. It is true that the infant becomes more social, but that is not the same as becoming less autistic. The infant never was autistic and cannot become less so. The process is rather the continuous unfolding of an intrinsically determined social nature.

Another problem with the "normal autistic" phase is that it is anchored by name, and partially by concept, with a condition that is pathological and that does not occur until later in development. This normal phase is thus referenced pathomorphically and retrospectively. These problems have been adequately commented on by others (Peterfreund 1978; Milton Klein 1980). (Dr. Mahler herself is well aware of the general problems of pathomorphic definitions and hoped to avoid some of them by speaking of "*normal* autism." She is also aware of many of the recent findings of infancy research and has somewhat modified her conceptualization of the normal autistic phase to accommodate these findings. In a recent discussion, she suggested that this initial phase might well have been called "awakening," which is very close to "emergence," as it has been called here [Mahler, personal communication, 1983].) In contrast to the concept of normal autism, the concept of emergent relatedness assumes that the infant from the moment of birth is deeply social in the sense of being designed to engage in and find uniquely salient interactions with other humans.

Orality

It may be a surprise for a clinical theorist to find himself or herself this far into a book on infancy without having encountered a single word about the special importance of the mouth for relatedness or as an organizing focus of a developmental phase. There are several reasons for this omission. The current methods of infancy research have been most readily adapted to vision and audition, the distance receptors. The notion of the mouth as specially endowed as an erotogenic zone, in the strict sense that Freud and later Erikson meant, has not borne up in general observation or in attempts to operationalize the concept of erotogenic zones as developmental realities. There has been a general historical trend toward seeing early relatedness of one kind or another as a primary goal in itself, one which does not need to grow out of or lean upon physiological needs and therefore is not secondary to some more primary physiological goal such as hunger (Bowlby 1958).

Even if one wishes to speak of orality as a mode of interaction rather than as an anatomical locus of charged action (Erikson 1950), the same questions about the special status of the mouth arise. Erikson focused on the interactional mode of "incorporation," which was a primitive form of internalization by way of the mouth. Adhering to Freud's timetable for erotogenic zones, he made the mouth the primary organ for initially conducting the crucial business of internalization. And the initial internalizations became tightly associated, in dynamically oriented thinking, with oral activity or fantasy. The current data show the infant to be at least equally engaged in visual and auditory "incorporation." It is striking that when Erikson revisited newborn babies in 1981, he was most impressed with their *visual* taking in of the world. Had that been his impression thirty years earlier, early internalization might have become more closely associated with visual activity. That too would have been a mistake. Erikson's internalization is little different from Piaget's assimilation/accommodation, and it is the domain of all modalities and all sensible body parts. No organ or mode appears to have special status with regard to it.

The recent evidence for cross-sensory coordination of information (amodal perception) highlights this point. The lack of emphasis on the mouth in engaging the world, compared with the eyes and ears, is partially to redress the previous imbalance of emphasis, not to mitigate the contribution of the mouth.

What about the role of feeding—the consummatory act and the concomitant feelings of satiation? How are they to be conceptualized during a period of emergent relatedness? The feelings of satiation in association with the perception of a person or a part of a person are unquestionably important, and we have dealt with them in part already.

Feeding is a vital activity for emergent relatedness for many reasons. It is one of the first major recurrent social activities, an occasion that repeatedly brings parent and infant into intimate face-to-face contact, during which the infant cycles through various states, including alert inactivity. (The newborn sees things best at a distance of about ten inches—the usual distance from a mother's eyes to the eyes of an infant positioned at the breast.) The feeding activity thus assures that the infant, when in an appropriate state to be attentive and attracted to stimulation, will be offered an engagement at appropriate distances with a full array of human stimulation, in the form of the parental social behavior that generally accompanies the feeding activities.

None of this so far has anything directly to do with eating or consummatory acts, although these are what brought the social occasion into being. What, then, about the fact and feelings of hunger and satiation? The role and place of the hunger-satiation experience has loomed very large as a metaphor for much theory-building. Its importance is unquestionable in the light of both common observation and the prevalence of oral symptomatology and fantasy in many clinical circumstances. A relativistic perspective is instructive, however. Much evidence about the feeding patterns of existent primitive societies and historical evidence on patterns in preindustrial societies suggest that throughout most of human history, infants were fed very frequently, on the slightest demand—as often as twice an hour. Since most infants were carried about with the mother, against her body, she would sense the infant getting even slightly restless and would initiate short and frequent feedings, maybe just a few sips to keep the level of activation low (DeVore and Konnor 1974).[2]

The import of this perspective is that the drama of feeding today is in part the product of our system of creating a great deal of stimulation and activation in the form of hunger build-up, followed by a steep fall-off of activation. Satiation becomes a phenomenon of intensity and drama equal to that of hunger, but in the opposite direction. It may well be that constant experience with exaggerated peaks and valleys of motivational and affective intensity is an adaptive advantage for the infant who is to enter the faster, more stimulating modern world. That question is beyond the scope of this book however. What is within our immediate scope is the question of how the perception of human stimuli will be affected by the experience of hunger and satiation. We have almost no evidence about the infant's capacity to take in external stimulation or to engage in any of the perceptual processes during the high activation states of distressful hunger or the very low activation states of somnolent satiation. Current methods of experimentation have not permitted access to these states. A discussion of infant sensibilities, and specifically of the ability to register events in states of very high and low excitation, will be addressed later in this chapter.

2. Among mammals one can predict the frequency of feeding for any species from the ratio of fat, protein, and carbohydrates in the milk. On the basis of the composition of human milk, human newborns should be fed every twenty to thirty minutes, as was once the custom, rather than every three or four hours, as is present practice (Klaus and Kennell 1976).

Instincts: Id and Ego

The actual observation of infants has caused a curious turnaround. One would expect, as Freud originally postulated, that in very young humans, the id would be pervasively evident and the ego barely present at all. Also, the pleasure principle (guiding the id) would precede, or at least strongly dominate, the reality principle (guiding the just-forming ego) in the first months of life.

The observed infant presents a different picture, however. Besides the regulation of hunger and sleep (no small dismissal), one is struck most by the functions that could have been called "ego-instincts" in the past—that is, the preemptive, stereotypic patterns of exploration, curiosity, perceptual preferences, search for cognitive novelty, pleasure in mastery, even attachment, that unfold developmentally.

By presenting us with a plethora of motivational systems that operate early, appear separable, and are backed by some imperative, the infant faces us again and in a new way with the longstanding arguments about the distinctions between id instincts and ego instincts. There are three related issues here. The first concerns the id instincts alone. Has classical libido theory, in assuming one or two basic drives that shift developmentally from one erotogenic zone to another and have a variety of viscissitudes during development, been helpful in viewing an actual infant? The consensus is no. The classical view of instinct has proven unoperationalizable and has not been of great heuristic value for the observed infant. Also, while there is no question that we need a concept of motivation, it clearly will have to be reconceptualized in terms of many discrete, but interrelated, motivational systems such as attachment, competence-mastery, curiosity and others. It is of no help to imagine that all of these are derivatives of a single unitary motivational system. In fact, what is now most needed is to understand how these motivational systems emerge and interrelate and which ones have higher or lower hierarchical standing during what conditions at what ages. The pursuit of such questions will be hampered if these motivational systems are assumed a priori to be derivatives of one or two basic, less definable instincts rather than more definable separate phenomena.

The second issue concerns "ego instincts." Infants have surprised us with their rich repertoire of immediately available or emergent mental functions: memory, perception, amodal representation, specification of invariants, and so on. The concept of autonomous ego functions went some way in resolving the longstanding problem of what to do about "ego instincts" as known in the 1950s, but it is nowhere near inclusive enough to contain all that we know in the 1980s. Because it is no longer reasonable to think in terms of the general drives of eros and thanatos, at least when encountering the infant as observed, the "autonomous" in autonomous ego function has lost much of its meaning. An adult patient can certainly use perception uncolored by dynamic conflict, but for an infant the act of perception has its own motive force and invariably creates pleasure or unpleasure. Until we can form a clearer picture of the separate motivational systems involved, the notion of "autonomous function" in an observed infant may only obfuscate the issue.

The third related issue is the classical developmental postulate that the id and the pleasure principle precede the ego and the reality principle. More recent evidence suggests that this proposed developmental sequence was theoretical and arbitrary. The evidence weighs far more on the side of a simultaneous dialectic between a pleasure principle and reality principle, an id and an ego, all operating from the beginning of life. Ego psychologists have come to accept that the pleasure principle works within the context of the reality principle from the beginning, and vice versa. The suggestion of Glover (1945) that ego nuclei are present from the start and Hartmann's (1958) description on an undifferentiated matrix of ego and id attest to this shift in ego psychology, towards a greater appreciation of the presence of ego functioning in young infants.

The observational findings of the past decade have reinforced this shift in thinking and perhaps moved it further, in the sense that these "ego" functions are now seen as discrete and rather highly developed functions that go well beyond both ego nuclei and an undifferentiated matrix. It seems apparent that the ability of infants to deal with reality has to be considered on a par with the ability to deal with hedonics and that ego formation is better differentiated and functioning that Glover or Hartman could have known. Furthermore, many of the corollaries that flowed from the basic assumption of id before ego, such as the idea that primary process (autistic) thinking precedes secondary process (reality or socialized) thinking, were also arbitrary. Vygotsky (1962), for example, makes a potent developmental case that secondary process thinking develops first. He further points out that Piaget borrowed the same assumption as did Freud in arriving at his cognitive sequences, which are no longer so widely accepted.

Many basic psychoanalytic conceptions about drive, the number of drives, their allegiance to id or ego (or even such a notion as allegiance), and their developmental sequencing all need to be reconceptualized when confronted with the infant as observed.

Undifferentiation and Some of its Corollaries: "Normal Symbiosis," Transition Phenomena, Self/Objects

The idea of a period of undifferentiation that is subjectively experienced by the infant as a form of merger and dual-unity with mother is very problematic, as we have seen, but at the same time it has great appeal. By locating at a specific point in lived time those powerful human feelings of a background sense of well-being in union with another, it gratifies the wish for an actual psychobiological wellspring from which such feelings originate and to which one could possibly return. Weil (1970) accomplishes the same with her "basic core."

Ultimately, this kind of notion is a statement of belief about whether the essential state of human existence is one of aloneness or togetherness (Hamilton 1982). It chooses togetherness, and in doing so it sets up the most basic sense of connectedness, affiliation, attachment, and security as givens. No active process is needed for the infant to acquire or develop towards this basic sense. Nor is a basic attachment theory with purposeful moving parts and stages a necessity. Only a theory of separation and individuation is required to move the infant on developmentally, which Mahler goes on to provide.[3]

3. Once "normal symbiosis" has been developmentally positioned, so to speak, even as an act of belief, then the schedule for the next phases of development has already been implied. Separation/individuation or something very like it must necessarily follow to undo or, at least, counterbalance the symbiotic phase in the sense of dialectically moving its work forward.

Attachment theory does the opposite. It makes the achievement of a basic sense of human connectedness the end point, not the starting point, of a long, active developmental course involving the interplay of predesigned and acquired behaviors.

From the point of view of core-relatedness, one assumes that pervasive feelings of connectedness and interpersonal well-being do occur during this period from two to seven months. One also assumes that these feelings do serve as an emotional reservoir of human connectedness. The process is not seen as a passive one, however, nor as one that is given a priori. It results from the infant's active construction of representations of interactions with self-regulating others (RIGs). The RIGs and their activated form of evoked companions become the repository of the feelings that Mahler describes so well but ascribes to dual-unity. The self-regulating other is not a given, however; it is an active construct, and it forms alongside the forming sense of self and other. In our view, the developmental tasks of Mahler's phase of normal symbiosis, together with her first phase of separation/individuation, are going on simultaneously during the period of core-relatedness. For Mahler, connectedness is the result of a failure in differentiation; for us it is a success of psychic functioning.

In a vein somewhat similar to Mahler's, the British object relations school also postulates an early undifferentiated phase, but with emphasis on initial relatedness. They assume that the infant "starts life in a state of total emotional identification with his mother" and gradually experiences separateness without losing the experience of relatedness (Guntrip 1971, p. 117). In a similar vein, Winnicott (1958) assumes that in the beginning the infant has not yet separated out the specific object from the "me." "In object relating, the subject allows certain alterations in the self to take place, of a kind that has caused us to invent the term cathexis. The object has become meaningful" (p. 72).

The object relations theorists make the same mistake as the ego psychologists in assuming an important initial period of undifferentiation, which they reify and imbue with subjective feelings of security and belongingness much as Mahler has done for her phase of symbiosis. In a sense, they push a symbiotic-like phase to the earliest point in life, where Mahler has placed autism. Unlike Mahler, however, they do not see the primary state of relatedness as something one grows out of during a separation/individuation-like phase. They see separateness and relatedness as concomitant and equal developmental lines. They thus avoid oscillating sequential phases in which one or the other (relatedness or separateness) is in dominance.

The developmental view of internalized objects put forward by Self Psychology is quite different from that described by classical psychoanalysis or ego psychology. Nonetheless, self psychologists either overtly or covertly also suggest that there exists an important phase of self/other undifferentiation during the first six months of life. Because of this view, they assume that one can speak only of a self emerging from a "self–selfobject *matrix*" or from a "self–self other *unit*" (Tolpin 1980, p. 49) or of the "emergence of a cohesive infantile self existing (initially) *within* a self object matrix" (Wolf 1980, p. 122). How different is this descriptively from the picture of normal autism and normal symbiosis, both of which are problematic as constructs and not supported by the observational data?

It is not clear why the theory of Self Psychology needs to adhere to the central tenets or timetable of traditional psychoanalytic developmental theory up through the first six months of life. Their theory clearly diverges from traditional theory after that point. (In fact, the notions of a sense of a core self and the construction of normal self-regulating others appears to be more in line with and useful to the general outlines of a theory of Self Psychology.)

The Developmental Fate of Self-Regulating Others

A central point of contention between Self Psychology and traditional psychoanalytic theory lies in the view that there is a lifelong need for "self-objects." Kohut emphasized the clinical reality of one person using some aspect of another person as a functional part of the self to provide a stabilizing structure against the fragmenting potential of stimulation and affect. That is what a selfobject is (1977). It is a catchall term for a variety of ongoing functional relationships with others that are necessary to provide the regulating structures that maintain and/or enhance self-cohesion. Kohut and others, in the course of their work, began to realize that the use of and need for "self-objects" was not limited to borderline disorders and manifest only in certain transference reactions seen in therapy. The users of "self-objects" included everyone, and the need for them became viewed as legitimate, healthy, and expectable at every stage of the normal life span.

It is this notion that places Self Psychology in opposition to traditional psychoanalytic accounts of development, which make the goal of maturity (in part) the achievement of a certain level of independence and autonomy from objects, by way of the processes of separation/individuation and internalization. The development of the "self-object," according to Self Psychology, is not a phase-specific product of normal symbiosis, but a lifelong developmental line (see Goldberg 1980). Both theoretical systems agree on the need for some functions and regulating structures that originally rely on another to become autonomous self functions. (In Self Psychology, "transmuting internalizations" accomplish the task that is the aim of "internalization" [Tolpin 1980].) The construction of the superego viewed as the repository of the prohibitions and moral standards of another is the extreme example of "structuralization." The difference between the two theories is not simply one of emphasis, Self Psychology stressing the development of self-objects that endure and even grow, and separation/individuation stressing those that dissolve and become autonomous self functions and structures. The difference is more one of the perceived nature of the self, or of humankind.

The theory developed here in the light of recent research considers these phenomena in terms of the memory of experiences of being with others and the ways in which these memories are retrieved and used. In the beginning, others exist "within" us only in the form of memories or imaginings, conscious or unconscious, of the experience of self being with them (RIGs). What, then, is needed to recall their presence from memory? And how abstract or automatic can the recall cue become? During the infancy period, before adequate symbolizing functions are available, the recall cue cannot be too abstract and the experience of being-with cannot be automatic; it must involve at least some degree of reliving the experience, the evoked companion. We are therefore necessarily concerned more with the development of memories of self-regulating-others (or, in Self Psychological terms, "self-objects"). Internalization of the type that superego functions represent is not yet at stake.

Teleologically, nature must create a baby whose capacity for this memory and recall of being with others can in later life adapt to the needs of varying cultures. A member of one society, such as a hunting-gathering group, may never be expected to be out of sight or earshot of close members of the group for more than minutes or hours, and then only rarely. In another society, the isolated person on the frontier may be the ideal. Similarly, there is a cultural range in the degree to which various roles, functions, feeling states, and so on are explicitly stated by the society or left more to individual invention for their internal and external form. This degree will determine how overt or abstract the recall cue can be.

Along a different line of approach, a group's overall reproductive pattern may have a great deal to do with the experience of falling in love, or it may have practically nothing to do with it. The capacity to fall in love greatly exercises the memorial and imagining capacity for being with another. To engage in sustained romantic love requires that the individual be given the opportunity through many life experiences to develop the ability to become imbued with the presence of an absent person, an almost constantly evoked companion.

In many ways, then, the need for and use of recall cues to call someone else into one's presence varies greatly. The infant therefore needs a memory system of being with others that is highly flexible, allowing for adaptation to life experience. Processes, rather than psychic structures, are required. The notion of becoming maturely independent of others and the notion of continually building and rebuilding a more extensive working set of "self-others" as a maturational goal are just opposite ends of the same spectrum. The infant must be equipped with the memorial capacities to do both or either as experience dictates.

Affect State–Dependent Experience

Psychoanalytic theory has implicitly given the very intense emotional states a special organizing role. Affects are privileged as attributes of experience, and high intensity affects are awarded an especially privileged status. It is not surprising that this should have happened, since Freud's original theories gave traumatic states the primary etiological role. In trauma, it was assumed, the intensity of experience disrupts the ability to cope with and assimilate information. It is this (often hidden) assumption that has guided so many theoreticians. Melanie Klein's (1952) designation of the "good" and "bad" breast and Kernberg's (1975, 1976) splitting of self-experience into "good" and "bad" are direct consequences. So is Pine's (1981) suggestion about the role of "intense moments." In a similar vein, Kohut (1977) speculates that if the empathic failures of parents are too large, the sense of a cohesive self will be thrown too far off balance and the infant will not be able to perform the needed internalization to restore equilibrium (see also Tolpin [1980]). The assumption behind this line of psychoanalytic thinking is that the most clinically important experiences (and their memory and representation) are affect state–dependent; in other words, the affect state acts as the cardinal organizing element, and the very intense affect states are the ones in which the most clinically relevant experiences are precipitated out. Extreme bliss or extreme frustration, for example, are more potent organizing experiences than mild or moderate contentment or frustration.

Some recent findings in memory research can be interpreted as partially supportive of this prevalent view. G. Bower (1981) demonstrated that mood influences the encoding and retrieval of memory, that what is remembered or recalled is affect state–dependent. Manic patients were taught a list of items. Much later, they were tested for recall. At the time of testing for recall, some of the patients were still manic while others were now depressed. The same procedure was followed for patients who were initially depressed during the learning phase and when tested for recall were either still depressed or now manic. The results showed that material learned in the manic state was more readily recalled when the patient was in the same mood state. Similar results applied to the depressed patients. For both groups, memory was mood-dependent to a significant extent. In another phase of the experiment, Bower altered the affect state through hypnosis and found essentially the same thing—that memory was partially affect state–dependent.

It is important to note that these experiments do not tell how "intense" an experience must be before it can exert significant "state-

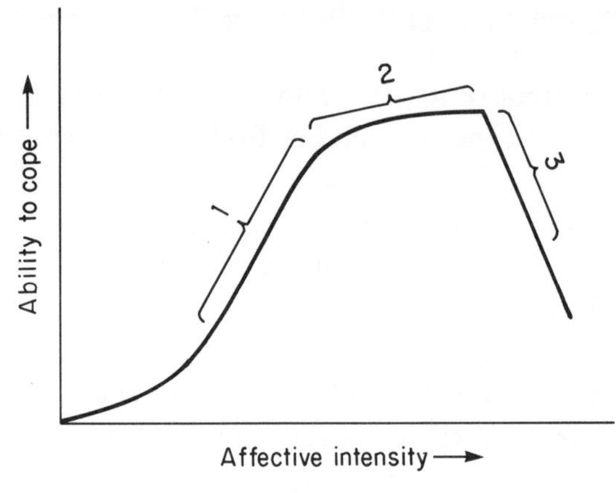

Figure 10.1

dependent" influences, nor do the psychoanalytic theories. Psychoanalytic theory usually makes the following distinctions: mild to moderate affect experience, intense affect experience, and traumatic affect experience. These could be schematized as in figure 10.1.

The mild to moderate intensity experiences (segment 1) are thought to play an insignificant role as organizers of memory. The intense experiences (segment 2) are thought to play an important role (compare Pine's "intense moment" [1981]). And the experiences that are so intense that the coping capacity to deal with them fails fall into the third segment of traumatic experiences. These may have particular potency as organizers of experience if they result in one-trial learning. (It is not always clear whether Klein and Kernberg see their formative experiences in segment 2 or segment 3.)

There are three main issues and problems with this conceptualization. The first is where to bound the segments. What constitute the boundary criteria for separate "states" that can produce *separate* state-dependent structures? Why could not this schematic be redrawn to show six, instead of three, separate and distinct segments? One then would end up with six separate state-dependent organizations of experience. On what basis can we divide the curve into discrete segments? There may be a natural break between segments 2 and 3, but even that is a supposition. Psychoanalytic theories more generally propose a discontinuity of experience between segments one and two. This issue is an empirical one. The separate states, however, may not be so discrete, and that leads to the second issue.

Can the different state-dependent experiences "speak to" one another? One of the classical notions of the traumatic state is that the traumatic experience is so state-dependent that it is entirely inaccessible under normal conditions and can only be re-experienced when the person is returned to the traumatic state, or close to it. Freud's original use of hypnosis was partially intended to permit patients to "revisit" experiences of trauma that were otherwise inaccessible.

Psychoanalytic theory has not been clear on the degree to which "intense moment"-dependent experiences are permeable. In other words, how available are such experiences to experiences in other states of affect intensity? Clearly, people do not create separate, impermeable states of experience that divide the intensity continuum into totally discontinuous, noncommunicating compartments like a string of pearls. Bower's experiment with mania and depression shows that these fairly intense mood states are not at all impermeable one to the other but are partially permeable; some information learned in one state can be recalled when in the other state. This issue, too, is an empirical one.

The third issue is that the more intense states are thought to have more state-dependent organizing power than the less intense states. This idea has intuitive appeal, but things may not be so simple as that. If intensity has reached the level of disorganizing adaptive capacities, the power to organize experience is dissipated. (Compare Sullivan's notion of the effect of extreme anxiety [1953].) The intense rather than the traumatic level might then be the most potent organizer. On the other hand, one can also argue that the capacity to take in the information to be organized would be best at a moderate rather than a high (let alone traumatic) level of intensity. In this case the moderate level of intensity would be the most potent organizer. This view is in accord with Demos's views:

> The bulk of psychic structure is created when both the "I" and the "we" experiences of the infant are going well. For example, the developmental literature is replete with descriptions of how the infant's behavior is enhanced in smooth interactions with a caregiver—interest is prolonged, variations on a theme and imitations of new behaviors occur, the infant's repertoire is expanded . . . At slightly later ages, Ainsworth has described how the securely attached infant will explore and play more freely in the presence of the attachment figure, and so on. Thus structure building is going on during good, empathic "we" experiences as well. What

> happens then, during an empathic break? I am suggesting that the empathic break could be seen as presenting the infant with a challenge to her adaptive capacities, which, by and large, have developed in more optimal situations. (Demos 1980, p. 6)

In a similar vein, it has recently been seen in our laboratory that rather ordinary and very moderate affective experiences can be well remembered one week later (MacKain et al. 1985).

Sander (1983a) has speculated that infants learn a great deal about themselves when there are neither pressing physiological inner needs nor external social need—that is, when they are alone and in equilibrium. It is then that they can begin to discover aspects of self. Similarly, Sander (1983b) has maintained that normal interactions, at both low and high levels of affect, are the stuff of representations.

In therapy, however, things may look different. The therapeutic experience may favor the recollection of the higher intensity affective experiences (for many reasons beyond a bias in selection of material on the basis of theory). The privileged role of such experiences for the clinical infant therefore remains unchallenged, although for the observed infant, these questions are still open and undecided.[4]

Splitting: "Good" and "Bad" Experiences

Psychoanalytic theorists assume that the infant's view of the world during the intense moments of affective experience is the most important factor in the construction of object relations. When this view is combined with the assumption that experiences of pleasure and unpleasure in early life are the most relevant, as the pleasure principle predicts, the result is the notion that the first dichotomy of the world that an infant will make is between pleasurable ("good") and unpleasurable ("bad") experiences. This hedonically based split is thought to occur before the self/other dichotomy is achieved. Many psychoanalytic theorists, among them Kernberg (1968, 1975,

4. This general issue has also contributed to the greatly exaggerated notion that the observed infant is really a "cognitive" infant, while the clinical infant is an "affective" infant.

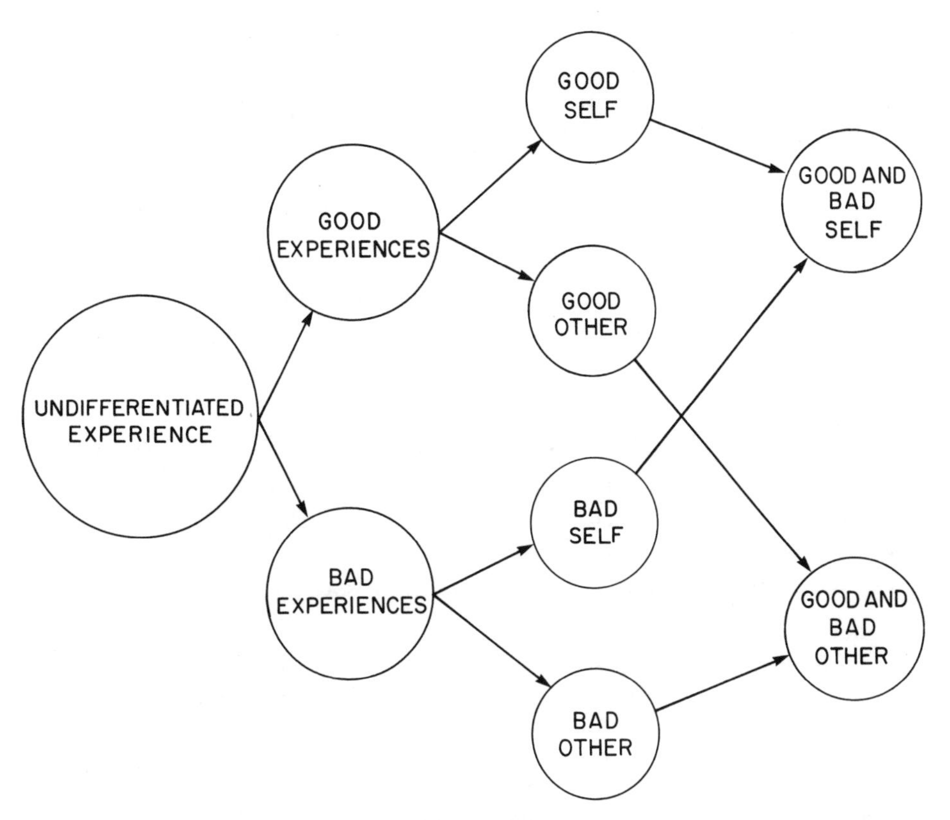

Figure 10.2

1976, 1982), would schematize the early developmental sequence as in figure 10.2.

The assumptions for this line of reasoning are as follows: (1) Hedonic experiences can and will override all other experiences and serve as the privileged organizing interpersonal event. (2) Infant experience is so hedonic tone–dependent that pleasurable and unpleasurable experiences cannot talk to each other, be cross-referenced, or integrated. Each is encapsulated from the other. (3) Accordingly, the infant is forced to do double bookkeeping with regard to experience and its memory. There is an interpersonal "world" that occurs or is re-evoked under the aegis of pleasurable feelings and another "world" under the aegis of unpleasurable feelings. There is also the cognitive interpersonal "world" that prevails under the conditions of neutral or less-than-peak states of hedonic tone. So the infant has to keep triple books, two affective and one cognitive. These three worlds cannot be mixed or integrated because of the impermeability of state-dependent experiences. (4) This splitting into pleasurable and unpleasurable occurs prior to the formation of self/other differentiation as dated by the Mahlerian timetable. So when self and other do appear, they do so under the prevailing splitting influence of this already present good/bad dichotomy. (5) "Good" can be equated with pleasurable and "bad" with unpleasurable.

This account of subjective development is well tailored to the needs of the clinical infant glimpsed in certain adult patients. There is no question that one sees the phenomenon of splitting, usually associated with the internalization of the "good" and the externalization or projection of the "bad," as an important entity in adult patients with borderline disorders. The question is, how does this particular pathomorphic reconstruction of the development of a clinical infant square with knowledge of the observed infant? This particular case is important, because the Kleinian view (1952) and the version of it elaborated by Kernberg (1984) are very widely used conceptualizations.

The problems with this "split" clinical infant as an observable reality are several. The hedonic tone of an experience is certainly a potent attribute, but it is certainly not the only one and not demonstrably the more potent. Perhaps more important, it probably does not create relatively encapsulated hedonic tone–dependent experiences and memories. Hedonic tone–dependent experiences are simply not impermeable. (The majority of experiences a person encounters while manic are recallable when the person is non-manic or even depressed.)

Another problem is even more telling. If an infant had only two experiences with a breast, a pleasurable one and an unpleasurable one, then the Kernbergian position of hedonically split experience might be more tenable. But the infant has four to six or so a day, every day. And each one differs slightly with regard to pleasurableness. Under these conditions it should be less of a task to discover the invariants of what a breast or face looks or feels like, across the many shades of pleasure/unpleasure that fall upon them. Certainly the current hedonic tone of an experience (say, a pleasurable feeding) will imbue all the other attributes of the experience (what the breast looks like and feels like, how the mother's face looks, and so on) with certain feelings. An unpleasurable experience will imbue all those attributes with different feelings. That much is consistent with current notions. The problem lies in the dichotomization of experience into two types and the experiential isolation of the two types one from the other.[5]

Yet another problem with Kernberg's position lies in the timing of things. He has inherited the traditional timetable for self/other differentiation. This view is not able to take into account the likelihood that affective experiences are one of the major sources of *self-invariance.* That is, they will promote the discrimination of the self from the breast ("I have experienced this affect state in myself many times before in many circumstances. It's part of how I can be and can feel, and it is independent of the presence of the breast"). In other words, affective tone should induce the self/other dichotomy as readily as the good/bad dichotomy.

In the sequence according to Kernberg, the self and the other as separate entities cannot come together—cohere—until the cognitive infant can encompass the separate good and bad selves, in other words, until the neutral perceptual invariants are as strong as or stronger than the affective ones, at least at times. When that happens the infant can solidify the second great dichotomy, between self and other. Once that is done, there is a "place," so to speak—a self and an other—where the good and bad selves can "reside" in alternating ambivalence and later in simultaneous ambivalence.

Such a sequence raises all sorts of other questions. How can one postulate a "good self" and a "bad self" before there is a "self?"

5. Infants must learn about the world of affects as subjectivity both experienced in themselves and as seen in others. To do this they must come to appreciate that affects vary along the dimension of intensity (in terms of both hedonic value and activation). In order for infants to gain an integrated view of subjective and objective affect experience, they must have available to them a perceptual and experiential view of the spectrum of affect dimension as a continuous gradient (Stern et al. 1980; Lichtenberg 1983). In drawing arbitrary thresholds, the psychoanalytic theorists would fracture the infant's experience of the world of affect.

There is no question that state-dependent perception and memory do exist and may prove very helpful in considering the enormous influence of affect on perception and memory. Psychoanalysis assumed this to be the case long before the notion of state-dependence in its current form arrived on the scene. It is one of the great strengths of the psychoanalytic view. However, for the purposes of further understanding, psychoanalytic theorists must begin to frame this polemic in terms of state-dependence or some other current explanatory mode. And future research must address the issue of the extent of permeability between state-dependent phenomena. It seems very unlikely that the continuous gradient from weak to strong in pleasure and unpleasure should be perceived discontinuously. There is no clear survival or communicative advantage in that. The weaker end of the spectrum could never be used as a "signal" in the psychoanalytic sense, or as an intentional "signal" in the ethological sense, if continuity between weak and strong were interrupted.

What would "self" mean? What would mark the distinction between a "good experience" and a "good self"? Or, how do the "good" and "bad" selves interact through the medium of a nonaffective self, that is, a cognitive self that has enough self-coherence and continuity to encompass the "good" and "bad" selves?

In this view, then, the affective dichotomy (good/bad) precedes the self/other dichotomy. Findings from the observed infant permit no such assumption about sequence of dichotomies or privileged status of affect over cognition. Rather, both proceed simultaneously and remain permeable one to the other.

The final problem concerns the notion of "good" and "bad" psychic entities. It seems unavoidable that "bad" derives from "unpleasurable" and "good" from "pleasurable." The question is, when does the infant make the leap? "Good" and "bad" imply either standards, intentions, and/or morality. The infant can in no way make the connection between "pleasurable" and "good" or "unpleasurable" and "bad" at the level of core-relatedness, as suggested. It is only at the level of intersubjective relatedness that infants begin to conceive of the other as having intentions toward them, let alone malign intentions. Accordingly, it is a distortion of the infant's likely experience even to use the terms "good" and "bad" as freely substitutable with pleasurable and unpleasurable. The ontogenetic line from pleasurable to good is of extreme importance, but it is an issue of a later period of development than the one we are considering. Once again, the need to find in the infant events that are part of adult experience is misleading. Good and bad as encountered in the splitting of borderline patients requires a level of symbolization beyond the infant's capacity. A complex reindexing of memories and reorganization of experience is needed to *conceptualize* as well as to divide interpersonal experience affectively into the good and the bad. The same would be true for "safe" versus "frightening" (Sandler 1960). Splitting is, however, a fairly universal experience. It occurs not only in pathological forms in patients, as Kernberg and others point out, but probably in all of us in less intense forms. The point of this critique is not to suggest that splitting is not a pervasive human phenomena. It is, and it is ready-made for pathological elaboration, but it is the product of a post-infancy mind capable of many symbolic transformations and condensations on an hedonic theme. It is not a likely experience of infants as observed.

In spite of this critique, I do believe that infants will group interpersonal experiences into various pleasurable and unpleasurable categories, that is, into hedonic clusters. The forming of hedonic clusters of experiences, however, is different from dichotomizing or splitting all interpersonal experience along hedonic lines. For instance, if we consider an unpleasurable cluster of interactive experiences with mother as an entity analogous to a particular type of "working model of mother," then this cluster can also be conceived of as an assemblage of RIGs, all of which have a common theme that brings and ties them together as a working model. The common theme is an attribute of the experience, namely a certain degree and even quality of unpleasure. We can then speak of a negatively toned mother. The difference, for our purposes, between a negatively toned mother and an avoidantly attached working model of mother (for example) is the different attribute that acts as the common theme to tie together the various RIGs that form the two different constructs. The RIGs that are assembled to create the negatively toned mother share a hedonic tone and quality as the common attribute. The RIGs that are assembled to create an avoidantly attached working model of mother share contextual and attachment activating and deactivating attributes. Let us call them both working models, but of different kinds. The infant is bound to form many such working models. At a later date, after verbal relatedness is well established, the child or adult can, with the aid of symbols, re-index RIGs and various working models to form two superordinate categories that are imbued with the full meanings of "good" or "bad." In this way, an older child or adult can indeed "split" their interpersonal experience, but it is in fact not a splitting but rather an integration into a higher order categorization.

Fantasy versus Reality as the Central Issue in Ontogenic Theories

When Freud realized the extent to which his patients had been seduced or sexually approached by their parents in their fantasies, but not in actuality, he cast his lot and that of psychoanalysis with fantasy. Fantasy—experience as distorted by wishes and defenses—

firmly became the arena of inquiry. Reality—what actually happened, as determinable by a third party—was relegated to a background position, even considered clinically irrelevant by many. Since Freud's clinical concerns were with a patient's life as experienced subjectively, not as enacted objectively, his decision is easily understandable. Coupled with the postulate that the pleasure principle preceded or at least dominated the reality principle in development, this theoretical clinical position resulted in an ontogenetic theory of experience as fantasy, not of experience as reality. The units making up the steps or stages of developmental theory came to be such phenomena as wishes, distortions, delusions, and defensive resolutions.

It is in this tradition that Mahler and Klein have worked. A basic assumption of the notion of "normal symbiosis" is that even if infants could tell self from other, their defenses would prevent their doing so, in order to ward off anxiety or stress. Mahler postulates that from birth until two months the infant ego is protected by the stimulus barrier. After the barrier is gone, infants would be left with all the stresses and threats of being on their own, unless they replaced the reality of their separateness and aloneness with the "delusion" of a fused-with mother and thus a protected state. "The libidinal cathexis vested in the symbiotic orbit replaces the unborn instinctual stimulus barrier and protects the rudimentary ego from premature phase-unspecific strain, from stress traumatic [and in doing so creates a] *delusion* of a common boundary" (Mahler et al. 1975, p. 451). Normal symbiosis theory thus is based on a belief in infantile fantasy or distortion rather than a belief in reality perception. In a similar vein, Klein postulates the infant's basic subjective experiences as consisting of paranoid, schizoid, and depressive positions. These assumed infantile experiences operate outside of ongoing reality perceptions. Here, too, the units of a genetic theory are fantasy-based. (This notion may permit these theorists to ignore selected observational findings, but at considerable expense.)

The basic assumption that the appropriate units of a genetic theory are fantasies is open to serious question. One cannot disagree that subjective experience is the appropriate stuff for genetic theory, but how firm is the assumption that the most relevant subjective experiences of the infant are reality-distorting fantasies? And here we restrike a chord sounded before. If current findings from infancy studies fly against the notion that the pleasure principle developmentally precedes the reality principle, then why must wishes and defenses against reality be given a privileged and prior developmental position? Why must the sense of reality be seen as secondary in time and derivation, growing out of the loss of the need for fantasy and defense?

The position taken here is based on the opposite assumption—namely, that infants from the beginning mainly experience reality. Their subjective experiences suffer no distortion by virtue of wishes or defenses, but only those made inevitable by perceptual or cognitive immaturity or overgeneralization. Further, I assume here that the capacity for defensive—that is, psychodynamic—distortions of reality is a later-developing capacity, requiring more cognitive processes than are initially available.[6] The views presented here suggest that the usual genetic sequence should be reversed and that reality experience precedes fantasy distortions in development. This position leaves the infant unapproachable by psychodynamic considerations for an initial period, resulting in a non-psychodynamic beginning of life in the sense that the infant's experience is not the product of reality altering conflict resolution. This position is far closer to Kohut's and Bowlby's contention that pre-Oedipal pathology is due to deficits or reality-based events—rather than to conflicts, in the psychodynamic sense.

Deficit is the wrong concept, however, for these reality-based events. From a normative and prospective vantage, the infant experiences only interpersonal realities, not deficits (which cannot be experienced until much later in life) and not conflict-resolving distortions. It is the actual shape of interpersonal reality, specified by the interpersonal invariants that really exist, that helps determine the developmental course. Coping operations occur as reality-based adaptations. Defensive operations of the type that distort reality occur only after symbolic thinking is available. From this position, we can now take up again the all-important task addressed by A. Freud and ask what may be the nature, form, and developmental timetable of the earliest-appearing defensive operations, now that they have been repositioned as secondary reworkings of the infant's initially fairly accurate experience of interpersonal reality.

6. A reading of A. Freud's (1965) view of the ontogeny of defensive operations is compatible with this claim.

Chapter 11

Implications for the Therapeutic Process of Reconstructing a Developmental Past

HOW MIGHT the developmental views presented here affect clinical practice? In particular, how might a therapist and a patient reconstruct a therapeutically effective narrative about the past? Two major features of this viewpoint have broad clinical implications. First, the traditional clinical-developmental issues such as orality, dependence, autonomy, and trust, have been disengaged from any one specific point or phase of origin in developmental time. These issues are seen here as developmental lines—that is, issues for life, not phases of life. They do not undergo a sensitive period, a presumed phase of ascendancy and predominance when relatively irreversible "fixations" could occur. It therefore can not be known in advance, on theoretical grounds, at what point in life a particular traditional clinical-developmental issue will receive its pathogenic origin.

Traditional theories assigned an age-specific sensitive phase of life for the initial impress of these issues. There was thus an actual moment in time toward which theory dictated we should direct our reconstructive inquiry. In fact, some understanding of the initial pathogenic events during the sensitive phase was not only practically desirable but theoretically essential for the fullest understanding of the pathology. From the point of view taken here, this situation no longer prevails. The actual point of origin for any of these traditional clinical-developmental issues could be anywhere along their continuous developmental line. No longer prescribed by theory, it poses a mystery and a challenge, and the therapist is freer to roam with the patient across the ages and through the domains of senses of the self, to discover where the reconstructive action will be most intense, unimpeded by too limiting theoretical prescriptions. This freedom permits the therapist to listen more evenly (much as Freud originally suggested) and to make the task of reconstruction more of a true adventure for both patient and therapist. There are fewer theoretical constraints on where they will arrive—in other words, fewer preconceptions about what the reconstructed clinical infant will look like.

The fact is that most experienced clinicians keep their developmental theories well in the background during active practice. They search with the patient through his or her remembered history to find the potent life-experience that provides the key therapeutic metaphor for understanding and changing the patient's life. This experience can be called the *narrative point of origin* of the pathology, regardless of when it occurred in actual developmental time. Once the metaphor has been found, the therapy proceeds forward and backward in time from that point of origin. And for the purposes of an effective therapeutic reconstruction, the therapy rarely if ever gets back to the preverbal ages, to an assumed *actual point of origin* of the pathology, even though there is theoretically supposed to be one. Most therapists would agree that one works with whatever reconstructive metaphor offers the most force and explanatory power about the patient's life, even though one can not get at the "original edition" of the metaphor. While the developmental theory is given lip service, the practice proceeds. There is widespread recognition that the developmental theories, when applied to a patient, do not deliver any reliable actual point of origin for the traditional clinical-developmental issues. Such actual points of origin of pathology apply only to theoretical infants, who do not exist.

The second major point with broad clinical implications is that the period of emergence of each sense of self is most likely a sensitive period, for reasons given in chapter 9. It is the different domains of self-experience, rather than the traditional clinical-developmental issues, that are given a strong formative impress during a particular, and specifiable, developmental time slot. This implication sets up clinical predictions that are testable.

We will begin with some of the possible consequences of disengaging the traditional clinical-developmental issues from age-specific sensitive periods and then address some of the consequences of putting the domains of sense of self in their developmental place.

Implications of Viewing Traditional Clinical-Developmental Issues as Issues for Life

STRATEGIES FOR FINDING THE NARRATIVE ORIGIN OF A PROBLEM

The notion of a layering of different senses of the self as different forms of ongoing experience is potentially helpful in locating an organizing therapeutic metaphor. Take, for example, a patient whose major concern focuses on control and autonomy. In search of a key metaphor, one explores the clinical "feel" of the problem. A first question in identifying the feel is, what domain of relatedness is most prominent or active? The patient's current life and transference reactions provide the clues. Patients readily indicate which sense of the self is most at stake in the issue of control. Imagine three different kinds of mother-child relationships with regard to autonomy. The first mother operates under the assumption that it is necessary and desirable to control Johnny's body—that is, his physical acts—but not his words or feeling states. Those are his own business. A second mother may contest only Jenny's feeling states and intentions. And a third mother's vital personal sphere of control lies neither in what Jimmy does or feels, but only in what he says. That becomes her business. Each of these situations will result in a different clinical feel as to what the problem of autonomy is about, or which sense of self is at risk in the struggle.

The following case illustrates the issue of where to look for the narrative origin and key metaphor. A professional woman in her thirties complained of feeling unable to cope by herself, to initiate her own wishes and goals. She had taken a passive role in the conduct of her life, following what for her (given her family background and mental resources) was the path of least resistance and the path that someone else had urged or initiated. It was in this way that she had become a lawyer and gotten married. Her current and most acute source of suffering was her sense of paralysis in her law career. She felt that she had no control over her present situation or future course and that her life was in the hands of others. She felt helpless and furious. She frequently overreacted, and the overreactions were placing her job in some jeopardy. When talking about her situation at work, she kept dwelling upon details that concerned her physical agency, especially the initiation and freedom of her *physical* acts: she wanted her office rearranged—flower pots, some books, a coffee table, all things she could move herself—and she had planned what was to be done, but somehow could not get herself to do it. She was furious with one of the senior partners for turning a common room into a special conference room, off-limits to all but senior partners. She seemed upset mainly at not being able to wander in there to see the view of the city, as she had before, not because it was any real inconvenience to her work or because she saw it as a demeaning statement about her lesser status. She most resented being deprived of her habitual walk and view.

Her concerns with her physical freedom to act made it feel as though the domain of core-relatedness and, in particular, the sense of agency were most involved. This impression was heightened by the fact that she felt no inability to initiate and control her life in the domains of intersubjective and verbal relatedness. She was very effective in addressing misunderstandings and empathic ruptures. With this in mind, we looked for any other times when her sense of a core self, and especially her physical agency, felt compromised. The life "moment" that made up the narrative point of origin for her therapy was found in a period of her life from age eight to ten, when she was largely bedridden with rheumatic fever and subacute bacterial endocarditis. This life period had been explored extensively earlier in treatment, when she had dwelled mainly on the depressive and depriving features of her illness. This time, however, we kept the therapeutic exploration closer to the feelings related to her sense of a core self. She then recalled that she had been ordered not to move about, even to walk to the window, and that even if she tried to do something or get somewhere, she was too physically fatigued. For anything physical to happen—to get upstairs or downstairs, to retrieve a book she wanted, to open the window—she had to wait for her mother or father to reappear and make it happen. She felt as though she had spent a lifelong season waiting for the "world to get activated and begin" at someone else's initiation.

This physically sick self, which had no agency and no capacity to initiate wished-for actions and which could not make "the world begin," became her narrative point of origin. It was this sense of self that she was now carrying about, and it became the pivotal metaphor for the "clinical infant" that was reconstructed. Once the metaphor was in place, she found it relatively easy to explore other manifestations of this historical event, and even some of its predispositions. Gradually, it helped her understand and deal with the acute distress she suffered at work. This metaphor acted as the fundamental referent for this aspect of her problems, and in her treatment she kept checking back to it, as to the North Star, to orient herself. This vignette makes several salient points for our purposes. First, the historical events ("traumatic" events) that served as the point of origin for the narrative occurred during the latency years. Regardless of her age, the major effect was in the domain of her sense of a core self. Because all senses of the self, once formed, remain active, growing, subjective processes throughout life, any one of them is vulnerable to deformations occurring at any life point. Similarly, since life issues such as autonomy or control are issues for the life span, they too are vulnerable at any life point.

The narrative point of origin can, and in this case probably does, correspond with the actual point of origin. The genesis of psychological problems may, but does not have to, have a developmental history that reaches back to infancy. Development of senses of the self is going on all the time, at all levels of "primitiveness." Development is not a succession of events left behind in history. It is a continuing process, constantly updated.

The second point to note is that the formative events that occurred during the patient's eighth to tenth years were the "first edition" of the problem. They were not necessarily a "re-edition" of earlier childhood events. We need not seek a theoretical actual origin point. One could then ask why she could not overcome the historical event, or trauma. Is it not necessary to look for earlier reasons that made her more susceptible to the trauma? Yes, it will be helpful to know about predispositions to susceptibility, but that is not the same as seeking an "original edition" in the earlier years.

Psychopathology when viewed from a developmental point of view is perhaps best seen on a continuum of pattern accumulation. At one extreme are actual neuroses, in which an isolated event (outside of the predictable and characteristic) impinges on the individual with pathogenic results. This kind of pathology has an actual point of origin that can occur at any point in development. And inevitably, the narrative point of origin and the actual point of origin are identical. There is no accumulation.

At the other extreme are the cumulative interactive patterns that can be observed very early, even at their initiation in infancy, and certainly during their continuation as development proceeds. These characteristic cumulative patterns result in character and personality types and, in the extreme, in personality disorders of the *DSM-III* Axis II types. These do not have an actual developmental point of origin in any meaningful sense. The insult (or pattern) is effectively present and acting at all developmental points. There is only accumulation. Naturally, the patterns start at only one point, the earliest point, but that does not assure that the contribution of this first point is more important quantitatively or even qualitatively than the contributions at later points.

Somewhere in the middle of the continuum is the situation in which characteristic cumulative developmental patterns are necessary but not sufficient to the pathogenic impact of an actual insult. In this case, the actual developmental point of origin is indeterminate and a matter for speculation.

This indeterminacy can be confusing for therapy. Most psychoanalysts would maintain that there is an earlier edition that either cannot be retrieved because of repression or cannot be recognized because of distortions or transformations between the primary and later editions. These postulations appear to be more theoretically than clinically based. It is certainly true that repression and distortions can hide an earlier edition; that is often the case in clinical work. It is not always the case, however, and even if it were, the unmasked earliest edition is rarely where theory predicts its origin point should be. To rescue this situation, theorists postulate an even earlier edition, hidden yet further in the past by repression and distortion. There is no end to the chase.[1]

When psychopathology is viewed from the clinical point of view, the primary task is to find the narrative point of origin—invariably, the key metaphor(s). Our theories about the actual point of origin tell us only how to conduct the therapeutic search for a narrative point of origin. Even in the case of character pathology, unless or until the therapy can come up with one narrative point of origin (even if it is actually no more important than a hundred other possible jump-in points), therapy will go more slowly. One of the major tasks of the therapist is to help the patient find a narrative point of origin, even as a working heuristic.

The third point of relevance to us is the way in which the domains of sense of self facilitate the identification of the narrative point of origin. The connection between the way the patient was feeling and acting in the present and the way she must have felt during her illness at age eight to ten seems so obvious that an astute clinician of almost any theoretical persuasion would soon enough have made the comparison: "Is the way you feel now at work at all like what it felt to be sick and limited in what you could do, when you were sick as a girl?" What then is the advantage of holding in mind a view of the development of senses of the self when listening to a patient? Speed and confidence in the therapeutic search process is one answer. With this patient, the connection made was not so obvious until after the fact, as is so often the case, because she had never been able to recover spontaneously the physical details of being sick and had dwelt in great detail on just the psychological features. Through the notion of domains of sense of self, it was easier and faster to find this narrative point of origin.

There is a final point to be noted in the vignette concerning the

1. The ultimate barrier to the "primary" editions of infancy may be the rendition into the verbal mode. This, however, is neither a repression nor a distortion in the dynamic sense.

lawyer. Sometimes the event that ought to constitute a narrative point of origin is clear to both therapist and patient, but the patient cannot get hold of it because the key experiences are not affectively available. The notion of different and coexisting levels of sense of self can inform the search for the affectively loaded experiences that, when recovered, can potentially serve as a narrative point of origin.

The affective component of the key experience usually resides primarily in one domain of relatedness (that is, in one sense of the self), and even in one feature of that domain—in the case of the lawyer, physical agency and freedom. The clinical question then becomes, what sense of the self carries the affect? And once the question is posed that way, a familiarity with the domains of self-experience can serve as a helpful guide. The procedure is no different from helping the patient to get or wander back "there"—into the experience—so that some part of the recalled event might trigger recall of the affective part, but it adds the particular sense of the self to the list of experienced components to use as a recall cue.

Another vignette will demonstrate how the process can work. A young man of nineteen had had a psychotic break three months earlier, precipitated by his girlfriend's leaving him. He acknowledged that this was the pivotal event. He could talk about his disappointment and sense of loss, but only rather intellectually. While he was clearly still mourning her loss, he had never cried or relived the pain or the pleasures of his relationship with her. He showed no feelings about the event. He even talked about the last night he saw her, before she finally wrote him a letter telling him it was over. They were necking in the back seat of a car, and she was sitting on his lap. Many questions were put to him to elicit his feelings towards her: "What happened the last night?" "Did you make out or just talk?" (general questions); "Did you sense a change in her?" "Was she behind her kiss?" (questions directed at the intersubjective domain); "What did it feel like to kiss her?" (a question directed at the domain of core-relatedness). None had unlocked his affect, but the next one was directed even deeper into his sense of a core self: "What was it like to have her full weight on your lap?" That question retrieved the affect and let him cry for the first time in three months. With a different patient, in whom, for instance, the shock and hurt were less in the loss and more in the sense of having been deceived, of being vulnerable, of not picking up the signals, and being angry about it, then a question such as "Was she behind her kiss?", which is addressed to a failure in intersubjectivity, might have unlocked the feeling of anger and humiliation.[2]

SEARCH STRATEGIES WHERE THE DIAGNOSIS IS ALREADY KNOWN

Different theories about a given diagnostic category have differing explanations of the central subjective experience of the illness and how it arises. For an example of widely differing views, let us look at what several authors have said about the state that Adler and Buie describe as an "experiential state of intensely painful aloneness" common to borderline patients (Adler and Buie 1979, p. 83). Each theory explains this feeling of loneliness differently.

Some authors have suggested that the experience of abandonment is the most critical to the borderline patient, that it engenders an aloneness that can only be alleviated by being held or fed or touched or "merged." Aloneness secondary to abandonment, then, is the primary experience that sets in motion various defenses (see Adler and Buie [1979]). In our view, this is the experience of aloneness at the level of core-relatedness.

Other authors (see Kohut [1971, 1977]) suggest that the fundamental determinant of aloneness in borderline patients is the absence

2. It may appear in the above description that uncovering the affect is more a problem of normal memory retrieval—did the therapist hit the right note (the effective retrieval cue) so that the patient resonated (recalled the lived episode with its attendant affect)?—rather than a problem of repression—a conflictually determined memory dysfunction. Two kinds of memory processes are involved, *involuntary memory* and *removing a repression.* Involuntary memory is perhaps best described by Proust in two well-known passages in *Swann's Way:* "And so it is with our own past. It is a labour in vain to attempt to recapture it: all the efforts of our intellect must prove futile. The past is hidden somewhere outside the realm, beyond the reach of intellect, in some material object (in the sensation which that material object will give us) which we do not suspect. And as for that object, it depends on chance whether we come upon it or not before we ourselves must die. . . . But when from a long-distant past nothing subsists, after the people are dead, after the things are broken and scattered, still, alone, more fragile, but with more vitality, more unsubstantial, more persistent, more faithful, the smell and taste of things remain poised a long time, like souls, ready to remind us, waiting and hoping for their moment, amid the ruins of all the rest; and bear unfaltering, in the tiny and almost impalpable drop of their essence, the vast structure of recollection" (Trans. C. K. Scott Moncrieff [New York: The Modern Library, 1928], pp. 61, 65).

Both processes of retrieval appear to be necessary, and complementary. It is the therapist's task to work on them simultaneously. For the "involuntary" component, this can best be done by leading the patient in the direction of that domain of self-experience where he or she is most likely to encounter the right "drop of . . . essence." For the repression, the usual therapeutic procedures are needed.

of empathic experience and/or the failure of a "sustaining object" that maintains psychological survival. Adler and Buie, in describing this kind of loneliness, refer to a patient who traced her "most unbearable loneliness" to her mother's empathic unavailability. In our view, this is the experience of aloneness at the level of intersubjective relatedness. (Adler and Buie focus on a failure of evocative memory as the underlying mechanism. This seems too limited.)

Still other authors have emphasized that it is the defenses against abandonment or against failures of gratification that provide the main explanation of the experience of aloneness. Meissner (1971) suggests that the desire to incorporate the object results in a fear of annihilating the object. A protective distance is set up to save the object from destruction, and it then becomes the secondary cause of the feeling of loneliness. Kernberg (1968, 1975, 1982, 1984) suggests that gratification failures lead to rage, which then forces the mechanism of splitting to occur to maintain both a "good" and a "bad" object. Splitting in turn results in a painful aloneness. In our view, these defense-based explanations of the loneliness experience belong at the level of verbal relatedness. Similarly, protecting the object from your own fury falls into the domain of a reorganized, verbally represented experience.

Probably all three views are correct, but none is all-inclusive. Each of these experiences of aloneness is the same feeling state experienced and elaborated in a different domain of self-experience. All are likely to happen, and three different qualities of feeling do not call for three different and mutually exclusive, dynamic etiologies. In order not to treat a patient with an inapplicable dynamic and in the wrong domain of relatedness, it is necessary to be alert to the clinical flavor of the feeling state, so that the patient, rather than an etiological theory, will guide the therapy to the sense of self that is most in pain.

All domains of relatedness will be involved in the illness, but usually one is experienced as more painful at any time. The therapist cannot know initially whether that domain is the most affected or whether it is the least affected and therefore the least defended. Some of the controversy over whether the empathic approach (as applied in Self Psychology) or the interpretive approach (as applied in traditional psychoanalysis) is more efficacious in the treatment of borderline patients is mitigated by the viewpoint taken here. An empathic approach will inevitably first encounter and address the failures in the domain of intersubjective relatedness. The patient usually experiences shock and then ultimately relief in discovering that someone is available who is capable and desirous of knowing what it feels like to be him or her. The relief and the opening up of interpersonal possibilities are enormous, almost irrespective of the particular content material that is discussed. (The literature is now replete with such examples other than Kohut's; for example, see Schwaber [1980b].) The content material, such as failure of gratification leading to rage, leading to splitting, resulting in loneliness, is in the domain of verbal relatedness and may be addressed only secondarily, as the background material through which the empathic understanding is achieved.

An interpretive approach, on the other hand, will inevitably first engage the content material as it exists in the domain of verbal relatedness. Any empathic understanding between patient and therapist falls to the background and is worked on almost secondarily in the course of interpretive work and usually later in the form of transference and countertransference.

In effect, the nature of the therapeutic approach determines which domain of experience will appear to be primarily distressed. Because one can expect problems in all the senses of self and in all domains of relatedness, the therapist will by virtue of the approach he or she chooses find the pathology predicted by the etiological theory that determined the choice of approach in the first place. The problem is that while all domains of relatedness will be affected, one is likely to be more severely compromised and will require not only more therapeutic attention but perhaps the initial attention that allows treatment to proceed. This fact requires the therapist to be flexible in approach. And most clinicians use neither approach exclusively; there is more flexibility in practice than their theoretical persuasion would suggest. All this suggests that instead of continuing to practice in apparent contradiction to the guiding theory, in order to treat patients more effectively, the guiding theories need to be more encompassing. The developmental lines presented here suggest one route.

SEARCH STRATEGIES WHERE THE AGE OF TRAUMA IS KNOWN

It is in the situation in which the age at which the trauma occurred has been identified that our developmental theories can be most helpful or harmful to therapy. To what extent are our clinical ears and minds pretuned by particular developmental theories to pick up only certain material and miss other material?

A case illustration serves best. A patient related that his mother was clinically depressed during the period of his life from twelve to thirty months and that his relatives said that at about that time he, an only child, had changed into a more somber and anxious child, needy but not always asking for assurance. His family recalled that he had occasional "silent tantrums" for which the triggering issue was his sudden, short-lived refusals to use words. These tantrums did not concern restrictions in his freedom of action. Speech development was normal. Mother stayed home with him during this time, occupied as a housewife. She was never hospitalized but was in treatment five days a week and quite "preoccupied with her problems." In spite of this, she was available enough that the boy appeared neither overly clingy nor resistant to her, and his exploratory behavior seemed normal as remembered by all. If anything, he appeared rather adventuresome.

At the age of thirty-four, when he first came to treatment, he was married with a two-year-old boy. He was functioning well enough at a junior level in a large corporation. His wife was a graduate student in the humanities and the more "intellectual" one. His presenting complaint was of a generalized depression, feelings of insecurity and not being understood, and episodes of enraged outbursts at his wife. The feelings of insecurity were experienced both at work and at home. For most of his life he had thought of himself as a risk-taker, but he was currently inhibited from taking a risk at work that involved an appropriate "betting on himself." He periodically yearned for a more stable job in which advancement would be less dependent on his initiations. Alternately, he wished that one of the more senior members would take him under his wing and serve as an unconditional patron. He had lost respect for himself for entertaining such wishes. He felt dependent on his wife and called her from work at least once a day, although she found the calls a nuisance. At times she complained that he would rather just hold her than make love with her.

It was mainly with his wife that he felt not understood. He felt that instead of just listening to him she always became defensive, so that he was confronted by an adversary rather than an ally. Even in issues that involved no criticism, when he simply wanted to explain how he felt about something, she would too quickly jump in with unasked-for suggestions about what to do or how to remedy a problem. When he wanted to be understood, he felt advised.

His explosions of temper arose most often in this context of not feeling understood. They took the form of a characteristic argument in which he would end up yelling something like, "You have words and labels and explanations for everything. And they are supposed to make sense, but they mean nothing to me. That's not what my life feels like to me." And while he raved, his wife would walk out of the room, shaken but saying coolly that he could not be talked to. He then would go after her in anger and fear, fear that he would strike her and that she would leave him. The fear was great enough that he backed off his position, retreating and apologizing to re-establish the previous level of contact with her. When this was accomplished, he felt less fearful and more secure, but sadder and more alone. At those moments, he burst out sobbing.

After one particularly explosive outburst on a Friday night, he came to my office Monday remarking that he had had a song in his head all weekend that he still could not get out. The song was "Reelin' in the Years," by Steely Dan, from the album "Can't Buy a Thrill." He remembered only some of the words:

> You wouldn't know a diamond
> If you held it in your hand
> The things you think are precious
> I can't understand . . .
>
> Are you gathering up the tears
> Have you had enough of mine . . .
>
> The things that pass for knowledge
> I can't understand

The therapeutic use of the known early history in such a case as this is determined by the features of the age period that seem most salient. And that is determined by what developmental theory is embraced.

Certain of this patient's problems—those in the area of security, fear of abandonment, wish for a patron, and inhibition of initiative—are readily accountable in the terminology of attachment theory or separation/individuation theory as patterns transformed across development. The comings and goings to and from mother during the twelve- to thirty-month age period make up a part of Mahler's practicing subphase of separation/individuation. They also exemplify the activation and deactivation of the attachment aim. For Mahler, the infant comes back to "refuel," or to get something that permits the infant to go back out and re-explore. What is the "something"? Mahler is not always clear, because the term "refueling" invites confusion with energic issues. But the metaphor implies a kind of ego infusion (via merging) that permits the infant to separate and explore again. For attachment theorists, these comings and goings help the infant to build up an internal working model of the mother that acts as a secure base to leave from and return to. In the terms used here, these are interactions with a self-regulating other that become generalized, represented, and activated. It is not difficult to imagine how a maternal depression could have an impact on these behavioral patterns and their representations. It remains to be traced how these early patterns survived the transformations of development, to present in the particular and not unrecognizable form that they assumed when this patient was thirty-four.

Mahler describes the appearance, around the middle of the second year, of a certain kind of seriousness, soberness, or deliberateness. A change in the infant's emotional and attitudinal aura occurs, away from the more carefree "world is my oyster" feeling previously given off. Mahler and her colleagues (Mahler, Pine, and Bergman 1975) have called this the "rapprochement crisis" that ushers in the "rapprochement subphase" of separation/individuation. They speculate that at this point infants have finally achieved enough separation/individuation from mother to realize that they are not in fact all-powerful, that they are still dependent. This realization brings about the emotional-attitudinal change and a partial, temporary resetting of the attachment balance toward more attachment than exploration. Infants partially lose their omnipotence.

The impact of the mother's depression on the son's "rapprochement crisis" is not precisely predictable. On the one hand, one could imagine that his omnipotence lasted longer but on a less secure base.

On the other hand, one could postulate that he had less opportunity to develop an appropriate sense of omnipotence and had to give it up earlier. In any event, it is not clear how this early patterning was transformed over the next thirty-two years. Whatever the reason, his belief in his own powers at age thirty-four was slightly impaired.

So far, attachment or separation/individuation theory, or the notions of a self-regulating other and its representation provide plausible bridges between the early insult and current behavior. These occur mainly in the domain of the sense of a core self with a core other. However, they fall short of explaining the other two features of the current clinical picture, namely, the sense and pain of not being understood and the particular form of the patient's outbursts of rage. A consideration of the domain of intersubjective relatedness is needed.

At the same time that the practicing subphase of separation/individuation and attachment behaviors and the overt use of a self-regulating other are much in evidence, the sense of a subjective self and the domain of intersubjective relatedness also begin to form. These cast a different light on the comings and goings that occur during this first half of the second year. When the infant returns to mother, it is not only to be "refueled" or to deactivate the attachment system. It is a reaffirmation that the infant and mother (as separate entities) are sharing in what the infant experiences. For instance, an infant experiencing fear after wandering too far needs to know that his or her state of fear has been heard. It is more than a need to be held or soothed; it is also an intersubjective need to be understood. On a more positive note, the infant may look at mother while returning to her after playing with a box, as if to say, "Do you also experience, as I do, that this box is surprising and wonderful?" The mother somehow indicates "Yes, I do," usually through attunements, and off and away the infant goes. Or the infant's returns to mother may be in the service of confirming that the reality and/or fantasy of intersubjectivity is being actively maintained ("Touching this castle of blocks is still scary-wonderful, isn't it, Mom?"). The creation of intersubjective sharing permits the exploration and pursuit of curiosity. Even the level of the infant's fear or distress in the situation is partially negotiated by social referencing signals that occur in the domain of intersubjectivity, since they use the mother's feeling state as a tuner of the infant's. ("Is the block castle more scary than wonderful, or the other way around?")

What appears to happen in the early locomotor behavior of the toddler is this. When the infant has wandered much too far away, has been hurt, has been scared by something unexpected, or has become tired, the experience of returning to mother is almost solely at the level of core-relatedness. This is the attachment theory's description of what other analytic theories call regression or refueling. In less extreme conditions, we see a majority of returns to mother as having to do with subjective sharings—the re-establishment of the intersubjective state, which is not a given experience but which must be actively maintained. And much of the time, returnings to mother occur in both domains simultaneously. In fact, we often see infants who appear near the verge of fear make up or grab onto a handy experience for intersubjective testing and return to mother with a multiple agenda, a core agenda and an intersubjective one.

The returning of infants with multiple agendas is potentially of clinical importance, because some mothers find one agenda more acceptable than another. If a mother is less ready to soothe the fear, the infant will find a surprising number of intersubjective "excuses" to return. The use of intersubjective relatedness in the service of physical security is hardly unknown to us as clinicians and parents. The opposite also happens: some mothers are less available for intersubjective sharing but readily accept their physical capacity to calm fear. Once again the use of physical relatedness in the service of fantasied intersubjectivity is also well known to us as clinicians and parents.

To return to the question of how the mother's depressed behavior during these events might have had an impact later in life, it is not surprising that this man had a very keen sense of not being understood. He experienced a painful rupture in intersubjective relatedness when his wife would not or could not enter into and share his subjective experience, so far as that is possible. It is likely that a heightened sensitivity to this form of interpersonal disjunction was established during the period when he was one to two-and-one-half years old. It is very likely that because of her depressive "preoccupations" his mother was relatively less available for intersubjective relatedness than for serving physically as a secure base of operations. The patient's painful feeling of not being understood seems to be most plausible and productively viewed in terms of intersubjective relatedness.

What then about the patient's particular form of enraged outbursts? During the period from eighteen to thirty months of age, the patient was in the formative phase of verbal relatedness. The advent of verbal relatedness permits the infant to begin to integrate experiences in the different domains of relatedness. For instance, the infant can now say the verbal equivalent of such core experiences as "I don't want to look at you," "I don't want you to look at me," and "I don't want to be near you." (Negativity begins around now.) The infant can also say the verbal equivalent of such intersubjective experiences as "Stay out of my excitement with this toy," and "I don't want to share my pleasure." The verbal equivalent may initially be something as impoverished as "NO!" or, some months later, "GO AWAY" or, even later, "I HATE YOU." The words are an attempt to tie together the infant's experiences in several domains. The verbal act of saying "NO!" is a statement of autonomy, separateness, and independence (Spitz 1957). At the same time it also refers to raw physical acts in the domain of core-relatedness, such as "I won't look at you," although the closest words the infant has to represent that personal knowledge residing in the core domain are "NO" or "GO AWAY."

This state of affairs both integrates and fractures experience and leads the infant into a crisis of self-comprehension. The self becomes a mystery. The infant is aware that there are levels and layers of self-experience that are to some extent estranged from the official experiences ratified by language. The previous harmony is broken.

I suggest that this crisis in self-comprehension is in large part responsible for the soberness seen at this period. This shift is a nonspecific consequence of a general crisis in self-comprehension and self-experience, brought about by the attempt (bound to partial failure) at the verbal representation of experience. It affects all life issues, with as many consequences for intimacy, trust, attachment, dependency, mastery, and so on as it has for separation or individuation.

This crisis in self-comprehension occurs because for the first time the infant experiences the self as divided, and rightly senses that no one else can rebind the division. The infant has not lost omnipotence but rather has lost experiential wholeness.

This version of what is going on is very different from Mahler's. It makes more comprehensible, however, the patient's outbursts at his wife when she insists on putting his subjective experiences into words. To him, his experiences somehow do not fit into her words. He is left confused, helpless, and infuriated. This is a current version of the crisis in infancy, when the need to verbalize preverbal experience results in fracturing. Parents are greatly needed for that buffering effect, and it is likely the patient's mother in her depression was not well disposed to help make this transition easier.

In sum, the greatest clinical value of the views put forth here lies in their suggesting search strategies to aid in the construction of therapeutically effective life narratives. The system presented urges a flexibility in theories about the developmental origin of pathology. It does so by offering some alternative explanations for well-known events, thus presenting a wider range of possibilities, and by emphasizing a developmental view that focuses on search strategies rather than answers about the timing of clinical origins.

Implications of Viewing the Different Senses of Self as the Subject Matter of Age-Specific Sensitive Periods

Each sense of the self has been allotted a formative phase when it first comes into existence—birth to two months for the sense of an emergent self, two to six months for the sense of a core self, seven to fifteen months for the sense of an intersubjective self, and eighteen to thirty months for the verbal sense of self. These formative phases can fruitfully be considered "sensitive periods" for the four senses of self, for reasons argued in chapter 9.

In the case of the lawyer cited earlier in this chapter, one would predict on theoretical grounds that there was, indeed, a predisposition for her problem, but that it occurred around the age of two to six months in the domain of a sense of a core self, especially agency, and not around age one to two-and-a-half years over the issues of autonomy and control. The battle is about the sense of core self-experience. The prize is self-agency; autonomy and control are only the local battlefields. The use of this clinical prediction is of limited value in a reconstruction, however, for the following reason. Even though the different domains of self-experience have replaced the traditional clinical-developmental issues as the subject matter for sensitive periods, they are less vulnerable to irreversible initial impresses, because all the domains of sense of self are viewed as active and still forming throughout life. They are not seen as the relics of past and finished developmental phases, as were the traditional clinical-developmental issues. The system stays more open to pathogenic insult, chronic or acute. Therefore, even in considering clinical problems in the different domains of self-experience, there are potentially many possible actual points of pathogenesis beyond the sensitive period. Again, the theory is less prescriptive with regard to actual points of pathological origin.

Nonetheless, this viewpoint does predict that environmental influences at formative periods of the different senses of self will result in relatively more pathology, or less easily reversible pathology, than later insults. In chapter 9 we discussed several of the more obvious predictions. In general, during the sensitive periods of formation answers to several questions about features of self-experience are being partially determined: What is the range of stimulations and events that will be subjectively perceived as self-experience? Which will be experienced as tolerable or disorganizing? What affective tones will be attached to all self-experiences in the different domains? How much actual interaction with self-regulating others is needed to maintain an undisturbed sense of self? Which self-experiences can be shared or communicated with ease and which with unease and foreboding? It is clear that a predictive working theory about these continuities would have considerable value in formulating the ontogeny of states of self pathology. It would also have much value within a traditional psychoanalytic approach, even if it were used only as a way of viewing and working with pre-Oedipal material and origins.

Epilogue

THE CENTRAL AIM of this book has been to describe the development of the infant's sense of self. I have tried to infer the infant's likely subjective experiences by considering the newly available experimental findings about infants in conjunction with clinical phenomena derived from practice. In this sense, it is a step towards a synthesis of the infant as observed and as clinically reconstructed, in the form of a working theory of the development of domains of self-experience.

The value of this working theory remains to be proved, and even its status as a hypothesis remains to be explored. Is it to be taken as a scientific hypothesis that can be evaluated by its confirming or invalidating current propositions, and by spawning studies that lead elsewhere? Or is it to be taken as a clinical metaphor to be used in practice, in which case the therapeutic efficacy of the metaphor can be determined?

It is my hope that it will prove to be both. As a hypothesis, this view calls attention to a variety of areas in which more experimentation is needed—in particular, studies on episodic memory and the role of affect in organizing experience, descriptive and theoretical efforts at providing a taxonomy of preverbal experience, and especially, renewed efforts to develop descriptive means to identify and trace interactive patterns across their developmental transformations. Also needed are prospective studies that test its hypothesis that age-specific insults will predict later pathology in specific domains of self-experience but will fail to predict pathology in specific traditional clinical-developmental issues. The scope of the field of inquiry that future experimentalists will find provocative, attractive, and challenging has, I hope, been expanded.

The view presented here is also intended to serve as a metaphor for clinical practice. It is likely that the clinical implications of this metaphor will come about slowly and indirectly. I suspect that the greatest force for change will happen through changing our view of who infants are, how they are related to others, what their subjective social experiences are likely to be, especially their sense of self, and how we search for past experience relevant for the creation of therapeutic narratives. Such a change filters its way through the thinking of therapists as they actively work with patients. As the picture of the reconstructed past of a patient's life becomes altered, the therapist finds it necessary to think and act differently. The constructs proposed in the last section of this book are intended to facilitate that process. Such a process of change takes many "generations" of patients. Exactly how this filtering and transforming process will translate into different techniques and theories of therapeutics is unpredictable. I have suggested some beginnings.

The second route for change is even more indirect and unpredictable, but perhaps the most potent. Besides being therapists or experimentalists, we are also parents, grandparents, and disseminators of information. The findings we relate and the theories we devise are ultimately information for new parents. Whether we intend it or not, the general educational nature of the work is inescapable. The process has already begun and is accelerating to alter the general view of the infant held by most people. Once parents see a different infant, that infant starts to become transformed by their new "sight" and ultimately becomes a different adult. Much of the book has described how such transformations between persons occur. Evolution as it is daily encountered in the guise of "human nature" acts as a conservative force in these matters, so that changing our general views of who infants are can change who they will become only to a certain degree. But it is exactly that degree of change that is at issue here. If seeing the infant as different begins to make the children, adolescents, and adults different enough a generation later, then we will be seeing different patients at that point—patients who will have experienced a somewhat different infancy and whose interpersonal worlds have developed slightly differently. The therapeutic encounter with this new patient will again require changes in clinical theory and search strategies.

Just as infants must develop, so must our theories about what they experience and who they are.

BIBLIOGRAPHY

Adler, G., and Buie, D. H. (1979). Aloneness and borderline psychopathology: The possible relevance of child developmental issues. *International Journal of Psychoanalysis, 60,* 83–96.

Ainsworth, M. D. S. (1969). Object relations, dependency and attachment: A theoretical review of the infant-mother relationship. *Child Development, 40,* 969–1026.

Ainsworth, M. D. S. (1979). Attachment as related to mother-infant interaction. In J. B. Rosenblatt, R. H. Hinde, C. Beer, and M. Bushell (Eds.), *Advances in the study of behavior* (pp. 1–51). New York: Academic Press.

Ainsworth, M. D. S., and Wittig, B. (1969). Attachment and exploratory behavior in one-year-olds in a stranger situation. In B. M. Foss (Ed.), *Determinants of infant behavior.* New York: Wiley.

Ainsworth, M. D. S., Blehar, M. C., Waters, E., and Wall, S. (1978). *Patterns of attachment.* Hillsdale, N.J.: Erlbaum.

Allen, T. W., Walker, K., Symonds, L., and Marcell, M. (1977). Intrasensory and intersensory perception of temporal sequences during infancy. *Developmental Psychology, 13,* 225–29.

Amsterdam, B. K. (1972). Mirror self-image reactions before age two. *Developmental Psychology, 5,* 297–305.

Arnold, M. G. (1970). *Feelings and emotions, the Loyola symposium.* New York: Academic Press.

Austin, J. (1962). *How to do things with words.* New York: Oxford University Press.

Baldwin, J. M. (1902). *Social and ethical interpretations in mental development.* New York: Macmillan.

Balint, M. (1937). Early developmental states of the ego primary object love. In M. Balint, *Primary love and psycho-analytic technique.* New York: Liveright.

Basch, M. F. (1983). Empathic understanding: A review of the concept and some theoretical considerations. *Journal of the American Psychoanalytic Association, 31*(1), 101–26.

Basch, M. F. (in press). The perception of reality and the disavowal of meaning. *Annals of Psychoanalysis, 11.*

Bates, E. (1976). *Language and context: The acquisition of pragmatics.* New York: Academic Press.

Bates, E. (1979). Intentions, conventions and symbols. In E. Bates (Ed.), *The emergence of symbols: Cognition and communication in infancy.* New York: Academic Press.

Bates, E., Benigni, L., Bretherton, I., Camaioni, L., and Volterra, V. (1979). Cognition and communication from nine to thirteen months: Correlational findings. In E. Bates (Ed.), *The emergence of symbols: Cognition and communication in infancy.* New York: Academic Press.

Bateson, G., Jackson, D., Haley, J., and Wakland, J. (1956). Toward a theory of schizophrenia. *Behavioral Science, 1,* 251–64.

Baudelaire, C. (1982). *Les fleurs du mal.* (R. Howard, Trans.). Boston: David R. Godine. (Original work published 1857)

Beebe, B. (1973). *Ontogeny of Positive Affect in the Third and Fourth Months of the Life of One Infant.* Doctoral dissertation, Columbia University, University Microfilms.

Beebe, B., and Gerstman, L. J. (1980). The "packaging" of maternal stimulation in relation to infant facial-visual engagement: A case study at four months. *Merrill-Palmer Quarterly, 26,* 321–39.

Beebe, B., and Kroner, J. (1985). Mother-infant facial mirroring. (In preparation)

Beebe, B., and Sloate, P. (1982). Assessment and treatment of difficulties in mother-infant attunement in the first three years of life: A case history. *Psychoanalytic Inquiry, 1*(4), 601–23.

Beebe, B., and Stern, D. N. (1977). Engagement-disengagement and early object experiences. In M. Freedman and S. Grand (Eds.), *Communicative structures and psychic structures.* New York: Plenum Press.

Bell, S. M. (1970). The development of the concept of object as related to infant-mother attachment. *Child Development, 41,* 291–313.

Benjamin, J. D. (1965). Developmental biology and psychoanalysis. In N. Greenfield and W. Lewis (Eds.), *Psychoanalysis and current biological thought.* Madison: University of Wisconsin Press.

Bennett, S. (1971). Infant-caretaker interactions. *Journal of the American Academy of Child Psychiatry, 10,* 321–35.

Berlyne, D. E. (1966). Curiosity and exploration. *Science, 153,* 25–33.

Bloom, L. (1973). *One word at a time: The use of single word utterances before syntax.* Hawthorne, N.Y.: Mouton.

Bloom, L. (1983). Of continuity and discontinuity, and the magic of language development. In R. Gollinkoff (Ed.), *The transition from pre-linguistic to linguistic communication.* Hillsdale, N.J.: Erlbaum.

Bower, G. (1981). Mood and memory. *American Psychologist, 36,* 129–48.

Bower, T. G. R. (1972). Object perception in the infant. *Perception, 1,* 15–30.

Bower, T. G. R. (1974). *Development in infancy.* San Francisco, Calif.: Freeman.

Bower, T. G. R. (1976). *The perceptual world of the child.* Cambridge, Mass.: Harvard University Press.

Bower, T. G. R. (1978). The infant's discovery of objects and mother. In E. Thoman (Ed.) *Origins of the infant's social responsiveness.* Hillsdale, N.J.: Erlbaum.

Bower, T. G. R., Broughton, J. M., and Moore, M. K. (1970). Demonstration of intention in the reaching behavior of neonate humans. *Nature, 228,* 679–80.

Bowlby, J. (1958). The nature of the child's tie to his mother. *International Journal of Psychoanalysis, 39,* 350–73.

Bowlby, J. (1960). Separation anxiety. *International Journal of Psychoanalysis, 41,* 89–113.

Bowlby, J. (1969). *Attachment and loss: Vol. 1. Attachment.* New York: Basic Books.

Bowlby, J. (1973). *Attachment and loss: Vol. 2. Separation: Anxiety and anger.* New York: Basic Books.

Bowlby, J. (1980). *Attachment and loss: Vol. 3. Loss: Sadness and depression.* New York: Basic Books.

Brazelton, T. B. (1980, May). *New knowledge about the infant from current research: Implications for psychoanalysis.* Paper presented at the American Psychoanalytic Association meeting, San Francisco, Calif.

Brazelton, T. B. (1982). Joint regulation of neonate-parent behavior. In E. Tronick (Ed.), *Social interchange in infancy.* Baltimore, Md.: University Park Press.

Brazelton, T. B., Koslowski, B., and Main, M. (1974). The origins of reciprocity: The early mother-infant interaction. In M. Lewis and L. A. Rosenblum (Eds.), *The effects of the infant on its caregiver.* New York: Wiley.

Brazelton, T. B., Yogman, M., Als, H., and Tronick, E. (1979). The infant as a focus for family reciprocity. In M. Lewis and L. A. Rosenblum (Eds.), *The child and its family.* New York: Plenum Press.

Bretherton, I. (in press). Attachment theory: Retrospect and prospect. In I. Bretherton and E. Waters (Eds.), *Monographs of the Society for Research in Child Development.*

Bretherton, I., and Bates, E. (1979). The emergence of intentional communication. In I. Uzgiris (Ed.), *New directions for child development, Vol. 4.* San Francisco, Calif.: Jossey-Bass.

Bretherton, I., McNew, S., and Beeghly-Smith, M. (1981). Early person knowledge as expressed in gestural and verbal communication: When do infants acquire a "theory of mind"? In M. E. Lamb and L. R. Sherrod (Eds.), *Infant social cognition.* Hillsdale, N.J.: Erlbaum.

Bretherton, I., and Waters, E. (in press). Growing points of attachment theory and research. *Monographs of the Society for Research in Child Development.*

Bronson, G. (1982). *Monographs on infancy: Vol. 2. The scanning patterns of human infants: implications for visual learning.* Norwood, N.J.: Ablex.

Brown, R. (1973). *A first language: The early stages.* Cambridge, Mass.: Harvard University Press.

Bruner, J. S. (1969). Modalities of memory. In G. Talland and N. Waugh (Eds.), *The pathology of memory.* New York: Academic Press.

Bruner, J. S. (1975). The ontogenesis of speech acts. *Journal of Child Language, 2,* 1–19.

Bruner, J. S. (1977). Early social interaction and language acquisition. In H. R. Schaffer (Ed.), *Studies in mother-infant interaction.* London: Academic Press.

Bruner, J. S. (1981). The social context of language acquisition. *Language and Communication, 1,* 155–78.

Bruner, J. S. (1983). *Child's talk: Learning to use language.* New York: Norton.

Burd, A. P., and Milewski, A. E. (1981, April). *Matching of facial gestures by young infants: Imitation or releasers?* Paper presented at the Meeting of the Society for Research in Child Development, Boston, Mass.

Butterworth, G., and Castello, M. (1976). Coordination of auditory and visual space in newborn human infants. *Perception, 5,* 155–60.

Call, J. D. (1980). Some prelinguistic aspects of language development. *Journal of American Psychoanalytic Association, 28,* 259–90.

Call, J. D., and Marschak, M. (1976). Styles and games in infancy. In E. Rexford, L. Sander, and A. Shapiro (Eds.), *Infant Psychiatry* (pp. 104–12). New Haven, Conn.: Yale University Press.

Call, J. D., Galenson, E., and Tyson, R. L. (Eds.). (1983). *Frontiers of infant psychiatry, Vol. 1.* New York: Basic Books.

Campos, J., and Stenberg, C. (1980). Perception of appraisal and emotion: The onset of social referencing. In M. E. Lamb and L. Sherrod (Eds.), *Infant social cognition.* Hillsdale, N.J.: Erlbaum.

Caron, A. J., and Caron, R. F. (1981). Processing of relational information as an index of infant risk. In S. L. Friedman and M. Sigman (Eds.), *Preterm birth and psychological development.* New York: Academic Press.

Cassirer, E. (1955). *The philosophy of symbolic forms of language, Vol. 1.* New Haven, Conn.: Yale University Press.

Cavell, M. (in press). *The self and separate minds.* New York: New York University Press.

Cicchetti, D., and Schneider-Rosen, K. (in press). An organizational approach to childhood depression. In M. Rutter, C. Izard, and P. Read (Eds.), *Depression in children: Developmental perspectives.* New York: Guilford.

Cicchetti, D., and Sroufe, L. A. (1978). An organizational view of affect: Illustration from the study of Down's syndrome infants. In M. Lewis and L. Rosenblum (Eds.), *The development of affect.* New York: Plenum Press.

Clarke-Stewart, K. A. (1973). Interactions between mothers and their young children: Characteristics and consequences. *Monographs of the Society of Research in Child Development, 37*(153).

Cohen, L. B., and Salapatek, P. (1975). *Infant perception: From sensation to cognition: Vol. 2. Perception of space, speech, and sound.* New York: Academic Press.

Collis, G. M., and Schaffer, H. R. (1975). Synchronization of visual attention in mother-infant pairs. *Journal of Child Psychiatry, 16,* 315–20.

Condon, W. S., and Ogston, W. D. (1967). A segmentation of behavior. *Journal of Psychiatric Research, 5,* 221–35.

Condon, W. S., and Sander, L. S. (1974). Neonate movement is synchronized with adult speech. *Science, 183,* 99–101.

Cooley, C. H. (1912). *Human nature and the social order.* New York: Scribner.

Cooper, A. M. (1980). *The place of self psychology in the history of depth psychology.* Paper presented at the Symposium on Reflections on Self Psychology, Boston Psychoanalytic Society and Institute, Boston, Mass.

Cramer, B. (1982a). Interaction réele, interaction fantasmatique: Réflections au sujet des thérapies et des observations de nourrissons. *Psychothérapies,* No. 1.

Cramer, B. (1982b). La psychiatrie du bébé. In R. Kreisler, M. Schappi, and M. Soule (Eds.). *La dynamique du nourrisson.* Paris: Editions E.S.F.

Cramer, B. (1984, September). *Modèles psychoanalytiques, modèles interactifs: Recoupment possible?* Paper presented at the International Symposium "Psychiatry-Psychoanalysis," Montreal, Canada.

Dahl, H., and Stengel, B. (1978). A classification of emotion words: A modification and partial test of De Rivera's decision theory of emotions. *Psychoanalysis and Contemporary Thought, 1*(2), 269–312.

Darwin, C. (1965). *The expression of the emotions in man and animals.* Chicago: University of Chicago Press. (Original work published 1872)

DeCasper, A. J. (1980, April). *Neonates perceive time just like adults.* Paper presented at the International Conference on Infancy Studies, New Haven, Conn.

DeCasper, A. J., and Fifer, W. P. (1980). Of human bonding: Newborns prefer their mothers' voices. *Science, 208,* 1174–76.

Defoe, D. (1964). *Moll Flanders.* New York: Signet Classics. (Original work published 1723)

Demany, L., McKenzie, B., and Vurpillot, E. (1977). Rhythm perception in early infancy. *Nature, 266,* 718–19.

Demos, V. (1980). Discussion of papers delivered by Drs. Sander and Stern. Presented at the Boston Symposium on the Psychology of the Self, Boston, Mass.

Demos, V. (1982a). Affect in early infancy: Physiology or psychology. *Psychoanalytic Inquiry, 1,* 533–74.

Demos, V. (1982b). The role of affect in early childhood. In E. Troneck (Ed.), *Social interchange in infancy.* Baltimore, Md.: University Park Press.

Demos, V. (1984). Empathy and affect: Reflections on infant experience. In J. Lichtenberg, M. Bernstein, and D. Silver (Eds.), *Empathy.* Hillsdale, N.J.: Erlbaum.

DeVore, I., and Konnor, M. J. (1974). Infancy in hunter-gatherer life: An ethological perspective. In N. White (Ed.), *Ethology and psychiatry.* Toronto: University of Toronto Press.

Dodd, B. (1979). Lip reading in infants: Attention to speech presented in- and out- of synchrony. *Cognitive Psychology, 11,* 478–84.

Donee, L. H. (1973, March). *Infants' development scanning patterns of face and non-face stimuli under various auditory conditions.* Paper presented at the Meeting of the Society for Research in Child Development, Philadelphia, Pa.

Dore, J. (1975). Holophrases, speech acts and language universals. *Journal of Child Language, 2,* 21–40.

Dore, J. (1979). Conversational acts and the acquisition of language. In E. Ochs and B. Schieffelin (Eds.), *Developmental pragmatics.* New York: Academic Press.

Dore, J. (1985). Holophases revisited, dialogically. In M. Barrett (Ed.), *Children's single word speech.* London: Wiley.

Dunn, J. (1982). Comment: Problems and promises in the study of affect and intention. In E. Tronick (Ed.), *Social interchange in infancy.* Baltimore, Md.: University Park Press.

Dunn, J., and Kendrick, C. (1979). Interaction between young siblings in the context of family relationships. In M. Lewis and L. Rosenblum (Eds.), *The child and its family: The genesis of behavior, Vol. 2.* New York: Plenum Press.

Dunn, J., and Kendrick, C. (1982). *Siblings: Love, envy and understanding.* Cambridge: Harvard University Press.

Easterbrook, M. A., and Lamb, M. E. (1979). The relationship between quality of infant-mother attachment and infant competence in initial encounters with peers. *Child Development, 50,* 380–87.

Eimas, P. D., Siqueland, E. R., Jusczyk, P., and Vigorito, J. (1971). Speech perception in infants, *Science, 171,* 303–306.

Eimas, P. D., Siqueland, E. R., Jusczyk, P., and Vigorito, J. (1978). Speech perception in infants. In L. Bloom (Ed.), *Readings in language development.* New York: Wiley.

Eisenstein, S. (1957). *Film form and the film sense.* (J. Leyda, Trans.). New York: Meridian Books.

Ekman, P. (1971). Universals and cultural differences in facial expressions of emotion. In J. K. Cole (Ed.), *Nebraska symposium on motivation, Vol. 19.* Lincoln: University of Nebraska Press.

Ekman, P., Levenson, R. W., Friesen, W. V. (1983). Autonomic nervous system activity distinguishes among emotions. *Science, 221,* 1208–10.

Emde, R. N. (1980a). Levels of meaning for infant emotions: A biosocial view. In W. A. Collins (Ed.), *Development of cognition, affect, and social relations.* Hillsdale, N.J.: Erlbaum.

Emde, R. N. (1980b). Toward a psychoanalytic theory of affect. In S. I. Greenspan and G. H. Pollock (Eds.), *Infancy and early childhood. The course of life: Psychoanalytic contributions towards understanding personality development, Vol. I.* Washington, D.C.: National Institute of Mental Health.

Emde, R. N. (1983, March). *The affective core.* Paper presented at the Second World Congress of Infant Psychiatry, Cannes, France.

Emde, R. N., Gaensbauer, T., and Harmon, R. (1976). Emotional expression in infancy: A biobehavioral study. *Psychological Issues Monograph Series, 10*(1), No. 37.

Emde, R. N., Klingman, D. H., Reich, J. H., and Wade, J. D. (1978). Emotional expression in infancy: I. Initial studies of social signaling and an emergent model. In M. Lewis and L. Rosenblum, (Eds.), *The development of affect.* New York: Plenum Press.

Emde, R. N., and Sorce, J. E. (1983). The rewards of infancy: Emotional availability and maternal referencing. In J. D. Call, E. Galenson, and R. Tyson (Eds.), *Frontiers of infant psychiatry, Vol. 2.* New York: Basic Books.

Erikson, E. H. (1950). *Childhood and society.* New York: Norton.

Escalona, S. K. (1953). Emotional development in the first year of life. In M. Senn (Ed.), *Problems of infancy and childhood.* Packawack Lake, N.J.: Foundation Press.

Escalona, S. K. (1968). *The roots of individuality.* Chicago: Aldine.

Esman, A. H. (1983). The "stimulus barrier": A review and reconsideration. In A. Solnit and R. Eissler (Eds.), *The psychoanalytic study of the child, Vol. 38* (pp. 193–207). New Haven, Conn.: Yale University Press.

Fagan, J. F. (1973). Infants' delayed recognition memory and forgetting. *Journal of Experimental Child Psychology, 16,* 424–50.

Fagan, J. F. (1976). Infants' recognition of invariant features of faces. *Child Development, 47,* 627–38.

Fagan, J. F. (1977). Infant's recognition of invariant features of faces. *Child Development, 48,* 68–78.

Fagan, J. F., and Singer, L. T. (1983). Infant recognition memory as a measure of intelligence. In L. P. Lipsitt and C. K. Rovee-Collier (Eds.), *Advances in infancy research, Vol. 2.* Norwood, N.J.: Ablex.

Fairbairn, W. R. D. (1954). *An object relations theory of the personality.* New York: Basic Books.

Fantz, R. (1963). Pattern vision in newborn infants. *Science, 140,* 296–97.

Ferguson, C. A. (1964). Baby talk in six languages. In J. Gumperz and D. Hymes (Eds.), *The Ethnography of Communication, 66,* 103–14.

Fernald, A. (1982). *Acoustic determinants of infant preferences for "motherese."* Unpublished doctoral dissertation, University of Oregon.

Fernald, A. (1984). The perceptual and affective salience of mother's speech to infants. In L. Fagans, C. Garvey, and R. Golinkoff (Eds.), *The origin and growth of communication.* Norwood, N.J.: Ablex.

Fernald, A., and Mazzie, C. (1983, April). *Pitch-marking of new and old information in mother's speech.* Paper presented at the Meeting of the Society for Research in Child Development, Detroit, Mich.

Field, T. M. (1977). Effects of early separation, interactive deficits and experimental manipulations on mother-infant face-to-face interaction. *Child Development, 48,* 763–71.

Field, T. M. (1978). The three R's of infant-adult interactions: Rhythms, repertoires and responsivity. *Journal of Pediatric Psychology, 3,* 131–36.

Field, T. M. (in press). Attachment as psychological attunement: Being on the same wavelength. In M. Reite and T. Field (Eds.), *The psychobiology of attachment.* New York: Academic Press.

Field, T. M., and Fox, N. (Eds.). (in press). *Social perception in infants.* Norwood, N.J.: Ablex.

Field, T. M., Woodson, R., Greenberg, R., and Cohen, D. (1982). Discrimination and imitation of facial expressions by neonates. *Science, 218,* 179–81.

Fogel, A. (1982). Affect dynamics in early infancy: Affective tolerance. In T. Field and A. Fogel (Eds.), *Emotions and interaction: Normal and high-risk infants.* Hillsdale, N.J.: Erlbaum.

Fogel, A. (1977). Temporal organization in mother-infant face-to-face interaction. In H. R. Schaffer (Ed.), *Studies in mother-infant interaction.* New York: Academic Press.

Fogel, A., Diamond, G. R., Langhorst, B. H., and Demas, V. (1981). Affective and cognitive aspects of the two-month-old's participation in face-to-face interaction with its mother. In E. Tronick (Ed.), *Joint regulation of behavior.* Cambridge, England: Cambridge University Press.

Fraiberg, S. H. (1969). Libidinal constancy and mental representation. In R. Eissler et al. (Eds.), *The psychoanalytic study of the child, Vol. 24* (pp. 9–47). New York: International Universities Press.

Fraiberg, S. H. (1971). Smiling and strange reactions in blind infants. In J. Hellmuth (Ed.), *Studies in abnormalities: Vol. 2. Exceptional infant* (pp. 110–27). New York: Brunner/Mazel.

Fraiberg, S. H. (1980). *Clinical studies in infant mental health: The first year of life.* New York: Basic Books.

Fraiberg, S. H., Adelson, E., and Shapiro, V. (1975). Ghosts in the nursery: A psychoanalytic approach to the problem of impaired infant-mother relationships. *Journal of American Academy of Child Psychiatry, 14,* 387–422.

Francis, P. L., Self, P. A., and Noble, C. A. (1981, March). *Imitation within the context of mother-newborn interaction.* Paper presented at the Annual Eastern Psychological Association, New York.

Freedman, D. (1964). Smiling in blind infants and the issue of innate vs. acquired. *Journal of Child Psychology and Psychiatry, 5,* 171–84.

Freud, A. (1966). *Writings of Anna Freud: Vol. 6. Normality and pathology in childhood: Assessments in development.* New York: International Universities Press.

Freud, S. (1955). *The interpretation of dreams,* (J. Strachey, Ed.). New York: Basic Books. (Original work published in 1900)

Freud, S. (1962). *Three essays on the theory of sexuality.* New York: Basic Books. (Original work published in 1905)

Freud, S. (1957). Repression. In *The standard edition of the complete psychological works of Sigmund Freud,* Vol. 14. (143–58). London: Hogarth Press. (Original work published in 1915)

Freud, S. (1959). Mourning and melancholia. In *Collected papers,* Vol. 4 (pp. 152–170). New York: Basic Books. (Original work published in 1917)

Freud, S. (1955). Beyond the pleasure principle. In *The standard edition of the complete psychological works of Sigmund Freud,* Vol. 18 (pp. 4–67). London: Hogarth Press. (Original work published in 1920)

Friedlander, B. Z. (1970). Receptive language development in infancy. *Merrill-Palmer Quarterly, 16,* 7–51.

Friedman, L. (1980). Barren prospect of a representational world. *Psychoanalytic Quarterly, 49,* 215–33.

Friedman, L. (1982). *The interplay of evocation.* Paper presented at the Postgraduate Center for Mental Health, New York.

Galenson, E., and Roiphe, H. (1974). The emergence of genital awareness during the second year of life. In R. Friedman, R. Richart, and R. Vandeivides (Eds.), *Sex differences in behavior* (pp. 223–31). New York: Wiley.

Garfinkel, H. (1967). *Studies in ethnomethodology.* Englewood Cliffs, N.J.: Prentice-Hall.

Garmenzy, N., and Rutter, M. (1983). *Stress, coping and development in children.* New York: McGraw Hill.

Gautier, Y. (1984, September). *De la psychoanalyse et la psychiatrie du nourrisson: Un long et difficile cheminement.* Paper presented at the International Symposium "Psychiatry-Psychoanalysis," Montreal, Canada.

Gediman, H. K. (1971). The concept of stimulus barrier. *International Journal of Psychoanalysis, 52,* 243–57.

Ghosh, R. K. (1979). *Aesthetic theory and art: A study in Susanne K. Langer* (p. 29). Delhi, India: Ajanta Publications.

Gibson, E. J. (1969). *Principles of perceptual learning and development.* New York: Appleton-Century-Crofts.

Gibson, E. J., Owsley, C., and Johnston, J. (1978). Perception of invariants by five-month-old infants: Differentiation of two types of motion. *Developmental Psychology, 14,* 407–15.

Gibson, J. J. (1950). *The perception of the visual world.* Boston: Houghton Mifflin.

Gibson, J. J. (1979). *The ecological approach to visual perception.* Boston: Houghton Mifflin.

Glick, J. (1983, March). *Piaget, Vygotsky and Werner.* Paper presented at the Meeting of the Society for Research in Child Development, Detroit, Mich.

Glover, E. (1945). Examination of the Klein system of child psychology. In R. Eissler et al. (Eds.), *The psychoanalytic study of the child, Vol. 1* (pp. 75–118). New York: International Universities Press.

Goldberg, A. (Ed.). (1980). *Advances in self psychology.* New York: International Universities Press.

Golinkoff, R. (Ed.). (1983). *The transition from pre-linguistic to linguistic communication.* Hillsdale, N.J.: Erlbaum.

Greenfield, P., and Smith, J. H. (1976). *Language beyond syntax: The development of semantic structure.* New York: Academic Press.

Greenspan, S. I. (1981). *Clinical infant reports: No. 1. Psychopathology and adaptation in infancy in early childhood.* New York: International Universities Press.

Greenspan, S. I., and Lourie, R. (1981). Developmental and structuralist approaches to the classification of adaptive and personality organizations: Infancy and early childhood. *American Journal of Psychiatry, 138,* 725–35.

Grossmann, K., and Grossmann, K. E. (in press). Maternal sensitivity and newborn orientation responses as related to quality of attachment in northern Germany. In I. Bretherton and E. Waterns (Eds.), *Monographs of the Society for Research in Child Development.*

Gunther, M. (1961). Infant behavior at the breast. In B. M. Foss (Ed.), *Determinants of infant behavior, Vol. 2.* London: Methuen.

Guntrip, J. S. (1971). *Psychoanalytic theory, therapy, and the self.* New York: Basic Books.

Habermas, T. (1972). *Knowledge and human interests.* London: Heinemann.

Hainline, L. (1978). Developmental changes in visual scanning of face and non-face patterns by infants. *Journal of Exceptional Child Psychology, 25,* 90–115.

Haith, M. M. (1966). Response of the human newborn to visual movement. *Journal of Experimental Child Psychology, 3,* 235–43.

Haith, M. M. (1980). *Rules that babies look by.* Hillsdale, N.J.: Erlbaum.

Haith, M. M., Bergman, T., and Moore, M. J. (1977). Eye contact and face scanning in early infancy. *Science, 198,* 853–55.

Halliday, M. A. (1975). *Learning how to mean: Exploration in the development of language.* London: Edward Arnold.

Hamilton, V. (1982). *Narcissus and Oedipus: The children of psychoanalysis.* London: Rutledge and Kegan Paul.

Hamlyn, D. W. (1974). Person-perception and our understanding of others. In T. Mischel (Ed.), *Understanding other persons.* Oxford: Blackwell.

Harding, C. G. (1982). Development of the intention to communicate. *Human Development, 25,* 140–51.

Harding, C. G., and Golinkoff, R. (1979). The origins of intentional vocalizations in prelinguistic infants. *Child Development, 50,* 33–40.

Harper, R. C., Kenigsberg, K., Sia, G., Horn, D., Stern, D. N., and Bongiovi, V. (1980). Ziphophagus conjoined twins: A 300 year review of the obstetric, morphopathologic neonatal and surgical parameters. *American Journal of Obstetrics and Gynecology, 137,* 617–29.

Hartmann, H. (1958). *Ego psychology and the problem of adaption* (D. Rapaport, Trans.). New York: International Universities Press.

Hartmann, H., Kris, E., and Lowenstein, R. M. (1946). Comments on the formation of psychic structure. In *Psychological issues monographs: No. 14. Papers on psychoanalytic psychology* (pp. 27–55). New York: International Universities Press.

Herzog, J. (1980). Sleep disturbances and father hunger in 18- to 20-month-old boys: The Erlkoenig Syndrome. In A. Solnit et al. (Eds.), *The Psychoanalytic Study of the Child, Vol. 35* (pp. 219–36). New Haven, Conn.: Yale University Press.

Hinde, R. A. (1979). *Towards understanding relationships.* London: Academic Press.

Hinde, R. A. (1982). Attachment: Some conceptual and biological issues. In C. M. Parks and J. Stevenson-Hinde (Eds.), *The place of attachment in human behavior.* New York: Basic Books.

Hinde, R. A., and Bateson, P. (1984). Discontinuities versus continuities in behavioral development and the neglect of process. *International Journal of Behavioral Development, 7,* 129–43.

Hofer, M. A. (1980). *The roots of human behavior.* San Francisco, Calif.: Freedman.

Hofer, M. A. (1983, March). Relationships as regulators: A psychobiological perspective on development. Presented (as the Presidential Address) to the American Psychosomatic Society, New York.

Hoffman, M. L. (1977). Empathy, its development and pre-social implications. *Nebraska Symposium on Motivation, 25,* 169–217.

Hoffman, M. L. (1978). Toward a theory of empathic arousal and development. In M. Lewis and L. A. Rosenblum (Eds.), *The development of affect.* New York: Plenum Press.

Holquist, M. (1982). The politics of representation. In S. J. Greenblatt (Ed.), *Allegory and representation.* Baltimore, Md.: John Hopkins University Press.

Humphrey, K., Tees, R. C., and Werker, J. (1979). Auditory-visual integration of temporal relations in infants. *Canadian Journal of Psychology, 33,* 347–52.

Hutt, C., and Ounsted, C. (1966). The biological significance of gaze aversion with particular reference to the syndrome of infantile autism. *Behavioral Science, 11,* 346–56.

Izard, C. E. (1971). *The face of emotion.* New York: Appleton-Century-Crofts.

Izard, C. E. (1977). *Human emotions.* New York: Plenum Press.

Izard, C. E. (1978). On the ontogenesis of emotions and emotion-cognition relationship in infancy. In M. Lewis and L. A. Rosenblum (Eds.), *The development of affect.* New York: Plenum Press.

Kagan, J. (1981). *The second year of life: The emergence of self awareness.* Cambridge, Mass.: Harvard University Press.

Kagan, J. (1984). *The nature of the child.* New York: Basic Books.

Kagan, J., Kearsley, R. B., and Zelazo, P. R. (1978). *Infancy: Its place in human development.* Cambridge, Mass.: Harvard University Press.

Karmel, B. Z., Hoffman, R., and Fegy, M. (1974). Processing of contour information by human infants evidenced by pattern dependent evoked potentials. *Child Development, 45,* 39–48.

Kaye, K. (1979). Thickening thin data: The maternal role in developing communication and language. In M. Bullowa (Ed.), *Before speech.* Cambridge: Cambridge University Press.

Kaye, K. (1982). *The mental and social life of babies.* Chicago: University of Chicago Press.

Kernberg, O. F. (1968). The treatment of patients with borderline personality organization. *International Journal of Psychoanalysis, 49,* 600–19.

Kernberg, O. F. (1975). *Borderline conditions and pathological narcissism.* New York: Aronson.

Kernberg, O. F. (1976). *Object relations theory and clinical psychoanalysis.* New York: Aronson.

Kernberg, O. F. (1980). *Internal world and external reality: Object relations theory applied.* New York: Aronson.

Kernberg, O. F. (1984). *Severe personality disorders: Psychotherapeutic strategies.* New Haven, Conn.: Yale University Press.

Kessen, W., Haith, M. M., and Salapatek, P. (1970). Human infancy: A bibliography and guide. In P. Mussen (Ed.), *Carmichael's manual of child psychology.* New York: Wiley.

Kestenberg, J. S., and Sossin, K. M. (1979). *Movement patterns in development, Vol. 2.* New York: Dance Notation Bureau Press.

Klaus, M., and Kennell, J. (1976). *Maternal-infant bonding.* St. Louis: Mosey.

Klein, D. F. (1982). Anxiety reconceptualized. In D. F. Klein and J. Robkin (Eds.), *Anxiety: New research and current concepts.* New York: Raven Press.

Klein, Melanie (1952). *Developments in psycho-analysis.* (J. Rivere, Ed.). London: Hogarth Press.

Klein, Milton (1980). On Mahler's autistic and symbiotic phases. An exposition and evolution. *Psychoanalysis and Contemporary Thought, 4*(1), 69–105.

Klinnert, M. D. (1978). *Facial expression and social referencing.* Unpublished doctoral dissertation prospectus. Psychology Department, University of Denver.

Klinnert, M. D., Campos, J. J., Sorce, J. F., Emde, R. N., and Svejda, M. (1983). Emotions as behavior regulators: Social referencing in infancy. In R. Plutchik and H. Kellerman (Eds.), *Emotion: Theory, research and experience, Vol. 2.* New York: Academic Press.

Kohut, H. (1971). *The analysis of the self.* New York: International Universities Press.

Kohut, H. (1977). *The restoration of the self.* New York: International Universities Press.

Kohut, H. (1983). Selected problems of self psychological theory. In J. Lichtenberg and S. Kaplan (Eds.), *Reflections on self psychology.* Hillsdale, N.J.: Analytic Press.

Kohut, H. (in press). Introspection, empathy, and the semi-circle of mental health. *International Journal of Psychoanalysis.*

Kreisler, L., and Cramer, B. (1981). Sur les bases cliniques de la psychiatrie du nourrisson. *La Psychiatrie de l'Enfant, 24,* 1–15.

Kreisler, L., Fair, M., and Soulé, M. (1974). *L'enfant et son corps.* Paris: Presse Universitaires de France.

Kuhl, P., and Meltzoff, A. (1982). The bimodal perception of speech in infancy. *Science, 218,* 1138–41.

Labov, W., and Fanshel, D. (1977). *Therapeutic discourse.* New York: Academic Press.

Lacan, J. (1977). *Ecrits* (pp. 1–7). New York: Norton.

Lamb, M. E., and Sherrod, L. R. (Eds.). (1981). *Infant social cognition.* Hillsdale, N.J.: Erlbaum.

Langer, S. K. (1967). *MIND: An essay on human feeling, Vol. 1.* Baltimore, Md.: Johns Hopkins Universities Press.

Lashley, K. S. (1951). The problem of serial order in behavior. In L. A. Jeffres (Ed.), *Cerebral mechanisms in behavior.* New York: Wiley.

Lawson, K. R. (1980). Spatial and temporal congruity and auditory-visual integration in infants. *Developmental Psychology, 16,* 185–192.

Lebovici, S. (1983). *Le nourrisson, La mère et le psychoanalyste: Les interactions precoces.* Paris: Editions du Centurion.

Lee, B., and Noam, G. G. (1983). *Developmental approaches to the self.* New York: Plenum Press.

Lewcowicz, D. J. (in press). Bisensory response to temporal frequency in four-month-old infants. *Developmental Psychology.*

Lewcowicz, D. J., and Turkewitz, G. (1980). Cross-modal equivalence in early infancy: Audio-visual intensity matching. *Developmental Psychology, 16,* 597–607.

Lewcowicz, D. J., and Turkewitz, G. (1981). Intersensory interaction in newborns: Modification of visual preference following exposure to sound. *Child Development, 52,* 327–32.

Lewis, M., and Brooks-Gunn, J. (1979). *Social cognition and the acquisition of self.* New York: Plenum Press.

Lewis, M., and Rosenblum, L. A. (Eds.). (1974). *The origins of fear.* New York: Wiley.

Lewis, M., and Rosenblum, L. A. (1978). *The development of affect.* New York: Plenum Press.

Lewis, M., Feiring, L., McGoffog, L., and Jaskin, J. (In press). Predicting psychopathology in six-year-olds from early social relations. *Child Development.*

Lichtenberg, J. D. (1981). Implications for psychoanalytic theory of research on the neonate. *International Review of Psychoanalysis, 8,* 35–52.

Lichtenberg, J. D. (1983). *Psychoanalysis and infant research.* Hillsdale, N.J.: Analytic Press.

Lichtenberg, J. D., and Kaplan, S. (Eds.). (1983). *Reflections on self psychology.* Hillsdale, N.J.: Analytic Press.

Lichtenstein, H. (1961). Identity and sexuality: A study of their interpersonal relationships in man. *Journal of American Psychoanalytic Association, 9,* 179–260.

Lieberman, A. F. (1977). Preschoolers' competence with a peer: Relations with attachment and peer experience. *Child Development, 48,* 1277–87.

Lipps, T. (1906). Das wissen von fremden ichen. *Psychologische Untersuchung, 1,* 694–722.

Lipsitt, L. P. (1976). Developmental psychobiology comes of age. In L. P. Lipsitt (Ed.), *Developmental psychobiology: The significance of infancy.* Hillsdale, N.J.: Erlbaum.

Lipsitt, L. P. (Ed.). (1983). *Advances in infancy research, Vol. 2.* Norwood, N.J.: Ablex.

Lutz, C. (1982). The domain of emotion words on Ifaluk. *American Ethnologist, 9,* 113–28.

Lyons-Ruth, K. (1977). Bimodal perception in infancy: Response to audio-visual incongruity. *Child Development, 48,* 820–27.

MacFarlane, J. (1975). Olfaction in the development of social preferences in the human neonate. In M. Hofer (Ed.), *Parent-infant interaction.* Amsterdam: Elsevier.

MacKain, K., Stern, D. N., Goldfield, A., and Moeller, B. (1985). *The identification of correspondence between an infant's internal affective state and the facial display of that affect by an other.* Unpublished manuscript.

MacKain, K., Studdert-Kennedy, M., Spieker, S., and Stern, D. N. (1982, March). *Infant perception of auditory-visual relations for speech.* Paper presented at the International Conference of Infancy Studies, Austin, Tex.

MacKain, K., Studdert-Kennedy, M., Spieker, S., and Stern, D. N. (1983). Infant intermodal speech perception is a left-hemisphere function. *Science, 219,* 1347–49.

MacMurray, J. (1961). *Persons in relation.* London: Faber and Faber.

McCall, R. B. (1979). Qualitative transitions in behavioral development in the first three years of life. In M. H. Bornstein and W. Kessen (Ed.), *Psychological development from infancy.* Hillsdale, N.J.: Erlbaum.

McCall, R. B., Eichhorn, D., and Hogarty, P. (1977). Transitions in early mental development. *Monographs of the Society for Research in Child Development, 42*(1177).

McDevitt, J. B. (1979). The role of internalization in the development of object relations during the separation-individuation phase. *Journal of American Psychoanalytic Association, 27,* 327–43.

McGurk, H., and MacDonald, J. (1976). Hearing lips and seeing voices. *Nature, 264*(5588), 746–48.

Mahler, M. S., and Furer, M. (1968). *On human symbiosis and the vicissitudes of individuation.* New York: International Universities Press.

Mahler, M. S., Pine, F., and Bergman, A. (1975). *The psychological birth of the human infant.* New York: Basic Books.

Main, M. (1977). Sicherheit und wissen. In K. E. Grossman (Ed.), *Entwicklung der Lernfahigkeit in der sozialen umwelt.* Munich: Kinder Verlag.

Main, M., and Kaplan, N. (in press). Security in infancy, childhood and adulthood: A move to the level of representation. In I. Bretherton and E. Waterns (Eds.), *Monographs of the Society for Research in Child Development.*

Main, M., and Weston, D. (1981). The quality of the toddler's relationships to mother and father: Related to conflict behavior and readiness to establish new relationships. *Child Development, 52,* 932–40.

Malatesta, C. Z., and Haviland, J. M. (1983). Learning display rules: The socialization of emotion in infancy. *Child Development, 53,* 991–1003.

Malatesta, C. Z., and Izard, C. E. (1982). The ontogenesis of human social signals: From biological imperative to symbol utilization. In N. Fox and R. J. Davidson (Eds.), *Affective development: A psychological perspective.* Hillsdale, N.J.: Erlbaum.

Mandler, G. (1975). *Mind and emotion.* New York: Wiley.

Maratos, O. (1973). *The origin and development of imitation in the first six months of life.* Unpublished doctoral dissertation, University of Geneva.

Marks, L. F. (1978). *The unity of the senses: Interrelations among the modalities.* New York: Academic Press.

Matas, L., Arend, R., and Sroufe, L. A. (1978). Continuity of adaptation in the second year: The relationship between quality of attachment and later competence. *Child Development, 49,* 547–56.

Mead, G. H. (1934). *Mind, self and society: From the standpoint of a social behaviorist.* Chicago: University of Chicago Press.

Meissner, W. W. (1971). Notes on identification: II. Clarification of related concepts. *Psychoanalytic Quarterly, 40,* 277–302.

Meltzoff, A. N. (1981). Imitation, intermodal co-ordination and representation in early infancy. In G. Butterworth (Ed.), *Infancy and epistemology.* London: Harvester Press.

Meltzoff, A. N., and Borton, W. (1979). Intermodal matching by human neonates. *Nature, 282,* 403–4.

Meltzoff, A. N., and Moore, M. K. (1977). Imitation of facial and manual gestures by human neonates. *Science, 198,* 75–78.

Meltzoff, A. N., and Moore, M. K. (1983). The origins of imitation in infancy: Paradigm, phenomena and theories. In L. P. Lipsitt (Ed.), *Advances in infancy research.* Norwood, N.J.: Ablex.

Mendelson, M. J., and Haith, M. M. (1976). The relation between audition and vision in the human newborn. *Monographs of the Society for Research in Child Development, 41*(167).

Messer, D. J., and Vietze, P. M. (in press). Timing and transitions in mother-infant gaze. *Child Development.*

Miller, C. L., and Byrne, J. M. (1984). The role of temporal cues in the development of language and communication. In L. Feagans, C. Garvey, and R. Golinkoff (Eds.), *The origin and growth of communication.* Norwood, N.J.: Ablex.

Miyake, K., Chen, S., and Campos, J. J. (in press). Infant temperament, mother's mode of interaction, and attachment. In I. Bretherton and E. Waterns (Eds.), *Monographs of the Society for Research in Child Development.*

Moes, E. J. (1980, April). *The nature of representation and the development of consciousness and language in infancy: A criticism of Moore and Meltzoff's "neo-Piagetian" approach.* Paper presented at the International Conference on Infant Studies, New Haven, Conn.

Moore, M. K., and Meltzoff, A. N. (1978). Object permanence, imitation and language development in infancy: Toward a neo-Piagetian perspective on communicative and cognitive development. In F. D. Minifie and L. L. Lloyd (Eds.), *Communicative and cognitive abilities: Early behavioral assessment.* Baltimore, Md.: University Park Press.

Morrongiello, B. A. (1984). Auditory temporal pattern perception in six- and twelve-month-old infants. *Developmental Psychology, 20,* 441–48.

Moss, H. A. (1967). Sex, age and state as determinant of mother-infant interaction. *Merrill-Palmer Quarterly, 13,* 19–36.

Murphy, C. M., and Messer, D. J. (1977). Mothers, infants and pointing: A study of a gesture. In H. R. Schaffer (Ed.), *Studies in mother-infant interaction.* London: Academic Press.

Nachman, P. (1982). Memory for stimuli reacted to with positive and neutral affect in seven-month-old infants. Unpublished doctoral dissertation, Columbia University.

Nachman, P., and Stern, D. N. (1983). *Recall memory for emotional experience in pre-linguistic infants.* Paper presented at the National Clinical Infancy Fellows Conference, Yale University, New Haven, Conn.

Nelson, K. (1973). Structure and strategy in learning to talk. *Monographs of the Society for Research in Child Development, 48*(149).

Nelson, K. (1978). How young children represent knowledge of their world in and out of language. In R. S. Siegler (Ed.), *Children's thinking: What develops?* Hillsdale, N.J.: Erlbaum.

Nelson, K., and Greundel, J. M. (1979). *From personal episode to social script.* Paper presented at the Biennial Meeting of the Society for Research in Child Development, San Francisco, Calif.

Nelson, K., and Greundel, J. M. (1981). Generalized event representations: Basic building blocks of cognitive development. In M. E. Lamb and A. L. Brown (Eds.), *Advances in developmental psychology, Vol. 1.* Hillsdale, N.J.: Erlbaum.

Nelson, K., and Ross, G. (1980). The generalities and specifics of long-term memory in infants and young children. *New Directions for Child Development, 10,* 87–101.

Newson, J. (1977). An intersubjective approach to the systematic description of mother-infant interaction. In H. R. Schaffer (Ed.), *Studies in mother-infant interaction.* New York: Academic Press.

Ninio, A., and Bruner, J. (1978). The achievement and antecedents of labelling. *Journal of Child Language, 5,* 1–15.

Olson, G. M., and Strauss, M. S. (1984). The development of infant memory. In M. Moscovitch (Ed.), *Infant memory.* New York: Plenum Press.

Ornstein, P. H. (1979). Remarks on the central position of empathy in psychoanalysis. *Bulletin of the Association of Psychoanalytic Medicine, 18,* 95–108.

Osofsky, J. D. (1985). *Attachment theory and research and the psychoanalytic process.* Unpublished manuscript.

Papoušek, H., and Papoušek, M. (1979). Early ontogeny of human social interaction: Its biological roots and social dimensions. In M. von Cranach, K. Foppa, W. Lepenies, and P. Ploog (Eds.), *Human ethology: Claims and limits of a new discipline.* Cambridge: Cambridge University Press.

Papoušek, M., and Papoušek, H. (1981). Musical elements in the infant's vocalization: Their significance for communication, cognition and creativity. In L. P. Lipsitt (Ed.), *Advances in Infancy Research.* Norwood, N.J.: Ablex.

Peterfreund, E. (1978). Some critical comments on psychoanalytic conceptualizations of infancy. *International Journal of Psychoanalysis, 59,* 427–41.

Piaget, J. (1952). *The origins of intelligence in children.* New York: International Universities Press.

Piaget, J. (1954). *The construction of reality in the child* (M. Cook, Trans.). New York: Basic Books. (Original work published 1937)

Pine, F. (1981). In the beginning: Contributions to a psychoanalytic developmental psychology. *International Review of Psychoanalysis, 8,* 15–33.

Pinol-Douriez, M. (1983, March). *Fantasy interactions or "proto representations"? The cognitive value of affect-sharing in early interactions.* Paper presented at the World Association of Infant Psychiatry, Cannes, France.

Plutchik, R. (1980). *The emotions: A psychoevolutionary synthesis.* New York: Harper & Row.

Reite, M., Short, R., Seiler, C., and Pauley, J. D. (1981). Attachment, loss and depression. *Journal of Child Psychology and Psychiatry, 22,* 141–69.

Ricoeur, P. (1977). The question of proof in Freud's psychoanalytic writings. *Journal of American Psychoanalytic Association, 25,* 835–71.

Rosch, E. (1978). Principle of categorization. In E. Rosch and B. B. Floyd (Eds.), *Cognition and categorization.* Hillsdale, N.J.: Erlbaum.

Rose, S. A. (1979). Cross-modal transfer in infants: Relationship to prematurity and socioeconomic background. *Developmental Psychology, 14,* 643–82.

Rose, S. A., Blank, M. S., and Bridger, W. H. (1972). Intermodal and intramodal retention of visual and tactual information in young children. *Developmental Psychology, 6,* 482–86.

Rovee-Collier, C. K., and Fagan, J. W. (1981). The retrieval of memory in early infancy. In L. P. Lipsitt (Ed.), *Advances in infancy research, Vol. 1.* Norwood, N.J.: Ablex.

Rovee-Collier, C. K., and Lipsitt, L. P. (1981). Learning, adaptation, and memory. In P. M. Stratton (Ed.), *Psychobiology of the human newborn.* New York: Wiley.

Rovee-Collier, C. K., Sullivan, M. W., Enright, M., Lucas, D., and Fagan, J. W. (1980). Reactivism of infant memory. *Science, 208,* 1159–61.

Ruff, H. A. (1980). The development of perception and recognition of objects. *Child Development, 51,* 981–92.

Sagi, A., and Hoffman, M. L. (1976). Empathic distress in the newborn. *Developmental Psychology, 12,* 175–76.

Salapatek, P. (1975). Pattern perception in early infancy. In I. Cohen and P. Salapatek (Eds.), *Infant perception: From sensation to cognition, Vol. 1.* New York: Academic Press.

Sameroff, A. J. (1983). Developmental systems: Context and evolution. In W. Kessen (Ed.), *Mussen's handbook of child psychology, Vol. 1.* New York: Wiley.

Sameroff, A. J. (1984, May). *Comparative perspectives on early motivation.* Paper presented at the Third Triennial Meeting of the Developmental Biology Research Group, Estes Park, Colo.

Sameroff, A. J., and Chandler, M. (1975). Reproductive risk and the continuum of caretaking casualty. In F. D. Horowitz (Ed.), *Review of child development research, Vol. 4.* Chicago: University of Chicago Press.

Sander, L. W. (1962). Issues in early mother-child interaction. *Journal of American Academy of Child Psychiatry, 1,* 141–66.

Sander, L. W. (1964). Adaptive relationships in early mother-child interaction. *Journal of the American Academy of Child Psychiatry, 3,* 231–64.

Sander, L. W. (1980). New knowledge about the infant from current research: Implications for psychoanalysis. *Journal of American Psychoanalytic Association, 28,* 181–98.

Sander, L. W. (1983a). Polarity, paradox, and the organizing process in development. In J. D. Call, E. Galenson, and R. L. Tyson (Eds.), *Frontiers of infant psychiatry,* Vol. 1. New York: Basic Books.

Sander, L. W. (1983b). To begin with—reflections on ontogeny. In J. Lichtenberg and S. Kaplan. *Reflection on self psychology.* Hillsdale, N.J.: Analytic Press.

Sandler, J. (1960). The background of safety. *International Journal of Psychoanalysis, 41,* 352–56.

Scaife, M., and Bruner, J. S. (1975). The capacity for joint visual attention in the infant. *Nature, 253,* 265–66.

Schafer, R. (1968). Generative empathy in the treatment situation. *Psychoanalytic Quarterly, 28,* 342–73.

Schafer, R. (1981). Narration in the psychoanalytic dialogue. In W. J. T. Mitchell (Ed.), *On narrative.* Chicago: University of Chicago Press.

Schaffer, H. R. (1977). *Studies in infancy.* London: Academic Press.

Schaffer, H. R., Collis, G. M., and Parsons, G. (1977). Vocal interchange and visual regard in verbal and pre-verbal children. In H. R. Schaffer (Ed.), *Studies in mother-infant interaction.* London: Academic Press.

Schaffer, H. R., Greenwood, A., and Parry, M. H. (1972). The onset of wariness. *Child Development, 43,* 65–75.

Scheflin, A. E. (1964). The significance of posture in communication systems. *Psychiatry, 27,* 4.

Scherer, K. (1979). Nonlinguistic vocal indicators of emotion and psychopathology. In C. E. Izard (Ed.), *Emotions in personality and psychopathology.* New York: Plenum Press.

Schneirla, T. C. (1959). An evolutionary and developmental theory of biphasic processes underlying approach and withdrawal. In M. R. Jones (Ed.), *Nebraska symposium on motivation.* Lincoln: University of Nebraska Press.

Schneirla, T. C. (1965). Aspects of stimulation and organization in approach/withdrawal processes underlying vertebrate behavioral development. In D. S. Lehrman, R. A. Hinde, and E. Shaw (Eds.), *Advances in the study of behavior, Vol. 1.* New York: Academic Press.

Schwaber, E. (1980a). Response to discussion of Paul Tolpin. In A. Goldberg (Ed.), *Advances in self psychology.* New York: International Universities Press.

Schwaber, E. (1980b). Self psychology and the concept of psychopathology: A case presentation.

In A. Goldberg (Ed.), *Advances in self psychology.* New York: International Universities Press.

Schwaber, E. (1981). Empathy: A mode of analytic listening. *Psychoanalytic Inquiry, 1,* 357–92.

Searle, J. R. (1969). *Speech acts: An essay in the philosophy of language.* New York: Cambridge University Press.

Shane, M., and Shane, E. (1980). Psychoanalytic developmental theories of the self: An integration. In A. Goldberg (Ed.), *Advances in self psychology.* New York: International Universities Press.

Shank, R. C. (1982). *Dynamic memory: A theory of reminding and learning in computers and people.* New York: Cambridge University Press.

Shank, R. C., and Abelson, R. (1975). *Scripts, plans and knowledge.* Proceedings of the Fourth International Joint Conference on Artificial Intelligence, Tbilis, U.S.S.R.

Shank, R. C., and Abelson, R. (1977). *Scripts, plans, goals, and understanding.* Hillsdale, N.J.: Erlbaum.

Sherrod, L. R. (1981). Issues in cognitive-perceptual development: The special case of social stimuli. In M. E. Lamb and L. R. Sherrod (Eds.), *Infant social cognition.* Hillsdale, N.J.: Erlbaum.

Shields, M. M. (1978). The child as psychologist: Contriving the social world. In A. Lock (Ed.), *Action, gesture and symbol.* New York: Academic Press.

Simner, M. (1971). Newborns' response to the cry of another infant. *Developmental Psychology, 5,* 136–50.

Siqueland, E. R., and Delucia, C. A. (1969). Visual reinforcement of non-nutritive sucking in human infants. *Science, 165,* 1144–46.

Snow, C. (1972). Mother's speech to children learning language. *Child Development, 43,* 549–65.

Sokolov, E. N. (1960). Neuronal models and the orienting reflex. In M. A. B. Brazier (Ed.), *The central nervous system and behavior.* New York: Josiah Macy, Jr. Foundation.

Spelke, E. S. (1976). Infants' intermodal perception of events. *Cognitive Psychology, 8,* 553–60.

Spelke, E. S. (1979). Perceiving bimodally specified events in infancy. *Developmental Psychology, 15,* 626–36.

Spelke, E. S. (1980). Innate constraints on intermodal perception. A discussion of E. J. Gibson, "The development of knowledge of intermodal unity: Two views," Paper presented to the Piaget Society.

Spelke, E. S. (1982). The development of intermodal perception. In L. B. Cohen and P. Salapatek (Eds.), *Handbook of infant perception.* New York: Academic Press.

Spelke, E. S. (1983). *The infant's perception of objects.* Paper presented at the New School for Social Research, New York.

Spelke, E. S., and Cortelyou, A. (1981). Perceptual aspects of social knowing: Looking and listening in infancy. In M. E. Lamb and L. R. Sherrod (Eds.), *Infant social cognition.* Hillsdale, N.J.: Erlbaum.

Spense, D. P. (1976). Clinical interpretation: Some comments on the nature of the evidence. *Psychoanalysis and Contemporary Science, 5,* 367–88.

Spieker, S. J. (1982). *Infant recognition of invariant categories of faces: Person, identity and facial expression.* Unpublished doctoral dissertation, Cornell University.

Spitz, R. A. (1950). Anxiety in infancy: A study of its manifestations in the first year of life. *International Journal of Psychoanalysis, 31,* 138–43.

Spitz, R. A. (1957). *No and yes: On the genesis of human communication.* New York: International Universities Press.

Spitz, R. A. (1959). *A genetic field theory of ego formation.* New York: International Universities Press.

Spitz, R. A. (1965). *The first year of life.* New York: International Universities Press.

Sroufe, L. A. (1979). The coherence of individual development: Early care, attachment and subsequent developmental issues. *American Psychologist, 34,* 834–41.

Sroufe, L. A. (1985). An organizational perspective on the self. Unpublished manuscript.

Sroufe, L. A. (in press). Attachment classification from the perspective of the infant-caregiver relationship and infant temperament. *Child Development.*

Sroufe, L. A., and Fleeson, J. (1984). Attachment and the construction of relationships. In W. W. Hartup and Z. Rubin, *Relationships and development.* New York: Cambridge University Press.

Sroufe, L. A., and Rutter, M. (1984). The Domain of developmental Psychopathology. *Child Development, 55*(1), 17–29.

Sroufe, L. A., and Waters, E. (1977). Attachment as an organizational construct. *Child Development, 48,* 1184–99.

Stechler, G., and Carpenter, G. (1967). A viewpoint on early affective development. In J. Hellmath (Ed.), *The exceptional infant, No. 1* (pp. 163–89). Seattle: Special Child Publications.

Stechler, G., and Kaplan, S. (1980). The development of the self: A psychoanalytic perspective. In A. Solnit et al. (Eds.), *The psychoanalytic study of the child, Vol. 35* (p. 35). New Haven: Yale University Press.

Stern, D. N. (1971). A micro-analysis of mother-infant interaction: Behaviors regulating social contact between a mother and her three-and-a-half-month-old twins. *Journal of American Academy of Child Psychiatry, 10,* 501–17.

Stern, D. N. (1974a). The goal and structure of mother-infant play. *Journal of American Academy of Child Psychiatry, 13,* 402–21.

Stern, D. N. (1974b). Mother and infant at play: The dyadic interaction involving facial, vocal and gaze behaviors. In M. Lewis and L. A. Rosenblum (Eds.), *The effect of the infant on its caregiver.* New York: Wiley.

Stern, D. N. (1977). *The first relationship: Infant and mother.* Cambridge, Mass.: Harvard University Press.

Stern, D. N. (1980). *The early development of schemas of self, of other, and of various experiences of "self with other."* Paper presented at the Symposium on Reflections on Self Psychology, Boston Psychoanalytic Society and Institute, Boston, Mass.

Stern, D. N. (1985). Affect attunement. In J. D. Call, E. Galenson, and R. L. Tyson (Eds.), *Frontiers of infant psychiatry, Vol. 2.* New York: Basic Books.

Stern, D. N., and Gibbon, J. (1978). Temporal expectancies of social behavior in mother-infant play. In E. B. Thoman (Ed.), *Origins of the infant's social responsiveness.* Hillsdale, N.J.: Erlbaum.

Stern, D. N., Barnett, R. K., and Spieker, S. (1983). Early transmission of affect: Some research issues. In J. D. Call, F. Galenson, and R. L. Tyson (Eds.), *Frontiers of infant psychiatry.* New York: Basic Books.

Stern, D. N., MacKain, K., and Spieker, S. (1982). Intonation contours as signals in maternal speech to prelinguistic infants. *Developmental Psychology, 18,* 727–35.

Stern, D. N., Beebe, B., Jaffe, J., and Bennett, S. L. (1977). The infant's stimulus world during social interaction: A study of caregiver behaviors with particular reference to repetition and timing. In H. R. Schaffer (Ed.), *Studies in mother-infant interaction.* London: Academic Press.

Stern, D. N., Hofer, L., Haft, W., and Dore, J. (in press). Affect attunement: The sharing of feeling states between mother and infant by means of inter-modal fluency. In T. Field and N. Fox (Eds.), *Social perception in infants.* Norwood, N.J.: Ablex.

Stern, D. N., Jaffe, J., Beebe, B., and Bennett, S. L. (1974). Vocalizing in unison and in alternation: Two modes of communication within the mother-infant dyad. *Annals of the New York Academy of Science, 263,* 89–100.

Stolerow, R. D., Brandhoft, B., and Atwood, G. E. (1983). Intersubjectivity in psychoanalytic treatment. *Bulletin of the Menninger Clinic, 47*(2), 117–28.

Strain, B., and Vietze, P. (1975, March). *Early dialogues: The structure of reciprocal infant-mother vocalizations.* Paper presented at the Meeting of the Society for Research in Child Development, Denver, Colo.

Strauss, M. S. (1979). Abstraction of proto typical information by adults and ten-month-old infants. *Journal of Experimental Psychology: Human Learning and Memory, 5,* 618–32.

Sullivan, H. S. (1953). *The interpersonal theory of psychiatry.* New York: Norton.

Sullivan, J. W., and Horowitz, F. D. (1983). Infant intermodal perception and maternal multimodal stimulation: Implications for language development. In L. P. Lipsitt (Ed.), *Advances in infancy research, Vol. 2.* Norwood, N.J.: Ablex.

Thoman, E. B., and Acebo, C. (1983). The first affections of infancy. In R. W. Bell, J. W. Elias, R. L. Greene, and J. H. Harvey (Eds.), *Texas Tech interfaces in psychology: I. Developmental psychobiology and neuropsychology.* Lubbock, Tex.: Texas Tech University Press.

Thomas, A., Chess, S., and Birch, H. G. (1970). The origins of personality. *Scientific American, 223,* 102–4.

Tolpin, M. (1971). On the beginning of a cohesive self. In R. Eissler et al. (Eds.), *The Psychoanalytic Study of the Child, Vol. 26* (pp. 316–54). New York: International Universities Press.

Tolpin, M. (1980). Discussion of psychoanalytic developmental theories of the self: An integration by M. Shane and E. Shane. In A. Goldberg (Ed.), *Advances in self psychology.* New York: International Universities Press.

Tomkins, S. S. (1962). *Affect, imagery and consciousness: Vol. I. The positive affects.* New York: Springer.

Tompkins, S. S. (1963). *Affect, imagery, consciousness: Vol. II. The negative affects.* New York: Springer.

Tompkins, S. S. (1981). The quest for primary motives: Biography and autobiography of an idea. *Journal of Personal Social Psychology, 41,* 306–29.

Trevarthan, C. (1974). Psychobiology of speech development. In E. Lenneberg (Ed.), Language and Brain: Developmental Aspects. *Neurobiology Sciences Research Program Bulletin, 12,* 570–85.

Trevarthan, C. (1977). Descriptive analyses of infant communicative behavior. In H. R. Schaffer (Ed.), *Studies in mother-infant interaction.* New York: Academic Press.

Trevarthan, C. (1979). Communication and cooperation in early infancy: A description of primary intersubjectivity. In M. M. Bullowa (Ed.), *Before speech: The beginning of interpersonal communication.* New York: Cambridge University Press.

Trevarthan, C. (1980). The foundations of intersubjectivity: Development of interpersonal and cooperative understanding in infants. In D. R. Olson (Ed.), *The social foundation of language and thought: Essays in honor of Jerome Bruner.* New York: Norton.

Trevarthan, C., and Hubley, P. (1978). Secondary intersubjectivity: Confidence, confiders and acts of meaning in the first year. In A. Lock (Ed.), *Action, gesture and symbol.* New York: Academic Press.

Tronick, E., Als, H., and Adamson, L. (1979). Structure of early face-to-face communicative interactions. In M. Bullowa (Ed.), *Before speech: The beginning of interpersonal communication.* New York: Cambridge University Press.

Tronick, E., Als, H., and Brazelton, T. B. (1977). The infant's capacity to regulate mutuality in face-to-face interaction. *Journal of Communication, 27,* 74–80.

Tronick, E., Als, H., Adamson, L., Wise, S., and Brazelton, T. B. (1978). The infant's response to intrapment between contradictory messages in face-to-face interaction. *Journal of Child Psychiatry, 17,* 1–13.

Tulving, E. (1972). Episodic and semantic memory. In E. Tulving and W. Donaldson (Eds.), *Organization of memory.* New York: Academic Press.

Ungerer, J. A., Brody, L. R., and Zelazo, P. (1978). Long term memory for speech in two- to four-week-old infants. *Infant Behavior and Development, 1,* 177–186.

Uzgiris, I. C. (1974). Patterns of vocal and gestural imitation in infants. In L. J. Stone, H. T. Smith, and L. B. Murphy (Eds.), *The competent infant.* London: Tavistock.

Uzgiris, I. C. (1981). Two functions of imitation during infancy. *International Journal of Behavioral Development, 4,* 1–12.

Uzgiris, I. C. (1984). Imitation in infancy: Its interpersonal aspects. In M. Perlmutter (Ed.), *Parent-child interaction in child development. The Minnesota symposium on child psychology, Vol. 17.* Hillsdale, N.J.: Erlbaum.

Vischer, F. T. (1863). *Kritische gange, Vol. 2.* (p. 86). (No. 5, second ed.).
Vygotsky, L. S. (1962). *Thought and language* (E. Haufmann and G. Vakar, Eds. and Trans.). Cambridge, Mass.: M.I.T. Press.
Vygotsky, L. S. (1966). Development of the higher mental functions. In A. N. Leontier (Ed.), *Psychological research in the U.S.S.R.* Moscow: Progress Publishers.
Waddington, C. H. (1940). *Organizers and genes.* Cambridge: Cambridge University Press.
Wagner, S., and Sakowitz, L. (1983, March). *Intersensory and intrasensory recognition: A quantitative and developmental evaluation.* Paper presented at the Meeting of the Society for Research in Child Development, Detroit, Mich.
Walker, A. S., Bahrick, L. E., and Neisser, U. (1980). *Selective looking to multimodal events by infants.* Paper presented at the International Conference on Infancy Studies, New Haven, Conn.
Walker-Andrews, A. S., and Lennon, E. M. (1984). *Auditory-visual perception of changing distance.* Paper presented at the International Conference of Infancy Studies, New York.
Wallon, H. (1949). *Les origines du caractère chez l'enfant: Les préludes du sentiment de personnalité* (2nd ed.). Paris: Presses Universitaires de France.
Washburn, K. J. (1984). *Development of categorization of rhythmic patterns in infancy.* Paper presented at the International Conference of Infant Studies, New York.
Waters, E. (1978). The reliability and stability of individual differences in infant-mother attachment. *Child Development, 49,* 483–94.
Waters, E., Wippman, J., and Sroufe, L. A. (1980). Attachment, positive affect and competence in the peer group: Two studies of construct validation. *Child Development, 51,* 208–16.
Watson, J. S. (1979). Perception of contingency as a determinant of social responsiveness. In E. Thomas (Ed.), *The origins of social responsiveness.* Hillsdale, N.J.: Erlbaum.
Watson, J. S. (1980). *Bases of causal inference in infancy: Time, space, and sensory relations.* Paper presented at the International Conference on Infant Studies, New Haven, Conn.
Weil, A. M. (1970). The basic core. In R. Eissler et al. (Eds.), *The Psychoanalytic Study of the Child, Vol. 25* (pp. 442–60). New York: International Universities Press.
Werner, H. (1948). *The comparative psychology of mental development.* New York: International Universities Press.
Werner, H., and Kaplan, B. (1963). *Symbol formation: An organismic-developmental approach to language and expression of thought.* New York: Wiley.
Winnicott, D. W. (1958). *Collected papers.* London: Tavistock.
Winnicott, D. W. (1965). *The maturational processes and the facilitating environment.* New York: International Universities Press.
Winnicott, D. W. (1971). *Playing and reality.* New York: Basic Books.
Wolf, E. S. (1980). Developmental line of self-object relations. In A. Goldberg (Ed.), *Advances in self psychology.* New York: International Universities Press.
Wolff, P. H. (1966). The causes, controls and organization of behavior in the neonate. *Psychological Issues, 5,* 17.
Wolff, P. H. (1969). The natural history of crying and other vocalizations in infancy. In B. M. Foss (Ed.), *Determinants of infant behavior, Vol. 4.* London: Methuen.
Worthheimer, M. (1961). Psychomotor coordination of auditory visual space at birth. *Science, 134,* 1692.
Yogman, M. W. (1982). Development of the father-infant relationship. In H. Fitzgerald, B. M. Lester, and M. W. Yogman (Eds.), *Theory and research in behavioral peadiatric, Vol. 1.* New York: Plenum Press.
Zajonc, R. B. (1980). Feeling and thinking: Preferences need no inferences. *American Psychologist, 35*(2), 151–75.
Zahn-Waxler, C., and Radke-Yarrow, M. (1982). The development of altruism: Alternative research strategies. In N. Eisenberg-Berg (Ed.), *The development of prosocial behavior.* New York: Academic Press.
Zahn-Waxler, C., Radke-Yarrow, M., and King, R. (1979). Child rearing and children's prosocial initiations towards victims of distress. *Child Development, 50,* 319–30.

INDEX